D0386519

STEP WARS

ALSO BY JEAN LIPMAN-BLUMEN

The Allure of Toxic Leaders: Why Followers Tolerate Bad Leadership

*Hot Groups: Seeding Them, Feeding Them, and
Using Them to Ignite Your Organization*

The Connective Edge: Leading in an Interdependent World

Gender Roles and Power

*Sex Roles and Social Policy: International Perspectives
on a Complex Social Science Equation*

STEP WARS

Overcoming the Perils and Making Peace in Adult Stepfamilies

GRACE GABE, M.D.,

AND

JEAN LIPMAN-BLUMEN, PH.D.

ST. MARTIN'S PRESS   NEW YORK

We dedicate this book to Warren and Hal and both of our families,
who inspired this book.

www.stmartins.com

Library of Congress Cataloging-in-Publication Data

Gabe, Grace.
    Step wars: overcoming the perils and making peace in adult stepfamilies /
Grace Gabe and Jean Lipman-Blumen.—1st U.S. ed.
        p. cm.
    ISBN 0-312-29099-3
    1. Stepfamilies.   2. Stepparents.   3. Remarriage.   4. Stepchildren.
5. Parent and adult child.   6. Intergenerational relations.
I. Lipman-Blumen, Jean.   II. Title.
HQ759.92.G33 2004
306.874—dc22

                                                                    2003015945

First Edition: April 2004

10 9 8 7 6 5 4 3 2 1

CONTENTS

ACKNOWLEDGMENTS

From the time we first began to explore and deliberate about writing this book, we have been encouraged and enlightened by so many people. Our munificent husbands, Warren Bennis and Hal Leavitt, inspired and galvanized us when we wavered, insisted it was worth doing, and advanced our thinking throughout this project. And, if all that were not more than enough, when we were in a crunch, Hal and Warren would come to the rescue with their marvelous editorial skills.

All of our children—biological, step, and in-law—encouraged and advised us all along the way. Lorna and Peter, Lesley and Marcello, Peter and Helena, Will, John B., David and Mark, John L. and Lynn, Emily and Steve, Liza and Michael, Nina and Joshua and Eden and Peter supported their moms'/step-moms'/step and biological mother-in-laws' efforts in taking on this complex and sometimes prickly project. Kate generously read and critiqued the manuscript in its early, middle, and late forms.

Conversations with Gerri Alpert, Marty Aronson, Nick Avery, Pat Biederman, Dorothy Braudy, Althea Brimm, Len Comess, Marilyn Curland, Nancy DeVille, Frank Dines, Susan Evans, Lillian Gallo, Sandy Goroff, Roger Gould, Myna Herscher, Selma Holo, Alice Levine, Connie Martinson, Donna Mitroff, Pat Palombo, Judith Rapoport, Ellen Sax, Bonnie Strauss, and Barbara Vinick helped us more than they probably knew at the time and had a major impact on our thinking in a variety of important ways. Robyn Letters put together our wonderful focus groups. Kevin Schneider created a Web page beyond compare.

Our dauntless agents, Denise Marcil and Margret McBride, gave us the momentum we needed and helped us to shape the book from the start. Our editor at St. Martin's Press, Jennifer Weis, had the confidence and courage to see what we wanted to accomplish from the beginning and guided us with her wisdom. Finally, without the extraordinary research and production assistance of Heather Fraschetti, the manuscript might never have metamorphosed miraculously into a book.

INTRODUCTION

We almost didn't write this book.

We had the idea ten years ago. A psychiatrist and a sociology professor, we had met for lunch at a restaurant near the beach in Santa Monica—two middle-aged professional women who knew how lucky we were to be happily remarried at a time in life when many people have given up any hope for that kind of happiness. As we leaned over our glasses of iced tea, we were shocked to discover that both of us had found life in an adult stepfamily surprisingly difficult at first. Here we were, professional students of human nature—one of us a therapist, the other a student of group behavior—and yet both of us had been stunned and hurt when our husbands' adult children hadn't warmed to us as quickly as we had hoped.

When we remarried, we had expected the adjustment to be easy—far easier than it would have been if we had had small children in tow. But an adult stepfamily, we quickly learned, has pitfalls of its own, tensions and problems that neither of us had anticipated. We laughed, a little guiltily, as we swapped stories about awkward holidays and tense conversations about finances. We confessed to feeling left out when our husbands reminisced about the past with their adult children or when our stepchildren failed to notice some especially thoughtful thing we had done just for them.

Meanwhile two women who appeared to be in their thirties were sitting nearby, quietly confiding in each other. Then, one of the young women raised her voice. "You have a stepmonster too?" she exclaimed to her friend, "and she's already gotten your father to put his IRA in her name!" They laughed conspiratorially as they swapped their own stories. Clearly bonding was going on at that table, too, as the young women described the sometimes bleak view from *their* side of the stepchild/stepparent divide.

Young remarried couples, trying to raise their youngsters from previous marriages under the same roof in "blended" families, receive much research attention and practical advice. By contrast, we noted the scarcity of good data on adult stepfamilies created when parents remarry after their children have become independent adults. In addition, there was certainly little or no practical advice for the person who needed help in dealing with the crises that seem to plague almost every adult stepfamily. We imagined a sort of Dr. Spock for these special stepfamilies, a book you could turn to, whether you were a parent, stepparent, or adult child, for answers to painful questions and strategies on how to cope. And we decided we were just the people to write it. That is, until we realized that our husbands and stepchildren would probably never forgive us for that one. So, we put the project on hold for almost a decade.

Both of us were busy with other things, including living the step life and working professionally. Yet we kept coming back to the adult stepfamilies project—in large part, because we realized the need was so great. Whenever one of us was at a party, if we mentioned adult stepfamilies, inevitably someone had a horror story to tell. Adult children told us how deeply they resented having a stepfamily forced upon them by a parent who seemed childishly, irresponsibly smitten late in life. Stepmothers griped about being treated like characters out of a Gothic fairy tale. Stepfathers, on the edge of tears, told us they were devastated when they realized an adult child cared more about his inheritance than about his father's happiness.

Some of the older couples we talked to were on the verge of divorce. One woman told us: "The only times I have thought seriously of getting out of the marriage have been in the heat of a fight about our adult children. . . . Their power to cause distress has been the biggest problem in our marriage. My fury escalates so fast when I feel that my husband is on his children's side and just won't allow himself to see how rejecting and mean-spirited they are to me or when he puts the worst interpretation on something my children have said. . . . I had predicted that our main problems would be health or job crises, but we always pull together on those issues. But when our disagreements are about our children, these arguments get truly dangerous to our commitment, loyalty, and trust of each other."

The adult children are suffering, too. One told us, "My father's new wife is the biggest threat our family has ever experienced. . . . It's the end of our family." Needless to say, we were shocked when we learned that Dad and his "new" wife had been married for almost thirty years.

Eventually, with the blessings of our husbands and our remarkable stepchildren, who encouraged us to be as candid as possible, we returned to the project and finally wrote this book.

THE ISSUES

Adult stepfamilies have been largely neglected, except by a small number of social and behavioral scientists. In fact, the problems of adult stepfamilies have been flying beneath the radar of census takers, most demographers, and other social and behavioral scientists, who don't even identify adult children as part of the "stepfamily." *The Encyclopedia of Marriage and the Family* (1995) defines stepfamilies as "consist(ing) of at least one minor child who is living with a biological parent and that parent's spouse—a stepparent—who is not the child's other biological parent.* The U.S. Census Bureau follows suit by counting as stepfamilies only those couples with children under eighteen years of age who are living at home.

As a result, adult stepfamilies remain all but invisible to everyone except the people in them. If we are not in an adult stepfamily, we tend not to think about them until one makes the headlines—as Paul McCartney's did not too long ago, when his children by the late Linda Eastman were said to be unhappy about his marriage to landmine activist and model Heather Mills.

Consequently, nobody knows exactly how many adult stepfamilies are created each year in the U.S.—that is, families that result from older couples who remarried when their children had already grown to adulthood and were no longer living with their parents. Although the U.S. Census Bureau collects vital statistics on marriage, divorce, death, and remarriage, it does not bother to collect data on how many older remarrying couples have adult children. At a minimum, we do know that at least 500,000 Americans age sixty-five and older get remarried each year, but there are many others younger than sixty-five who start adult stepfamilies. Unfortunately there is no direct way of determining how old their spouses are or how many children, children-in-law, and grandchildren they are bringing into their new families. Nonetheless, we know that the numbers will continue to increase as we all live longer, healthier lives and more people remarry later in life.

When a divorced or widowed parent remarries, no one is really prepared for what lies ahead—not the parent, not the spouse, not the adult children. The first shock is usually the stark contrast between the joy of the older bride and groom and the response of virtually everyone else in both their families. The couple usually sees the marriage as a great, unexpected gift and a last chance to savor love. The adult children rarely share the parent's unalloyed pleasure. The children often resist the change they know the marriage will bring. And they intensely resent being expected to act enthusiastic about it.

No one expects to become a stepchild, especially as an adult. To their surprise and chagrin, adult stepchildren quickly discover that they experience many of the same fears and other painful emotions as young stepchildren. They fear losing their parent's love. They fear being demoted to second place by a stepparent, who may try to limit the child's access to Mom or Dad. Whether spoken of or not, money usually becomes a huge issue, especially when the children fear that they will be denied an inheritance they expected to receive someday.

At first, most new couples don't worry about their grown children. They assume their offspring are now mature adults, who live independently, often with families of their own. It rarely occurs to the newlyweds that the marriage will be such a big deal for their adult children or that the children may act like angry ten-year-olds. In fact, the starry-eyed couple often figures that the kids will feel relieved, knowing that someone will be there to take care of their aging parent, in sickness and in health.

The torrent of emotions set off by the marriage typically stuns everyone. The couple usually has failed to think about the possibility that the children may be unhappy, if only because they did not choose this new arrangement. Unfortunately, few people in adult stepfamilies are willing or able to lay all the important issues on the table.

Angry silence is the enemy of happy stepfamilies, and it is too often the norm. Adult children are embarrassed to admit that they have concerns about whom Mom or Dad loves best, and they often can't admit, even to themselves, that they are counting on a generous share of the family money or property. Then, even as the children are being roiled emotionally, they have another unexpected jolt to adjust to—the arrival of a whole passel of new people whom they are expected to treat like family.

Don't even ask how embarrassing it can be for an adult child to see a parent suddenly acting like a loopy teenager over some white-haired Romeo or Juliet. Who is this person sneaking kisses in the kitchen and doing all sorts of other unseemly things?

Ours is not the first book written for people who live in adult stepfamilies; however, it is the first to deal with the issues they face in a comprehensive, multidisciplinary, and pragmatic way. There are hundreds of books on blended families with young children. In many ways, however, the problems of older families are even more complex and painful, if only because the older couple may be simultaneously confronting health problems, retirement, and other issues relating to aging.

METHODOLOGY

Let us tell you something about the methodology we used. This book is based upon 111 interviews with people in all the major roles in adult stepfamilies: stepmother, stepfather, stepchildren, stepgrandchildren, ex-spouses. Somewhat more than half of our stepfamilies were created after divorce. The rest occurred following the death of a spouse.

We interviewed sixty people one-on-one, for one to three hours. Each of us interviewed different subjects, and some people were interviewed more than once. When we were able, we interviewed both the couple and the adult children in the family.

In addition, we conducted and audiotaped four focus groups, each with ten to sixteen people. Two of these groups we also videotaped. These focus group members also completed extensive questionnaires just before the groups began. In that way, we collected as much detailed information on each focus group participant as we had from our individual interviewees. These fifty-one people were strangers to one another, but shared one characteristic: membership in an adult stepfamily. Some had been members of several such families because they or their parents had remarried more than once. Some were seasoned members of stepfamilies; others were brand-new.

The late-in-life marriages in the stepfamilies we studied varied in duration from one to thirty years. About 60 percent of our subjects were women—our belief is that women are, on the whole, more willing to be interviewed on intimate subjects than are men. Nonetheless, the men we interviewed were very forthcoming. Sixty-five percent of our subjects were stepparents. Since most parents bring the median two children to their stepfamilies, we know that there are many more stepchildren than stepparents out there. Still, we encountered far more stepparents than offspring, in large part, we speculated, because we are of the stepparent generation. The stepparents in our study ranged in age from thirty-seven to eighty-five, the stepchildren from twenty-two to sixty-two.

Most of our subjects are American citizens, although a few family members from Asia and Europe were interviewed, as well. We included people of many different racial and ethnic backgrounds, religious affiliations, and socioeconomic groups—Caucasian, Afro-American, Hispanic, Chinese, Japanese, Mexican, Irish, German, Polish, British, Catholic, Protestant, Jewish, Buddhist, and Shinto, upper middle class through upper blue collar. We used the so-called snowball technique to find participants, asking acquaintances, colleagues, and friends to identify likely candidates. We then asked the people we interviewed to suggest others living the step life.

After transcribing the taped individual interviews and the videotaped conversations of the focus groups, we pored over the transcripts, looking for recurring themes. As a sociologist and a psychiatrist, each of us committed to a multidisciplinary approach and each of us with more than thirty years in her respective field, we brought diverse perspectives to the material we studied. We are convinced that the complexity of adult stepfamilies calls for a multidisciplinary, multilayered approach.

We should add that, before our first interview, we combed the literature on adult stepfamilies, as well as on stepfamilies in general. We learned much from that review, including what remained to be explored.

THE GOAL

The goal of this book is to raise the profile of adult stepfamilies and provide practical help in dealing with the problems that arise in them time after time. There will be much in the pages that lie ahead about pain, anger, and other negative emotions. So we want to make clear right at the start that there is an upside to adult stepfamilies as well.

Becoming part of a stepfamily can enrich your life in ways you never imagined. It can result in new friendships, new alliances, new growth, and new sources of support—emotional, social, and even financial. Some stepfamilies manage to create a climate that is happier and healthier than the biological family ever had. More family members can mean more people to laugh with, more people to delight, more people to learn from, more people to teach, and more people to comfort one another. These new resources can outweigh the angst and emotional turmoil in which most adult stepfamilies begin.

Step Wars: Overcoming the Perils and Finding Peace in Adult Stepfamilies is designed as a handbook for every member of the adult stepfamily. It is filled with stories told from both sides—the new couple's and the adult children's. We hope it will help readers deal more effectively with the confusion, the pain, the absurdity, and, yes, the joy of adult stepfamilies. We hope you will keep it nearby, perhaps on your nightstand, and turn to it when troubled by something in your adult stepfamily, just as you would turn to a trusted friend.

THE STRUCTURE OF THE BOOK

The book is roughly chronological. It deals with the issues as they are typically encountered in adult stepfamilies, starting with the wedding and ending with chapters on health and last things. We do not deal with the dissolution of the stepfamily by divorce, since that complex set of circumstances deserves a study in its own right. Real-life stories told to us by our interviewees are the starting point for discussions in most chapters. In our research, we found that certain problems seem to dog every family. We call these the Five Furies because, to some degree, they bedevil every adult stepfamily. We'll describe them in detail later, but, for now, let us name them: Fears of Abandonment and Isolation, Fidelity to Family, Favoritism, Finances, and Focus on Self to the Exclusion of Others. Throughout the book, we shall tell you how to spot the Five Furies and how to bring them under control. We'll equip you with strategies for dealing with the Furies—strategies that we call Tact and Tacking skills. We'll also point you toward the Saving Graces—the often hidden rewards that lie within every adult stepfamily.

This book, we hope, will help you empathize with members of your stepfamily for your mutual benefit and structure what you say before you say it. We'll let you peek at the probable thoughts of other stepfamily members so that you can deal with them more compassionately and effectively.

We believe that most of the struggles that go on inside adult stepfamilies have little to do with personal chemistry. Instead, most of the problems are systemic, related to the structured roles and dynamics of adult stepfamilies. Once you understand how stepfamilies work, including the roles that people play in them, you can learn how to reduce tension in the system instead of escalating it. You can also learn how to change things for the better, rather than blaming yourself and others. Using these new insights and practical strategies, we hope you will find peace, even joy and step love.

As stepmothers, both of us face the same complexities and challenges that our interviewees and many of our readers face, day in and day out. This book is rooted in our professional expertise, but it was written from our hearts. We dedicate the book to our own stepfamilies, who inspired us, as well as to adult stepfamilies everywhere.

---

*Levinson, David, ed. (1995). *The Encyclopedia of Marriage and the Family* (New York, NY: MacMillan Library Reference).

PART I

Entering a Foreign Land:
Some Travel Necessities

CHAPTER 1

Announcing the Good News:
Why Isn't Everybody Happy?

I was so ecstatic when Arthur asked me to marry him, I could barely contain myself! I felt alive again, in a way that I never expected. When Roger died fifteen years ago, I thought my life was over. Of course, I had the kids and the grandkids, but I mean my own life. Now I feel like a schoolgirl again.

To tell you the truth, I wasn't expecting my kids' reactions. After all, they've all known Arthur for more than forty years. He and his late wife, Jan, were like an aunt and uncle to my kids while they were growing up. We were very close friends, family really. We went on trips together and everything. Both sets of kids played together all the time. It was like one big family.

When Jan died, Roger and I tried to console Arthur and keep him company. We spent a lot of time with him and his kids. They came to all our family events, just as before. When Roger died so unexpectedly, it was a huge shock. I felt so grateful and lucky that Arthur was there to help with everything. We just naturally began to keep each other company. The kids seemed okay with that.

Arthur and I have been together for fourteen years now. We have our own places, but we go on trips together, we baby-sit for the grandkids together, we go out dancing and to the movies. We keep each other company. So I really was shocked by my oldest daughter, Mary's, reaction. She asked, "Why do you have to get married?" My sister Annie, who was there at the time, jumped in and tried to explain how I felt, but Mary inter-rupted her, and said, "I'm asking my mother for an explanation." I didn't really know what to say. I thought she already understood. After all, she has a husband and children herself.

When I phoned my son in Chicago, he was out, so I told Joanne, his wife, the good news. She was all excited and asked when the wedding was going to be. I told her we were getting married in six months. She said she would tell Jim when he came in, and he'd call back. She asked if Hilda, their six-year old daughter, could be in the wedding. I thought I'd get a call from Jim that day, but I didn't. Not the next day, and not the next. That made me wonder what was going on.

When I finally called Jim again on the third day, he answered the phone. He said he'd forgotten to call and apologized casually. How do you forget to call your mother when she's called to say she's getting mar-ried? After all, that doesn't happen every day. I didn't say anything about that. But it was his next words that really shocked me. He said, "You're getting married in six months. This is so impetuous. What's the big hurry?" He acted as if we were teenagers who had just met! I reminded him we'd been together for the last fourteen years and had known one another for forty. That didn't seem so impetuous to me.

Finally he said, "Well, I hope you know what you're doing." We talked a little longer about other things. Just as Jim was about to hang up, he added, "Incidentally, don't forget to get him to sign a prenuptial agree-ment. Remember, there's your house and the land at the beach." I didn't know what to say.

These are the words of Mary, a middle-class Irish-American Catholic, aged sixty-five, mother of six, and grandmother of nine. But they could be the words of *any* of the men and women we interviewed, who spanned a broad ethnic, economic, and social spectrum. They all had adult children no longer living at home. This is how we define adult stepfamilies, to distinguish them from step-families with young children, sometimes called "blended families." Some of the parents had been divorced, others widowed. For several, this was their first marriage. Everyone else was remarried or living with a partner.

Back to Mary: She had entered an enchanted new world—where happiness reigned. She and the other soon-to-be-remarrieds we interviewed all felt that they were living in a magical moment, about to embark on a journey to a new, some-what foreign land. They looked forward to traveling in this unfamiliar territory, with its distinctive architecture and customs, even its own language, whose vocab-ulary did not yet roll smoothly off their tongues. They welcomed the challenge.

Most of our interviewees were charmed by the prospect of a new life filled with love, intimacy, and companionship. They felt increased emotional security and, for some, greater financial security, as well. Their enchantment often made it difficult for them to see that others did not necessarily share their joy. The very people whom they most wanted to join in their happy new odyssey— their own adult children—were often unable to celebrate their bliss.

In fact, whenever older people remarry, there is a strong possibility that their adult children will be decidedly unhappy at this turn of events, one that forces them into the unanticipated role of adult stepchild. There is also a good chance that this will be the beginning of a protracted struggle, unless all the parties have the requisite tools to work through the issues that inevitably arise. These tools don't always come naturally: our aim is to provide readers with the tools they need to survive in this increasingly common phenomenon—the adult stepfamily.

This is how Frank, a forty-five-year-old white Protestant upper-middle-class married man with two grown children, described the moment of truth, when his father announced his plans to remarry.

When my father called and said he had something important he wanted to tell me, my heart sank. At the time, he was seventy-two, living alone as he had since my mother died two years before. His voice was so serious that I thought he was going to tell me he had cancer. Instead, he said he and his girlfriend, Edith, had decided to get married. To tell you the truth, that didn't make me feel all that much better. None of us, my brothers and I, really likes Edith. She's so different from my mother. She's a little too stylish, in good taste of course, but still she seems to spend a lot on herself. Besides, my mother's only been gone barely two years. You'd think he'd have a little more respect for her memory. I said, "You're not really over Mother's death. Do you think this is a good idea?"

According to the adult stepchildren whom we interviewed, the sinking feel-ing that Frank reports is quite normal, or at least extremely common, for adult children of divorced or widowed parents who never imagined that they would become stepchildren. For adult children who have gotten used to their parent's single existence, the whole idea of remarriage may catch them off their emo-tional guard—even after many years of seeing the parent in a romantic relation-ship with the intended spouse.

THE ANNOUNCEMENT CRISIS: NEW CHANCES
AND RISKS FOR EVERYONE

The announcement of the decision to remarry sets off an avalanche of feelings. (We'll talk later about parents who decide simply to live together.) There is no avoiding it. If you are an adult child who learns that your parent is getting remarried, you are going to be thrown. As a result, you will learn things about yourself and your family that you never imagined, whether you like it or not. Even several professional therapists whom we interviewed reported being upset by a parent's plan to remarry. No wonder. As an adult child, you didn't ask for a new family. You never dreamed that you would have to deal so intimately with so many new people, each of whom has his or her own opinions and self-interests. In fact, the only real choice you have is whether to stew and be miserable or to grow stronger, wiser, and more independent as a result of your parent's remarriage.

You have two basic options, whether you are an adult stepchild or a remarrying parent. The first option is to take a passive role, letting it all happen to you or silently hoping it will just go away. If that is your choice, you could remain muddled about how to behave. You'd also be more likely to feel rejected and become less confident. In addition, you'd probably resign yourself to chronic pain and frustration about your new family situation.

If you remain passive, you avoid determining what you want in your new circumstances and what decisions you must make. You let others decide how the new family will develop. As a result, you are likely to resent the choices others make and become disgruntled and unhappy.

The alternative is for you to work your way proactively through this family drama. Selecting this option helps you to become stronger, more realistic, and more certain about what is really important to you. You will have to decide which way to go, because even if you refuse to recognize your stepfamily, you cannot divorce your own family. In this second, more active and effective option, you will develop new skills that will help you understand your own fears and other emotions and will maximize your chances of getting positive results.

We are not advocating either acceptance or rejection of your stepfamily. That's up to you. Instead, we shall try to help you determine what *you* want. Once you are clear about that, we'll help you find effective ways of achieving your goals. We'll also teach you valuable new strategies for communicating with members of your new family—strategies that lessen tensions and misunderstandings.

The unadorned truth is that something very basic within a family changes when a parent remarries. Even when the children are adults with children of their own, they are forced to reexamine their often complex feelings about their parent. Ultimately, a parent's remarriage forces the adult children to become *much more* independent of their parents. The parents, too, must learn to be *much more* independent of their adult children.

If this process founders, the fearful parents may slip into a clinging dependency on their adult children. For adult children, it may mean backsliding into the dependency of childhood. After all, whether you need constant approval or if you are always furious at your parent or adult child, it boils down to the same thing. Being furious is just hanging on to that person through anger, rather than affection. This produces the same result: increased dependency coupled with decreased self-reliance and self-esteem. Is this the direction you want for yourself?

As a remarried parent or an adult stepchild, you have an important role in determining how your original family maintains itself while simultaneously making new connections. You will have to determine what you want to hold on to and where you can comfortably loosen your grip. From the beginning, focusing on the long view, the bigger picture, is key to finding your best direction. You carve your path with your first moves and decisions. It's hard—but not impossible—to go back and take another path once you start down that initial road.

New chances and risks emerge for everyone. You will have to choose to be courageous or cowardly, honest or deceptive, realistic or deluded about achieving your desires in your stepfamily. Will you approach this new, unfamiliar land as dangerous territory to be avoided or as an exciting foreign country begging for intrepid exploration? That's what this book is about. So let's suit up. This will be quite a journey!

THE FIVE FURIES

Although the adult stepfamily members we interviewed told many different stories, a set of common problems emerged. One or more of the following five concerns came up time and again. These five recurrent issues, which we call the Five Furies, will reappear throughout the book. Both parental couples and adult children had these same five basic fears and concerns, although they often had opposing views of who was causing the problem. The Five Furies are:

1. **Fear of Abandonment and Isolation:** the fear that you will lose a relationship that you depend upon for emotional and/or financial support and the fear that you will be pushed aside and left in a lonely limbo.

2. **Fidelity to Family:** worry about changes in loyalty. Fidelity problems occur when members of the original family worry that the parent will lose his/her old loyalty after remarriage. The children may also feel that they themselves are demonstrating a lack of fidelity by sup-

porting their remarrying parent. In the new stepfamily, other concerns surface. Either spouse may feel that the new partner is overly committed to his or her old family. Stepchildren also may feel that the new stepparent's biological family has too much influence.

3. **Favoritism:** concern about who is now number one. Whose wishes get top priority when choices have to be made?

4. **Finances:** for adult children, fear that they may lose money and/or property that they expected to be theirs; for parents, fear that their children care more about their inheritance than about the parent.

5. **Focus on Self to the Exclusion of Others:** anger that a parent or adult child is concerned only about himself or herself and no longer cares about the needs of others.

We have one initial piece of advice that is too important to put off any longer. One of the most valuable things you can do in dealing with your new stepfamily is to distinguish between what you *think* and what you actually *say*. What goes on inside your mind is your business. But we strongly caution you against blurting out the first thing that pops into your head. Words can be terribly destructive, especially when either the speaker or the one spoken to is in an agitated or a fragile state. Instead, make a habit of thinking about what you want to say before you say it. And remember, what you say invariably will elicit a response in the other person. In fashioning your words, you want to remember what you hope to achieve, as well as the information you wish to convey. Something more tactful and less inflammatory than detailed candor usually works best.

Here are some examples of what you might *feel* in situations involving the Five Furies, and, later, what you might *say*.

Mary, who was marrying her companion of fourteen years, and Frank, whose widowed father was remarrying, were reacting to several of the Furies—the fears and potential dangers that are usually lurking inside adult stepfamilies. As a first step in taming the Furies, you must recognize and identify each Fury accurately and honestly. Only then will you be able to construct an appropriate response.

FIVE FURIES FOR PARENTS WHO ARE REMARRYING

Let's go back to the first story about Mary, widowed for fifteen years, and see how the Five Furies come into play. Surprised that her children don't share her happiness at the prospect of her remarriage, Mary might *feel* the following:

Fury #1: Fear of Abandonment and Isolation

It's hard for me to believe that my own grown-up children are reacting as though my getting married means abandoning them. This is crazy. And they are parents themselves. I know it's the right thing for me to do, even though they might not like it and even though I might really need them in the future. They are behaving as if my getting married means I'm deserting them. I'm worried. Could this really cause a permanent rift between us?

Fury #2: Fidelity to Family

I've given my children and their children so much consideration all their lives and never dreamed they would treat me so harshly. My daughter has no right to demand an explanation from me. She's treating me like a teenager, instead of like her mother. Fourteen years is not sudden. Jim's got a problem with that? It would almost be funny if it weren't so disloyal.

Fury #3: Favoritism

My marriage does mean that Arthur has priority for me, but when my kids had to make a choice between me and their spouses, I didn't have to guess whom they would pick.

Fury #4: Finances

My son's first thought is about protecting his inheritance. After all, it is my money. Why can't he trust me? I have a pretty good track record.

Fury #5: Focus on Self

For the first time in my life, we are not part of the same team. Suddenly, I'm seeing a pair of tough, self-interested children whose first reaction is to look out for themselves. You would think they'd care more about my happiness. When I became a widow, it was all "poor dear Mom, we'll always be here for you." But now that I'm taking my life in my own hands and making a change, I've got to deal with their disapproval and stick up for what I want. We don't want the same thing. After all, I didn't just automatically love the people they chose for mates, but I learned to adjust.

WHAT A PARENT MIGHT *SAY* IN RESPONSE TO THE FIVE FURIES

So often we think of what we should have said only after the moment has passed. We may hesitate to speak because we don't want to do permanent harm to a relationship while we are still shocked or uncertain about what is happening. Thinking before we speak is a good thing: We need time to process our intense feelings.

Very early in the game, however, you need to decide what you want your new life to be like. You have to get a grip on your new parenting role. Being vague simply postpones the inevitable. Yes, you are still and forever the parent, so it's up to *you* to make your new role clear. So, give these issues serious thought *before* the announcement. Remember, if someone you love is being angrily confrontational or putting pressure on you to respond in a certain way, you don't have to *say* anything at the moment. It's okay, even advisable, to call back and take up the conversation again after you have had time to think through your response.

Here are some things you might *say* in a situation like Mary's:

Fury #1: Fear of Abandonment and Isolation

I'm having a difficult time with your reaction. It bothers me that you aren't encouraging me to make what I consider such a positive change in my life. I wonder if you might not always feel it was too soon for me to get remarried. Maybe you feel like I'm deserting you by remarrying. I don't believe this has to separate us. I'm getting married because I love Arthur, and it will make me happy and secure to be his wife. We know each other well and want to spend together the years we have left to us.

Fury #2: Fidelity to Family

I am bringing Arthur into the family as my husband. You are my son and daughter, and my marriage does not change my loyalty to you as my children.

Fury #3: Favoritism

Arthur has to be my first priority now, just as your father was during all those years when we were married. When you got married, I understood that your priorities would have to change.

Fury #4: Finances

I shall be fair to you about money and property. I have in the past, and I shall in the future.

Fury #5: Focus on Self

I know it's right for me to marry even though you may not like it very much right now. I understand your feelings, because, as a parent, I didn't automatically love the mates that you children brought home, but I learned to adjust. I kept an open mind and heart, and eventually I began to see in your mates what you saw in them. In time, I trust you will feel similarly.

THE FIVE FURIES FOR ADULT CHILDREN

For Mary's adult children and many others, a parent's remarriage is the second biggest challenge after becoming parents themselves. Because of their parent's unilateral decision, their own childhood has ended now in a crucial way, and no one is ever really prepared for this.

Even when you have children yourself, there is still the comfort of having your own parent in the background. We don't expect parents to step out of that role until they die. Yet, all at once, the remarrying parent is acting not primarily as your parent, but as just another adult.

A parent's remarriage forces adult children to reconsider familiar roles, even identity. In this new context, are you an adult or a child? What are your rights, and what are your responsibilities now? While you didn't choose to have the Furies enter your life, you are probably stuck now with at least some of them. Maybe this is how you would *feel* if you were in the shoes of Mary's adult children:

Fury #1: Fear of Abandonment and Isolation

My mother is going to be angry with me if I question her decision to get married. I don't want to lose her love. I don't want her to cut off our relationship.

Fury #2: Fidelity to Family

Why must my mother and Arthur get married rather than just live together if they really love each other? It doesn't make sense at their age. After all, they are not going to have children. That's the only real reason to marry. Arthur has been a friend, but now she is making him family. She's changing something so fundamental so late in her life. What about loyalty to us?

Fury #3: Favoritism

Her new husband might become more important to my mother than we are. Will all that legitimacy of a formal marriage forge a stronger bond between them than the one she has with us? Ours goes back to when we were born. How can someone just walk into her life and become so important to my mother just like that? This marriage will make her new husband take the place of my real father. It changes my life overnight. I thought my mother would always be there for me, and now I don't know if she will care as much. She's really rejecting us by taking this step.

Fury #4: Finances

What will happen to my inheritance? My mother is so in love she will do whatever her husband wants and not what is important to me. He shouldn't be allowed to use up what is rightfully mine.

Fury #5: Focus on Self

For the first time in my life, I'm seeing my mother in a completely different way. She is just a determined woman who is making decisions to please herself and not taking her children's interests into account. She's not at all concerned with what is going to make my life better. It's only her life that is important now. How long will this go on?

Remember, you don't want to say what occurs to you in the heat of the moment until you are able to think through what you really want to say. Even in a threatening situation, intense emotions usually cool down after you have decided how to respond.

After cooling off, here is what you might *say* if you were one of Mary's adult children:

Fury #1: Fear of Abandonment and Isolation

Being alone can't be all that much fun. Having Arthur in your life has certainly made a difference. I can see why you believe you are changing your life for the better.

Fury #2: Fidelity to Family

Not everyone knows how to take surprises. It feels sudden, so give us some time. I need to know that you still feel the loyalty to me that I feel to you. I don't want that to change just because you are getting married.

Fury #3: Favoritism

It's difficult thinking of you marrying and replacing my father with another man. It's even hard to think he's now number one. It's a lot for me to take in, even though I know and like Arthur.

Fury #4: Finances

The marriage ceremony changes things legally, and that makes me feel insecure about any property you had been planning to leave to me or my siblings. Of course, this is your own business, and I make my own income and expect to continue to support myself. Still, I want to be honest and put things on the table. Perhaps, we can discuss this at a later, not too distant time.

Fury #5: Focus on Self

You have devoted so much of your life to us and your grandchildren. It's going to be hard to give up any of that.

MORE FURIES FOR ADULT CHILDREN

Let's return to the story told by Frank, the adult child whose widowed father is remarrying. Like Frank, you may be shocked by your immediate reaction to your parent's news, even though you thought you knew yourself pretty well.

You may have to deal with disappointment, resistance, depression, or outright anger. You may also perceive issues of trust, loyalty, and finances in a new light. None of these emotional matters need be settled at once, however. Perhaps, this is how you would *feel* if you were Frank.

Fury #1: Fear of Abandonment and Isolation

I feel as though my mother is dying for the second time. From now on my father won't need me. He'll have Edith fluttering around him all the time. I'll never get to do anything alone with him anymore.

Fury #2: Fidelity to Family

This is too fast. It's not respectful to Mother. Two years later and thirty years of marriage are erased just like that. I haven't gotten over her death, and he's not only forgotten her, he's writing over her memory with a new wife.

Fury #3: Favoritism

He'll be afraid to do anything for me or my children without consulting Edith. He's so weak. He'll be under her thumb.

Fury #4: Finances

Edith is just the type of person who will spend my inheritance buying expensive clothes.

Fury #5: Focus on Self

My father always sees to it that he gets what he wants. He's pretty quick to take care of his own needs. He was that way even when my mother was alive.

Each family member will react differently when a parent announces that he/she is remarrying. As an adult stepchild, forgive yourself if you are shocked at the moment, even though you should have seen the signs that it was coming.

If the announcement completely stuns you, don't even try to respond. Simply say it's a big surprise and that you will call back. Cut yourself some slack. None of the Furies can be tamed in a single day.

When Frank is ready, he might *say:*

Fury #1: Fear of Abandonment and Isolation

Dad, I know you have been so lonely since Mom died. You haven't lived alone since before you and Mom married more than thirty years ago. I'm glad you have companionship.

Fury #2: Fidelity to Family

I still haven't gotten over Mom's death, so it will be hard for me to see her shoes filled so soon. I'm sure you understand. Give me some time.

Fury #3: Favoritism

Let's plan a time to get together and talk about the changes for the family that your remarriage will bring.

Fury #4: Finances

I guess I'm a little worried about you changing your lifestyle so dramatically. I guess, however, that you are both savvy financial planners. [At that time, if it seems right, Frank and his father can discuss inheritance issues. Frank might ask if his father has made a prenuptial agreement.]

Fury #5: Focus on Self

Dad, I'm sorry if I seem so caught up in my own sense of loss for Mom. I realize you've had more time to adjust, since you lived it every day of her illness. I need time to catch up.

FURIES FOR THE REMARRYING PARENT

If you were Frank's father, you might *feel:*

Fury #1: Fear of Abandonment and Isolation

Where is his concern about me? Why isn't he happy that I have found a wonderful partner to enjoy and do things with and who will be there for me when I am ill? He'll just phone or visit, but Edith will be at my side no matter what happens.

Fury #2: Fidelity to Family

He's talking as if I'm the child, and he's the parent. He's lecturing me as if he's carrying the "loyalty" torch and I'm abandoning the family.

Fury #3: Favoritism

Edith will be number one for me, and Frank won't like that.

Fury #4: Finances

I wonder if he is concerned that Edith and I will spend some of his inheritance? But, after all, I earned it!

Fury #5: Focus on Self

My son isn't thinking about anything but his own feelings. What nerve he has to tell me I'm not finished grieving over my wife's death. I know all about grief. I felt it every day from the time she was diagnosed until the day she died. I know what it is like to have death in the house for years.

He's still young. He can't understand how I feel about time running out at my age. Every day I live is a blessing, and now I can share it with someone I love.

If you are a parent making the announcement, you can say that you have given much thought to the concerns your children might have about your remarrying. You are prepared to hear them out, and you are confident that you can deal with each other in a constructive way.

Upon reflection, Frank's father might *say:*

Fury #1: Fear of Abandonment and Isolation

I'm glad to get your honest input, because it's important to me for us always to be frank with each other, but my decision makes sense to me.

Fury #2: Fidelity to Family

It's difficult for all of us to get over Mother's death. She will always be in my heart. But having been with her every day from the time she was diagnosed until the day she died, I had a long time to go through my grief and mourning and finally accept my loss.
I think you are at a different place in the grieving process, and I don't expect that you can accept my new wife until you are further along.

Fury #3: Favoritism

At my age, what may seem "too soon" and "impulsive" to you is quite reasonable to me. You may not understand that fully until you are at my point in life. So, it may look like I'm charging off with no concern for you, but that's not the case. You'll always have a special place in my heart.

Fury #4: Finances

Frank, Edith and I have given a lot of thought to the difference in our lifestyles. We plan to live with an eye on our financial future. So, don't worry.

Fury #5: Focus on Self

From the outside, I know this might look like a selfish, silly decision, but I've been thinking about this for a while. After your mother got sick, I realized how easily life can be taken away. So, I'm making the most mature choice I can: to take the opportunity for life and happiness while I'm still healthy enough to do so. I hope you'll support my chance for a full life.

These "might think" and "might say" scenarios are simply examples—you can adapt them or use them as springboards for your own appropriate responses.

As you can see, the bride and groom's joyous announcement often boomerangs, striking different family members in unexpected ways. The announcement often triggers fears in the adult child. Will I lose my parent's love and attention or my long-expected inheritance? How will the new spouse, an outsider, affect the family? Who gets priority now? Late-life courtship may be the first time a parent has acted entirely out of self-interest, or it can be a reminder of how selfish a parent has always been. Did you really expect your parent to ask your permission to marry? In fact, some families do reverse roles that way, although it is a role reversal that often spells disaster for the new marriage.

When a parent decides to remarry, some family members manage very well; most have to struggle. The struggle is often worse because there is little help, either from within or outside the family. Stepfamilies occupy largely undiscovered territory. Outsiders rarely understand what the family members are going through, and the family members themselves are often lost at first.

The announcement is the prologue to a whole new life for everyone in the family. In the next chapter, we raise the curtain on Act I . . . the wedding.

CHAPTER 2

The Wedding: Here Comes the Bride, Here Comes Complexity

Planning a wedding creates a human minefield. Everyone tenses up. Unexpected explosions leave the participants dazed and wounded. Wedding planning becomes a projective test. The key relatives play out their worries about how the upcoming marriage will change their relationship with the member of the couple who "belongs" to them. So why is anyone surprised when the weddings of older couples with adult children sometimes become battle zones?

The bride and groom, of course, want everybody to be as happy as they are. They're envisioning a joyous celebration. The new couple wants all their adult children to feel included. So, they often make a great effort to ensure that the wedding is, indeed, a family affair.

Maryanne, a forty-six-year-old entrepreneur, told us:

I guess I was very naïve. Since this was my first marriage, and I've missed out on having kids, I was very excited about inheriting a "real" family with a grown child. This seemed like the best of all worlds, a grown-up kid you didn't have to diaper, with a life of her own, but still a real part of the family. Well, I was in for a shock.

Michael's daughter, Sally, was off in graduate school and working part-time, but she was used to being her daddy's best girl, particularly since the divorce. She hadn't gotten along with her own mother, so I thought maybe she would be able to see me in a different light. I guess she did, but not quite the light I was hoping for. Instead, she looked at me as an intruder on her private preserve. After all, she had her mother under control. Sally kept her distance from me, but she clung even closer to her father.

I felt sorry for Michael, because I could see that he felt trapped, even embarrassed. I think his guilt about the divorce, long before I was on the scene, made him very vulnerable. We couldn't really talk about it, but I could see how awkward he felt. We tried to plan the wedding for the summer to avoid conflicts with Sally's school calendar, but Sally kept telling us each date we picked wouldn't work for her. We finally agreed upon a date. Then, at the last minute, she had a work assignment overseas and couldn't make it. I couldn't believe it. Michael was very disappointed, but he kept up a brave front and took the work assignment at face value.

THE FIVE FURIES FOR THE ADULT CHILD

Sally, the adult stepchild, appears to be the bad guy here, spoiling her father's wedding plans. But who is the true spoiler? Look at it from Sally's point of view. Once Maryanne linked up with her father, Sally began losing her primacy to him. Is she supposed to be thrilled by that? Adult children commonly see the impending marriage as making a bad situation both worse and permanent. While the parent is singing, "Here comes the bride," the children may be humming, "Here comes the wicked stepmother or father."

Let's consider what Sally, might *feel*:

Fury #1: Fear of Abandonment and Isolation

Ever since Maryanne has come into my dad's life, he has been acting as if being a father isn't that important to him anymore. When she's around, he can't even sit on the couch and talk without holding her hand or cuddling and looking into her eyes. It's as if I don't exist when they are together. And, of course, I can't say a word about it.

Fury #2: Fidelity to Family

Maryanne is falling all over herself trying to be my friend or surrogate mother or aunt or something. Why doesn't she cool it? I've got a mother.

Fury #3: Favoritism

My father used to be thrilled to hear from me whenever I telephoned him. He would want to keep on talking, and I always had to be the one to say I had to go. Now he rushes to get off the phone because they are "on their way out" or "just sitting down to dinner."

Fury #4: Finances

Between the new home they are buying and the trips they take, they won't have a problem spending his money.

Fury #5: Focus on Self

Dad wants to tie me down to a date for his wedding ceremony, not thinking about how much I have to do between work and school. Well, if it works out with my schedule, okay. But if it doesn't, they'll just have to do the wedding themselves, just like they are managing to do everything else.

These are all very legitimate, understandable, and normal emotional responses. Nonetheless, if Sally were to express these feelings to her father and Maryanne, there would be explosive consequences. If you feel the way Sally does and you feel that you must articulate your fears and concerns, okay. But say them only to your most trustworthy friend. It would be a terrible mistake to present your emotions in their raw form to your parent.

Howl and punch a pillow in private, but don't self-destruct by telling all. Take as long as you need to vent emotionally. Then, when you are ready, get down to work on taming the Five Furies. To do that, you will need to draw on your integrity and your wisdom. Disciplined brainwork is necessary in order to change undigested emotion into a successful action plan. But having such a game plan will make you feel less emotional and more in control.

THE EIGHT TACT AND TACKING SKILLS

This is one of the most important parts of this book. It will provide you with the essential skills that you need to be happier in your new stepfamily as you learn to deal with the Five Furies. But, more important, it will provide you with skills that will help you whenever you are involved in a difficult transaction with another person.

There are at least eight strategies that you can use to resolve conflicts. We call the eight skills, or principles, needed to resolve conflict "Tact and Tacking skills." The term *tact* you already know: it means diplomacy, doing things in a thoughtful, nonabrasive way. Virtually any message is more likely to be heard if said with tact, as well as conviction. *Tacking* is a term that sailors know. It means getting to your destination in a series of moves, each at an angle, rather than in a straight line.

Some of these Tact and Tacking strategies are meant to be applied quickly. They function as emotional Band-Aids. You can teach yourself to use them reflexively when you find yourself in a social emergency. Other Tact and Tacking strategies are useful over longer periods of time.

The eight Tact and Tacking strategies are:

1. **Reframe the Issue. Turn a sow's ear into a silk purse. Look for a kinder interpretation of negative behavior.** This strategy helps you to see the same set of facts, originally viewed as negative, in a more positive way. By reframing, a parent may understand an adult child's anger about the remarriage as demonstrating an excessive attachment to the parent instead of excessive resentment. This strategy requires you to accentuate the positive. Practice seeing your own failures and the failures of others in a more positive light as a necessary step in learning how to be successful.

2. **Let Time Pass.** This strategy involves letting the passage of time decrease the intensity of negative feelings. In the short term, it might mean giving yourself a twenty-four-hour cooling off period instead of blurting out an angry response. Remember, "The tongue is the enemy of the neck." Try not to criticize impulsively. Some tips for dealing with emotional crises:

   • Do not engage in serious discussions when you are tired. Schedule another time to talk when you are well rested.

   • Don't offer criticism without having a constructive reason for offering it, particularly about your partner's children.

   • Write down immediate uncensored feelings and lock them up in a drawer or file them under electronic lock and key on your computer. Or, better yet, simply file them more safely in your mind.

   Usually, these passions diminish in strength over the months and years. There are plenty of exceptions, though: in stepfamilies, sometimes each meeting exacerbates the old bad feelings. In such cases, limiting the frequency and length of contact may make the most sense.

3. **Become an Observer, then a participant observer. Get some emotional distance on your new stepfamily by assuming the role of a cultural anthropologist.** Observe how the two tribes approach each other. Take notes. Talk with a friend who is in a similar situation. Besides giving you emotional distance, this strategy helps you get a coherent, holistic view of the family situation. This strategy allows you to look at everyone's behavior, including your own, in a more dispassionate, objective way and helps you keep track of what is happening.

   Notice the habits of each clan as it gather for meals, holidays, and vacations. Record attempts at inclusion and exclusion. In the long term, this approach will allow you to anticipate predictable hot spots (holidays, visits, illnesses, etc.).

   In stepfamilies, prevention is worth a thousand cures. Make a serious effort to honor old rituals, as well as create new traditions and loyalties that bond the two families together over time. Recognize the universality of family issues and become less judgmental.

4. **Use Tenacity; stick up for what you believe.** This strategy requires you to maintain and defend your core values (the personal rules of behavior that allow you to maintain your integrity). This includes managing the impulse to please everyone.

5. **Trade and Negotiate; give and take.** This strategy involves learning how to negotiate until you both achieve win-win results.

6. **Use Forgiveness, Empathy, Apology, and Tolerance (FEAT):** This strategy involves the attitudes and behaviors directed toward others. We devised the mnemonic FEAT to help you remember the elements of this strategy. *Forgiveness* is maintenance of a positive relationship despite your having been treated in an unfair or harmful way. Remember that forgiving the person does not mean you have to forgive the behavior. *Empathy* is the capacity to identify with and show compassion for another person. This involves generosity in all its manifestations—emotional, spiritual, and financial. *Apology* is acknowledgment and admission that your own behavior has been wrong. Apologize without reservation and directly to the person you have mistreated. *Tolerance* is the ability to see that views contrary to your own may have validity.

7. **Practice Transformation Through Wisdom.** This strategy calls for making changes within yourself as a result of new insights and understanding. It requires a process of maturation that allows you to accept your own frailties, as well as those of others. Wisdom often consists of managing your own expectations in a realistic way.

8. **Practice Turning Away from the Problem and Letting It Go.** Sometimes, the best and only strategy is to recognize that you cannot solve a particular problem. Then, find ways to keep it from influencing your present thoughts and feelings. Recognize what cannot be changed, and don't allow it to dominate your life.

These eight strategies can help you manage all situations of conflict. We found they were repeatedly used by the most successful stepfamilies we studied.

TACT AND TACKING SKILLS FOR THE ADULT CHILD

If you are in a situation like Sally's, the about-to-be stepdaughter, here are some suggestions for what you might say, using the eight Tact and Tacking skills. This is not a script to follow point by point. This is what Sally might *say* to her dad:

Tact and Tacking #1: Reframe the Issue

Dad, this is a very special time in your life. It seems to me that we used to be closer when you were alone, but now you'll have a wife. I have to admit that I'll be relieved to have somebody to take care of you so I won't have to worry about you so much.

Tact and Tacking #2: Time

I'm really not yet over your divorce from my mother, so it's hard for me to get used to your getting remarried. I need to give it time.

Tact and Taking #3: Become an Observer

Your marriage puts you and your new wife and me into new roles. We may bump up against each other until the three of us learn the best way of working out our new relationships.

Tact and Tacking #4: Tenacity

I don't want to be part of the decision about the wedding date because I really don't know if I'll be able to keep my promise. Right now, I have to work on my own life and be free to take advantage of opportunities that come my way. I'll come if I'm able, but you have to understand what has to come first for me at my age.

Tact and Tacking #5: Trade and Negotiate

It's hard to go from being very close to you to being more distant. When you and Mom got divorced, you needed me a lot, and I got used to it. Now, of course, Maryanne is the most important person in your life, and you don't need to be with me nearly as much. Later on, I hope we can come back to somewhere in the middle.

Tact and Tacking #6: Forgiveness, Empathy, Apology, and Tolerance

Having a stepmother is not a big plus in my life. On the other hand, I can understand why you are getting married. I'm sorry that I am not able to celebrate something so important as this with you. I'll try to arrange my work so I can come to future events. I hope we can maintain our basic love and trust even though my decision is not what you probably wish it to be.

Tact and Tacking #7: Transformation Through Wisdom

We can't force togetherness. We can't make a family on demand. Let's wait and see how it goes. I have to accept that, and you do, too.

Tact and Tacking #8: Turn Away

Let's try not to be too resentful of each other about the wedding. I'm trying to drop it. I really don't want to keep holding on to negative feelings.

FIVE FURIES FOR THE PARENT

Let's look at how Michael, the father, might *feel:*

Fury #1: Fear of Abandonment and Isolation

I can't believe this is happening. This is my darling daughter, the light of my life. Sally was the single best thing to come out of my marriage. Now, I feel that she's threatening to divorce me as her father.

Fury #2: Fidelity to Family

I've never turned her down on anything that really mattered to her. Where's her loyalty to me?

Fury #3: Favoritism

Now she might join forces with her mother and turn me into a monster.

Fury #4: Finances

She always has had time for me when she needed financial help. Funny she hasn't time now.

Fury #5: Focus on Self

Sally has made it so difficult to plan my wedding date. We bent over backward to accommodate her. How can she be so self-centered?

Michael might *say* to Sally:

Tact & Tacking #1: Reframe the Issue

My getting married is turning out to be a test for you and me to learn to tolerate our differences. This is the first time in quite a while that we haven't seen eye to eye on something so important. It's a test of our love, and, if we make it, our relationship will be that much stronger.

Tact and Tacking #2: Time

Years from now, we'll see this whole thing in better perspective.

Tact and Tacking #3: Become an Observer

I am going to try to step away from my own exclusive point of view and regard this as a three-person issue with no right or wrong answer.

Tact and Tacking #4: Tenacity

As your father, I want to continue to give you many things, but I can't give you the power to hurt me so much. It's clear to me, from the number of dates I suggested that don't work out for you, that coming to my wedding is not at the top of your list. I'm trying to accept that.

Tact and Tacking #5: Trade and Negotiate

I know that you didn't choose to have a new person—an outsider—injected into the family. I can see how this time of great joy for me is a time of disruption for you. Is there some way for me to make it easier for you? Do you think we can both give a little?

Tact and Tacking #6: Tolerance and Forgiveness

I'd hoped you would be an important part of my wedding, but sometimes you just don't get everything you want. If things change for you at the last minute, we would love to have you there.

Tact and Tacking #7: Transformation Through Wisdom

You are a grown-up, but you will always be my beloved daughter, now and forever. No one can ever replace you, and Maryanne has no intention of doing so. Right now, you probably feel squeezed out a little, and you have been a good sport. Let's plan for us to have time alone soon to do some of the things that we enjoy together.

Tact and Tacking #8: Turn Away

I'm not going to focus on something like your attending the wedding ceremony, which cannot be resolved. I'm willing to let it go.

FIVE FURIES FOR THE NEW STEPMOTHER

Maryanne, Michael's new wife, might *feel:*

Fury #1: Fear of Abandonment and Isolation

From what Michael says, Sally and her mother are estranged. Michael is like a father and a mother to her. He's all she's got; however, he's all I've got too. I feel like Sally doesn't want to let me in.

Fury #2: Fidelity to Family

I wanted so much for us to be one family. Instead of that, I'm going to be cast as the wicked stepmother. Had I known how their loyalty to each other would play out, I might have thought longer about marrying him.

Fury #3: Favoritism

I feel as though I'm competing with Sally for Michael. Sally was his favorite before I came into the picture. I can't wait until she gets a boyfriend of her own. I think her dependency on Michael has held her back from that.

Fury #4: Finances

Michael is overly guilty about feeling that he's deserted Sally by getting married. As a result, he spoils her and feels he has to fulfill her every whim.

Fury #5: Focus on Self

Sally is being selfish. She doesn't want the wedding to happen at all, and she is not considering how much her presence at the ceremony means to her father.

TACT AND TACKING SKILLS FOR STEPPARENTS

Maryanne may damage her fledgling marriage if she doesn't use all her wisdom and skill to deal with her new stepfamily. If she wants her marriage to succeed, Maryanne might *say* to her husband-to-be:

Tact and Tacking #1: Reframe the Issue

I'm glad Sally had the courage to tell us she won't be at the wedding. That way, we won't be waiting on our wedding day and worrying about whether we should go ahead with the ceremony.

Tact and Tacking #2: Time

You've been so close and always there for Sally. She doesn't want her relationship with you to change. It could take a while for her to accept me. Let's not try to rush it.

Tact and Tacking #3: Become an Observer

I'm going to step back and observe without judging anyone. I think we are just learning our new roles.

Tact and Tacking #4: Tenacity

This is a blow for you and me. We'll probably have to face other disappointments together in the future, and we must make sure this kind of thing doesn't divide the two of us. We are the role models here, and we can teach Sally what a really good partnership in marriage is like.

Tact and Tacking #5: Trade and Negotiate

When I think about it realistically, there isn't any reason why Sally should feel she has to go out of her way to please me by coming to our wedding. I'm going to have to work on building a relationship with her before expecting her to do something like that for me.

Tact and Tacking #6: Tolerance and Forgiveness

I hadn't counted on Sally's power to reject us and hurt our feelings that way, but that's part of sharing our lives. She might be reacting to feeling rejected by us. I'll try to learn not to let her behavior affect my caring for her.

Tact and Tacking #7: Transformation Through Wisdom

I might have overstepped my bounds by having a fantasy of Sally becoming a surrogate daughter. I've been trying to replace what I thought was a void in her life and mine by offering her something positive that she and her mother don't have right now. Maybe, that is too much of a reach for now. Experiences that we have together will gradually form whatever relationship we ought to have.

Tact and Tacking #8: Turn Away

I can't let my disappointment about Sally's rejection of me be a negative in my life and harm our marriage. I need to let go of it.

Many of those we interviewed raised similar issues. For example, someone whom we'll call Mark, a twenty-two-year-old computer scientist, described how he felt when he had to decide whether or not to attend his father's wedding.

I spent the whole day before my dad's wedding talking on the phone with my mother. She had left town because she couldn't stand being here, knowing this was really the end of their relationship. They were married twenty-five years, and they split up five years ago. At first, my mother was so angry with him I think she was relieved. But when my father hooked up with this other woman, things began to change. My mother really wanted to reconcile, and my brother and I were hoping they would. But things just went from bad to worse. My father and Andrea, his girlfriend, decided to get married. My brother and I were invited to the wedding, but we didn't know what to do. I love my dad, but I think he's made a terrible mistake.

So, you can see why I felt torn in two directions about the wedding. I want my dad to be part of my life, but I hated seeing my mother in such misery. My mother spent a lot of time on the long-distance line with me the day before the wedding. We spoke about six different times. She was trying to comfort me, but I could tell she would be very hurt if I went to the wedding. I finally decided not to go.

THE FIVE FURIES FOR ADULT CHILDREN

What Mark might *feel:*

Fury #1: Fear of Abandonment and Isolation

I'm not going to get on my mother's enemies list of all the people who betrayed her. I'm not going to pay the price of going to the wedding, no matter how bad my father feels. But I know he will never forget that I didn't stand up there with him at the ceremony. I don't want to lose him, either. How can I show him that I love him too?

Fury #2: Fidelity to Family

Now, my dad is causing even more problems for me by deciding that it's not enough just to live with his girlfriend, but he's got to marry her. That's really the end of any chance of my folks getting back together. Now, I have to hold my mother's hand while she goes through that.

Fury #3: Favoritism

From now on, Dad's new wife will come first.

Fury #4: Finances

I wonder if Dad will have a second family with Andrea? She's twenty years younger than he is. That'll certainly drain his pocketbook.

Fury #5: Focus on Self

Ever since my dad left my mother, my brother and I have been the ones who have had to deal with all of her misery. We had to listen to her complaining about his bad behavior, and we had to comfort her when she was crying. Since they split, my brother and I have had to take over my dad's job of being her protector. The marriage vow Dad made thirty years ago has become our responsibility.

TACT AND TACKING SKILLS FOR ADULT CHILDREN

Mark might *say* the following:

Tact and Tacking #1: Reframe the Issue

Dad, you taught me to stand by my principles, and that's what I'm doing.

Tact and Tacking #2: Time

This will be hard to forget, but it won't hurt so much a year from now.

Tact and Tacking #3: Become an Observer

We are in a situation where there is more than one valid point of view.

Tact and Tacking #4: Tenacity

Dad, I'm sorry I'm not going to be by your side at your wedding, but I have to do what I think is best. I'm being forced to decide between your needs and Mother's needs. I finally decided not to attend your wedding as a way of showing my support to Mother on a day that will be very rough for her.

Tact and Tacking #5: Trade and Negotiate

I'd like to make a date for me to take you and Andrea to dinner so we can celebrate your marriage. I know it's not the same thing as attending your wedding, but I'd like to start there to show you my love and commitment.

Tact and Tacking #6: Tolerance and Forgiveness

I can see your point of view, and I hope you will forgive me.

Tact and Tacking #7: Transformation Through Wisdom

I truly want you to be happy with Andrea, and I wish you all the best.

Tact and Tacking #8: Turn Away

This could permanently damage our relationship. I don't want to discuss that. Let's both try hard to get over it.

THE FIVE FURIES FOR PARENTS

Mark's dad might *feel:*

Fury #1: Fear of Abandonment and Isolation

Mark is letting me down just when I was counting on him. I am always there for him.

Fury #2: Fidelity to Family

The divorce was final five years ago, for crying out loud. He should be a son to me and stand up for me on a day that's so important in my life.

Fury #3: Favoritism

He was always his mother's favorite. He's twenty-two years old, and he's still trying to please his mother. He's ignoring the fact that his mother was the one who wanted out, but then never accepted the consequences.

Fury #4: Finances

He's always the first to ask questions about money. He's not a dependent child anymore so why can't he accept financial responsibility for his own life?

Fury #5: Focus on Self

He's so worried about his own problems. He can't step up like a man to accept his responsibility to me.

TACT AND TACKING SKILLS FOR THE PARENT

What Mark's dad might *say* to Mark:

Tact and Tacking #1: Reframe the Issue

I guess the problem is that families who love each other also know how to hurt each other.

Tact and Tacking #2: Time

Let's both give it some time and see if the intensity of feeling hurt gets less. There's still time to talk later when we'll probably be better able to do it.

Tact and Tacking #3: Become an Observer

This situation seems like a huge knot, with each of us pulling on our own end and making it tighter. Neither of us is getting what he wants. Each of us has to figure out what it is about the role we are in that makes us pull so hard.

Tact and Tacking #4: Tenacity

I'm very disappointed that you won't be at the wedding. I love you very much and want my sons at my side.

Tact and Tacking #5: Trade and Negotiate

Remember, it was your mother's decision to divorce. Attending my wedding is not being disloyal to your mother. It is punishing me. Can you figure out some other way to celebrate my marriage with Andrea after our wedding?

Tact and Tacking #6: Tolerance and Forgiveness

I guess I wasn't thinking much about your mother's feelings. She's probably hurting a lot, without much to offset those feelings. I'll feel sorry that you won't be there, but I don't want you getting caught in the middle. I know you'll be there with me in spirit.

Tact and Tacking #7: Transformation Through Wisdom

It would be great if you could get to know Andrea better. Over the past few years, she's been a very positive part of my life. I hope you will learn to appreciate her.

Tact and Tacking #8: Turn Away

Now I'd like to put this conversation behind us and go forward.

THE WEDDING DILEMMA

For adult children whose entire lives have been spent within the enduring structure of their parents' long-term marriage, a divorced or widowed parent's decision to remarry may seem to threaten the very foundation of the child's existence. The old family shared all the important events that make a life—birthdays, holidays, graduations, marriages, and perhaps the births of grandchildren. The new marriage threatens to eradicate that shared history. It's not surprising that the child feels disoriented—the remarriage feels not like a joyous event but more like the loss of everything the child knows. Who will continue to remember and treasure the family's past and all its rituals?

Betty Jo, the fifty-five-year-old daughter of a couple who divorced after thirty years of marriage, described her emotions as she watched her father exchange vows with his new wife:

My parents had been married for thirty years. Of course, they had their disagreements, but who doesn't? I couldn't imagine their getting divorced. Maybe if they had gotten divorced when I was younger, their marriage wouldn't have been such a big part of my own entire life. So, it was very hard for me to accept the divorce. I think it was harder than if it had happened when I was younger. I think it was even harder because my mother didn't want it.

At my father's wedding to his new wife, I couldn't stop crying. I kept thinking, "But he made all those same vows to my mother! How can he be making those promises again?" I was pretty terrible to my stepmother for a long time. I felt I could dump on her, vent the anger that I really felt toward my father without risking my relationship with him. After a number of years, I finally apologized to her, but I have never confronted my father about the divorce.

Staying away from the wedding, however, creates another set of problems. Thirty-year-old Erika put it this way:

It feels more comfortable at that moment not to go to the wedding, but it makes things harder in the long run. One of the main fears is that you are going to be edged out. By not going, you edge yourself out.

Watching your parent marry someone new is strong stuff. If your other parent is still living, remarriage ends any hope for reconciliation. If that parent has died, it may feel like the last trace of his or her existence is being obliterated. The marriage ceremony begins to record the music of a new life over an earlier melody that will never be heard again. The wedding ushers in a new and unknown era.

Adult stepchildren whose other parent died long ago may experience an especially powerful sense of loss. The children may have grown very close to the surviving parent, far closer than they were when the other biological parent was living. The appearance of the new spouse inevitably changes the relationship between the parent and adult child. Since the child didn't ask for this change, he or she may have a hard time seeing it as anything other than a change for the worse.

WHAT IF THE CHILDREN STAY AWAY?

After listening to dozens of stories about "the wedding," we began to think differently about these events. Usually in first marriages, the children are not yet a factor. Think about it. Most of the time, children do not witness the wedding of their biological parents. Ordinarily, children only hear about their parents' wedding and see pictures, maybe a video, of it. It is a distant happy event experienced through gauzy layers of nostalgia and time.

If the Great Matchmaker thought that children should attend their parents' wedding, the kids would be at the first one. So, why do we think the children have to attend their parent's wedding the second, third, or fourth time around?

Our advice: Think very carefully about the wedding and how strongly you feel that the children must be there. There's much more to marriage than having a picture-perfect wedding with the smiling children arrayed around you. A marriage is made up of many shared moments, not just watching a parent say, "I do." Don't fall into the trap of thinking that an adult child's reluctance to attend the wedding means your new stepfamily is doomed. The wedding may be too emotionally charged an event for some family members, and it might be best for everyone if those who felt they couldn't handle it didn't attend. Don't make attendance at the wedding a make-it-or-break-it symbol of anyone's loyalty or love. Better to wish a family member were at the wedding than to rue the day he or she came and spoiled it. A wedding full of tension and resentment serves neither the newlyweds nor their adult children.

WHAT IF THE PARENTS SLIP AWAY?

We've focused on the children's choice not to attend the wedding. What happens—and it occasionally does—when the couple decides to elope or "just slip away and do it" without the children? This may come as a shock to the adult children, who had no idea marriage was in the offing. It may also surprise those who expected it, but also assumed they'd be invited. We spoke to several adult stepfamily members who found themselves in both of these situations. In every case, the children were upset. It was only a matter of *how* upset they were.

Jodi and her brother, Jim, were each married with families of their own. Their mother had died three years before, and their father lived 1,500 miles away. They were in touch, but they didn't see much of him. This is how Jodi described the situation:

My father was always a very difficult person, for my mother and for us, too. But we love him, and he is our father, whatever his faults. He never told us much about his social life after my mother died, so we didn't think he even had a girlfriend. So, you can imagine how we felt when we received a postcard—I said "postcard"—marked Las Vegas, with six words: "Just got married. See you soon." We couldn't believe it. We were hurt and furious. We were ready to hate Isabelle, his new wife. How could they both be so thoughtless? As it turned out, when we met Isabelle, we liked her. She was a good woman. We both thought she was probably too good for him. We turned out to be correct. She hung out with him for five

years, and they were in counseling most of the time. She finally left him,
and we don't blame her one bit.

In this case, both Jodi and Jim eventually understood their exclusion as consistent with their father's typical behavior. They were able to separate their feelings about the wedding from their opinion of their stepmother, whom they came to like and respect. Their anger over the wedding gradually subsided.

In many of the other couples who made the decision to get married without the children present, both partners were seen by their children as sharing responsibility for the decision. Occasionally, however, it was initially seen as a decision imposed by the new stepparent. That interpretation often led to short-term, sometimes long-term, friction with the stepparent.

In one family, with eight children living in four countries, the choice was clearly a joint decision by the new couple. They simply decided things would get too complicated if they invited their children, all of whom were married, with a total of fifteen children of their own. It was wintertime, travel was difficult, and the kids were in school. Bud and Heather knew that no one date would be convenient for everyone, unless they planned the wedding at least a year in advance. And they didn't want to wait that long. Here is Bud's description of what happened:

Heather and I had gone back and forth about getting married versus living together. We've been living together, more or less, for the last few years. Finally, we decided we wanted to get married. As we talked about planning a wedding, it became very obvious to us—and we don't even know their schedules in detail—that it would be difficult to get all the kids together on any single date soon, or maybe in our lifetimes. And we didn't want to get hung up waiting for their schedules to clear. Once we made up our minds, we really wanted to do it right away. We didn't want to wait a year to do this. We're older. Time means something different to us. So, we decided we'd do it very quietly and simply and then later have a wedding reception with enough notice so that everyone—or most everyone—could come.

We just went to the town hall and were married by a justice of the peace. The witnesses were the justice's staff people. We didn't tell anyone. We felt like teenagers eloping. Then, we went to Hawaii, where it was nice and warm, for ten days. We've been away together longer than that at other times, so the children didn't notice anything unusual. When we got back, we called each of our children. Some of them were okay with it; others weren't. But that's okay with us. It's our life. They have pretty full lives of their own, and we don't expect them to consult us in advance about decisions they make. We're all grown-ups. I think my kids like Heather, and Heather's kids like me. So, it's no big deal. And if any of them doesn't like it, they'll just have to get used to it. It wasn't meant as an insult to them. It was meant as a happy decision for us.

Their children, as you might have guessed, tended to see it somewhat differently. Their reactions ranged from outright indignation and intense hurt to resigned acceptance. Several were quite content that their parent had married, but still felt some residual anger or hurt about not being invited to the wedding.

When we interviewed Bud's and Heather's adult children, the wedding had taken place the previous year. By then, the two children whom we interviewed (one of Bud's and one of Heather's) assured us they were happy with the results, if not the wedding arrangements, *per se*. They reported that only one of their siblings was still quite angry. In fact, three of the children (two of Heather's and one of Bud's) had joined forces to throw the newlyweds a postwedding reception that spring. Although not all of the adult stepchildren and grandchildren could attend, many of Bud's and Heather's friends were there to celebrate with them.

Deciding not to have the children attend has built-in costs and benefits. These are the most obvious ones:

BENEFITS

- allows flexibility to arrange the wedding and honeymoon to suit the new couple's own pleasure, needs, and timetable;

- avoids arguments, complaints, and debates about *everything*—from why are you marrying that person to why are you having such a big/small wedding and why aren't you inviting all the cousins. These are all the same questions that might be raised with a first marriage;

- avoids creating a "command performance" event, which may be impossible for some children to attend, leaving them with both guilt and hurt feelings;

- avoids the time and financial expense of a family-style wedding for parents, as well as adult children;

- creates an opportunity for the adult children to demonstrate that they are mature, understanding, welcoming, and generous adults.

COSTS

- the likelihood of hurting the adult children's and stepchildren's feelings;

- the possibility of each set of biological children blaming the new step-parent for the decision.

- the chance of evoking lingering negative effects on the stepchildren's (and maybe stepgrandchildren's) relationships with their new stepparent (or stepgrandparent).

One last recommendation about the wedding to everyone concerned: Try to remember that this is a special time of happiness for the new couple. It's their treasured moment. Don't spoil it, and don't let anyone else rain on their parade, either. If you are the bride or groom, be kind and fair—not only to the kids, but to yourselves. And there is another important point: Everyone needs to remember that the parents are grown-ups, and they're entitled to do what they want with their own lives.

To the children: Try to remember how much your parent has done to bring you happiness throughout your life, even when it meant sacrificing his or her own needs. If you are a parent yourself, you'll know what we mean. Besides, this is a good time to reduce that "diaper account" (all the countless times your parent got up in the middle of the night to answer your cry, change your diapers, or give you your antibiotic, etc.). You can never quite zero out your diaper account, but this situation at least offers you the chance to make a nice dent in it.

Now that the marriage has taken place, significant new relationships have been created. Your next step is to determine how close you want to be to your new steprelatives. In the next chapter, we'll look at family roles and other important step matters.

CHAPTER 3

Step Matters: Which Role Will You Play?

We have known for decades the roles we play in our birth families, whether we like those roles or not. But what roles shall we assume as adults in our new stepfamilies? Which roles shall we choose, and which roles will be thrust upon us? Uncertainty about these important step matters, as we call them, caused anxiety in almost every stepfamily we studied.

In this chapter, we'll describe six roles that we have seen in almost all the adult stepfamilies we met. Each of these roles consists of a cluster of attitudes and behaviors, and, in real life, people play a mixture of these parts. The six roles that we have observed are: the Joiner, the Guardian Angel, the Unifier, the Indifferent, the Distancer, and the Destabilizer. Each of the first three roles, starting with the Joiner, is characterized by an increasing desire to affiliate with the new stepfamily. The last three, beginning with the Indifferent, are characterized by an escalating desire to distance oneself from or, in the case of the Destabilizer, to undermine the new stepfamily. Most people decide intuitively and largely unconsciously whether they are for or against the new family. In this chapter, we shall describe these roles and how they affect the dynamics of stepfamilies in ways that may help you better understand your own feelings and behavior and those of your new relatives.

How you relate to your stepfamily appears to be a consequence of several related factors: your genes, your basic view of human nature, and your prior cultural and psychological experiences with family life. But whatever your past, the role you will play in your new family is not carved in stone. Your role in your birth family probably changed over the years, as you matured and weathered various life crises. Your role in your new family can also be expected to change over time. In the meantime, we believe there is a mathematics of family life. In any given stepfamily, the sum of positive and negative roles is a good measure of its cohesiveness and contentment. If the majority are Indifferent and the remainder are mostly Distancers, one Unifier is not likely to prevail, no matter how desperately he or she tries.

It is our experience with adult stepfamilies that there is no single response to becoming a member of a stepfamily. The events themselves—a parent's remarriage, the addition of stepchildren, the acquisition of new stepsisters or stepbrothers—are ambiguous. The meaning of each of these events is the one that the participant assigns to it. The events can be perceived as positive, negative, and anything in between. The meaning is what you make it.

Like nations, some families have porous boundaries and open borders. The family members have a culture of inclusiveness, which welcomes outsiders. They are adventurous, curious about people, and seek new relationships.

Other families have tighter, less penetrable boundaries. The family members are more likely to be exclusive, suspicious, or simply uninterested in outsiders. They tend to view the world as one in which the family is on one side and everyone else is on the other. These attitudes may stem from a pessimistic view of human nature based on unpleasant experiences, or they may reflect cultural traditions. Or they may flow from strong positive feelings about the importance of loyalty to blood relations.

WHAT SHOULD YOU EXPECT OF YOURSELF IN YOUR ADULT STEPFAMILY ROLE?

You are better off if you know at the outset what type of involvement you want with your stepfamily. Most of us, however, don't know right away. If you have been in a stepfamily for some time and feel that you are too close, or not close enough, to your new relatives, you are probably ready for a change. You may not be able single-handedly to bring about the exact degree of connection or intimacy you want, but at least you'll be clear-eyed about your goal. Each of the roles we identified has its own rights and responsibilities, and each reflects the investment the individual is willing to make in the lives of other stepfamily members.

FOR THE OLDER COUPLE

We have not observed any gender difference in how much intrafamilial involvement is considered optimal by the older couple. Husbands, however, think it will happen naturally. Wives tend to feel much more responsible than their husbands for actively creating one big happy stepfamily. In their work on late-in-life marriages, Barbara Vinick and Susan Lanspery find that stepmothers are the "carpenters" in the new stepfamily—the ones who try to build relationships that work out right.*

Women may feel compelled to accomplish this ambitious task, in part, because they want to counter the negative image of the stepmother. Remarrying women are painfully aware of the stereotype of the cruel stepmother—after all, they, too, heard the story of Cinderella while growing up. One new stepmother told us she had been advised by another, "Keep your mouth shut and your wallet open"—in other words, don't criticize and be generous.

The role of stepfather carries less cultural baggage, despite considerable evidence of stepfathers' violence toward younger children. The lack of negative stepfather stereotypes may be one reason why stepfathers feel less pressure to make the two families into one. Besides, until recently, fathers commonly ceded emotional responsibility for the family to their wives.

Let's examine more closely each of the six roles we found in the course of our study (the numbers that follow each name indicate the degree of affiliation with or distance from the new family each role represents). Can you recognize yourself in one of the following roles?

1. **The Joiner—plus 1:** a proactive stepfamily member who wants connectedness with the new stepfamily. The spouse or adult stepchild who chooses this role tries to make a place for himself or herself in the other biological family.

2. **The Guardian Angel—plus 2:** a Joiner who, in addition, helps a new stepfamily member to become a part of his/her family.

3. **Unifier—plus 3:** a stepparent or adult stepchild who goes even further and attempts to create a situation in which all members of both families feel they belong to a single, larger family. The Unifier wants the two families to become one.

4. **The Indifferent—minus 1:** a stepfamily member who has little interest in becoming part of a stepfamily. He or she is usually preoccupied with his or her own life and isn't thinking much about the stepfamily at all.

5. **The Distancer—minus 2:** a stepfamily member who consciously chooses to have no involvement with the new stepfamily. There are

several variations. The parental couple may decide that they do not wish to create any relationship with each other's adult children. Or the adult children may decide not to establish a relationship with their stepparent or stepsiblings. Or both may be true.

6. **The Destabilizer—minus 3:** a stepfamily member who actively attempts to disrupt the building of new bonds between the two stepfamilies. Usually, this person is convinced that he/she has everything to lose and nothing to gain from being a part of the new stepfamily. People who adopt this role may try to break up the marriage or undermine friendships among the stepsiblings and between stepparent and stepchildren. If the Destabilizer is a remarried parent, that person may want to disrupt preexisting bonds within his/her spouse's biological family.

CHANGES OFTEN OCCUR WITH TIME

Family members are rarely fixed rigidly and for all time in just one of these roles. Over time, family members can and do change their involvement with each other. These role changes often depend on the individual's stage in life and the length of time he or she has been in a stepfamily.

When adult stepchildren change roles, it is often because of major developments in their own lives. These may include marriage and parenthood or crises, such as divorce or illness. For both parents and children, financial reverses and illness may change how much involvement family members want or need. For example, we interviewed an adult stepchild who had tried to undermine his father's remarriage for many years. The son's behavior was that of a classic Destabilizer. Later, when he married a woman who had several children of her own and became a stepparent himself, he began to view his father and stepmother differently. Once, at a large family party, his stepmother gave him some good advice after she observed that his own stepchildren were treating him poorly. As a result, he developed a new understanding of, and even affection for, his stepmother. As a consequence, he was able to become a Joiner and finally a Guardian Angel for his stepmother in his own biological family.

These Six Roles are useful ways of conceptualizing members of stepfamilies and help predict how stable the stepfamily will be. Now, let's look more closely at how stepfamily members function in each role.

EXAMPLES OF POSITIVE ROLES IN AN EVOLVING STEPFAMILY

The Joiner

We can look at Joiners as outsiders to the other biological family who are determined to become insiders. The Joiner wants to make a psychological investment in the new family for the long term. If the stepparent or adult stepchild succeeds, he or she becomes an adopted member of the other family. That means being included in family celebrations, holidays, and memorials, being privy to personal news, and becoming an active stepgrandparent, step-aunt, and the like. The responsibilities of the outsider-become-insider, or Joiner, include having respect for and communicating with all stepfamily members and keeping track of the important events in their lives. Such Joiners often develop warm relationships with those steprelatives who make it a point to include them.

For a stepparent, being a Joiner usually means spending time with your spouse that is focused on his/her children and advising, consulting, and doing whatever needs to be done in a generous way. Because of your seniority, being a Joiner may mean serving as a quasi parent, insofar as you are invited to do so and wish to do so.

For adult stepchildren, the Joiner's long-term rights of inclusion might involve being treated in a quasi sisterly or brotherly way by your stepsiblings. Your parent's spouse might become a friend, mentor, advisor, and additional grandparent to your children. The responsibilities are to treat your stepparent and stepsiblings with respect and concerned interest.

Joiner Kathy, age fifty-two, told us:

Marriage was a big step for me. I thought about getting married again for a long time before I actually married Jack. I knew how close he was to his children and that they were part of the whole package. By the time we married, I made up my mind to go the whole way and become a part of his grown children's lives, too. When I met them, they were perfectly polite to me, but that was all. I decided I would reach out and see what happened. I would invite all of them to our home for dinners and holiday meals and after that I continued to call one or the other to get together alone and have lunch or go shopping for the grandchildren or baby-sit. It was like a long campaign. Nothing came back to me for years, but finally I think I worked my way in, and slowly I realized that I was a permanent part of their lives.

Not everyone has the time to devote to such a campaign, and some family members can't persevere that long without acceptance. But even if they fail, Joiners have the satisfaction of knowing they tried to make things better for everyone.

Certain cultures expect all family members—biological and step—to be Joiners. The Mediterranean cultures, Italian or Greek, for example, have time-honored rules for inclusion after families are joined by marriage. The culture does not allow you to remain angry with or distant from your parents or siblings or stepfamily. Everyone has a given place in this type of Joiner-Unifier culture, and everyone also has responsibilities, like showing up for every important family affair.

Fifty-year-old Sandy told us:

My husband's cousin invited us to Sunday dinner shortly after we married. I thanked her for the invitation but said that we had already planned to go to my son's house. She said, "Why can't your son and his family come here? We have plenty of food. Bring them with you." She kept on insisting that we come and bring everyone with us. We didn't really want to go there, but she wouldn't take no for an answer. I'd never been in a family like that, where it was almost an insult to refuse an invitation, even though we had made other plans.

If you are entering a family whose culture is different from your own, you will serve yourself well by finding out what that culture expects of you. Some cultures expect family to be Distancers. In such cultures, family membership may be expressed in subtle ways—some so subtle that the newcomer feels unwelcome.

Seventy-year-old Maria said:

My husband's son and wife treat us coldly as if we were some kind of business associates. They invite us to their home in Florida once a year for a weekend, and the visit is always exactly the same. They take us out for dinner the first night, then the men go to play golf the next day, after which they invite the same neighbors over for cocktails from six to eight. The next morning, we go out for brunch, and they take us to the airport. Aside from this, they never see us at all. At Christmas, there is the five-minute phone call. At first, I felt very rejected. I thought it might have to do with their feeling that they missed their deceased mother so much that they didn't want to be reminded of her absence by seeing me with their father.

*As time went on, I got the courage to ask. I found out from my husband
that it was their typical family behavior going way back.*

Stepfamily members may change their minds about how much familial distance they want as circumstances change, even years after the marriage.

Thirty-five-year-old Louise told us:

*I think I made a mistake to be so distant from my father's wife, Frances.
They had been married for five years. I just hadn't adjusted to the reality
that my dad had replaced my mother with someone else and that if I didn't
want to lose my dad I had to face up to developing some kind of real relationship with Frances. I know it hurt him that I hadn't been kind to her.
But I knew what I had to do, and, last year, I just pulled up my socks and
did it. Now, my dad is much warmer to me.*

With some exceptions, among the adult stepchildren we interviewed, those
with the healthiest bonds to their remarrying biological parent were the most
likely to be Joiners. If they experienced rejection, however, they often felt they
had to become more distant to protect themselves from further disappointment.
Adult stepchildren who were favored or only children in their biological families
sometimes felt they were being pushed aside. For them, it took time to draw
closer.

You may want to be a Joiner, but, remember, you can't do it alone. The family
you wish to join may have a tight emotional rubber band around it. If you are a
stepparent in a family created after a divorce, be careful not to elbow yourself into
the parental role. If your stepchildren's other parent has died, the family may be
equally touchy, feeling that you are somehow violating a sacred memory. In both
cases, the passage of time helps. So does a big dose of patience. And we mean *big*.

The Guardian Angel

The Guardian Angel goes beyond being a Joiner by helping outsiders from
the stepfamily to become insiders in his/her biological family. A remarrying
parent, stepchild, or stepsibling can be a Guardian Angel. First Guardian Angels
find out whether their spouse or stepchild really wants to be included in their
biological family. They need to determine whether the spouse or stepchild
wants to share the responsibilities that are part of the Guardian Angel's particu-

lar family culture. These responsibilities may require a major investment of time and other resources. If the new members do want to participate, being a Guardian Angel means helping your spouse or stepchild to become a genuine insider in your biological family. To do this, the Guardian Angel makes the others aware of the newcomer's positive aspects, encourages inclusion, and refuses to allow hostility directed toward the newcomer.

An adult stepchild can become a Guardian Angel by making a place for a stepsibling or stepparent in his/her biological family and monitoring the newcomer's comfort level. A stepparent can do the same for a spouse or stepchild.

Continuing vigilance is often part of what makes stepfamilies successful. Sometimes this means being aware of and rebuffing repeated attempts by your other family members to reject the newcomer. Such vigilance requires real dedication on the part of the Guardian Angel to helping the outsider achieve permanent inclusion.

Being a Guardian Angel gives you no additional rights, but requires you to accept ongoing responsibility for monitoring your biological family's behavior toward the newcomer. And being a Guardian Angel means intervening directly if the outsider is not treated fairly. The rewards may include enhancing your marital relationship or stepsibling relationship because of the newcomer's deep appreciation of your ongoing help.

As forty-nine-year-old Nancy said:

Henry was great at picking up any sign of hostility his children showed toward me and saying something that took the sting out of the situation for me. He let them know in a humorous, but firm, way that unkindness toward me was just not going to be tolerated by him. Ever. So, they stopped doing it.

The Guardian Angel is alert to situations that may make a stepfamily member feel excluded. Marilyn, a sixty-nine-year-old stepparent, told us:

I had been a stepparent for ten years when my stepdaughter, Jill, got married. She and I are really good friends, and so I was surprised to find myself becoming apprehensive about how I would feel at her wedding. I knew I was worried about how I would handle my feelings of being excluded. I am overly sensitive. How would I hold up when Jill, her mom, her sisters, and my husband would be a tight group again talking about old times, marching down the aisle together, toasting each other and making family jokes. Well, Jill did the most loving thing. She pulled me into the family picture taking after the ceremony and then, right after that, she asked the photographer to take several of just her and me together. She made me feel that I was important to her, and she showed her family that I was, as well.

If there is no Guardian Angel, many potential Joiners told us that they felt discouraged and were very aware that they had no advocate to help ease their way into the new stepfamily. Some finally gave up trying to become insiders.

Forty-two-year-old Steven told us:

I want my father to be happy. But he never says to his wife or her children, "Wait a minute. How is this going to affect my kids? If you don't have a good relationship with my kids then I can't have a good relationship with you." He loves us to death. He'd die for us. But when it comes to his wife, he always agrees to just what she wants him to do. He never really thinks about helping our relationship by being firm about including us.

We recommend that Joiners identify and enroll an influential stepfamily member to be their Guardian Angel, once they decide to try to join the group. Sometimes, the main job of the Guardian Angel is to say what should be obvious to everyone, but still needs to be said.

For five years after they were married, sixty-seven-year-old Fred hadn't felt it necessary to intervene directly to help Ronnie, his wife, become a part of his biological family.

Up until that time, I thought it was best to bring Ronnie and my children closer simply by our spending time together with them in our home and having them join us at our vacation place on holidays. But Ronnie didn't feel accepted. She's a very proud person, and she was always on guard about being "odd man out"! Recently, I decided that even after all this time had passed, perhaps what I had assumed was obvious to my children hadn't occurred to them. I needed to put it into words.

I sat down with them at the next opportunity and told them that I wanted their help. I said that Ronnie and I had had a late start in life as a couple, although we were making up for it by the good fortune of the deep love we felt for each other. I told them that although she had lots of her own friends, she also has a shy side. I said that it was up to them to make room for her in our family.

I think my saying that surprised them and shook them up. But it had a positive effect. Their behavior changed, and they started to pay more attention to her. For my part, it's important to remember to tell them that it makes me feel good to see them reaching out to her. They can't read my mind. It's never too late to make things better. I've got to keep on top of this until it becomes a habit for them.

The Unifier

Our next role is the Unifier, who is a Guardian Angel plus 1. Unifiers want everyone in the stepfamily to become insiders in a new, larger family. Unifiers want the two families to become one genuine, fully integrated extended family to which all the members are committed by choice. This is an enormous undertaking, and it assumes that the rights of the members will extend beyond mutual interest, respect, and consideration, to an exchange of loyalty, trust, tenderness, even affection and love.

Carol, age fifty-six, told us:

We really feel we are one family, but it has taken us something like ten years. We are even thinking of starting a family business together, selling vitamin supplements.

My husband's ex-wife was an alcoholic who moved away to Idaho after their divorce. They had two children, who were both married. I had none. His kids and I had a cool relationship at first. I think the turning point was when we were visiting my stepdaughter and her husband shortly before their first baby was due. When her biological mother canceled out at the last minute, my stepdaughter asked me to be with her when their first baby was born. I said "Okay, I'll just go home and get some clothes and come back." I didn't have to be told what to do. I just did it. Make the food, hold the baby, sit up at night with the baby . . . With her second baby, she said, "I was waiting for you to say you'd come out and help."

It was different with my stepson, who was more identified with his mother and less friendly towards me out of loyalty to her. But things got much better when he got married to a woman with two children.

One of the best ideas we had was to ask everyone in the family to contribute to renting a place where we could have Christmas or maybe a summer vacation week together. Then, nobody felt put out by doing all the work in their own home. Somehow, having a third place, not a hotel or somebody's home, but a place where we all feel equal responsibility, is a good way to prevent resentment.

Barbara, age forty, told us:

It's gotten pretty easy for us to function as one large family. I think one factor that helped was that my mother and stepfather remarried before most of us adult kids had gotten married. So, when we brought our new spouses into the family and realized how much we wanted them to be accepted, we didn't think it was fair to treat our stepfather as an outsider, either.

One other thing that helps is that we all understand and respect that both biological families have some times that they want to spend alone. You can't completely do away with the importance of original family because my brothers and sisters and I formed bonds in our childhood that can't be replaced. And that we don't want to replace.

It's often more difficult to evolve into one unified family if the adult children have been married before the parent remarries. In this circumstance, the stepparent is the last to arrive in a group that has usually already established cohesion and boundaries. The birth of grandchildren, however, can provide another window of opportunity. Stepsiblings with young children may help each other out with advice and support and become Unifiers. Similarly, the stepgrandparents' relationship to new grandchildren can also strengthen connections.

The Unifier must develop the ability to identify opportunities for making the new family closer. Besides, most Unifiers are very good at selling the idea to others.

WHEN STEPFAMILIES REACT NEGATIVELY

Now, let's consider family members whose reaction to being in a stepfamily spans the full spectrum of resistance. But before doing so, it's important to remember that, at first, many family members may simply not know the degree of affiliation they want. At any point, they may decide to assume one of the six roles we have described.

Those who remain undecided for a long time generally know more about what they *don't* want than what they *do* want in their new family situation. They may act with civility and apparent good humor, but may only be going through the motions. From the outside, they may be indistinguishable from Indifferent family members.

The Indifferent

Of the three roles that reflect a rejection of the stepfamily, the least negative is the Indifferent. These family members aren't really thinking about the stepfamily at all. They are not invested emotionally. They are often very busy with their own work and family life and just don't have any time or energy left over to invest in step matters. Geographic distance and infrequent contact often sustain Indifference.

Frank, age sixty-seven, told us:

> *I'd have to say my son Hank has been really indifferent to the whole step-family thing. He has been on the road working for a new company that sells dental instruments and appliances. It's a good job, and they value him in the company, and they are grooming him for something important. He's dating a few women but nobody seriously yet. When we see him three times a year, he is pleasant to everyone, and that's that. On the phone, he always sends his regards to my wife but never asks to speak with her. He's never asked me anything about his inheritance or anything about my wife's children.*

Ten years after the families are joined, Indifferent members may be as little known by other stepfamily members as they were at the outset. They do not initiate contact, but they usually attend stepfamily functions, however perfunctorily, when invited.

Distancers

Distancers chose a more negative role. They are *outsiders* to each other's biological families and choose to remain that way. As a result, they have the most limited responsibilities and rights in the stepfamily. In the case of the remarrying couple, this may mean neither husband nor wife wishes to get involved with his or her spouse's adult children. Sometimes, only one spouse wants to be a Distancer. In such cases, the couple needs to reach agreement on how to relate to the stepfamily. Unilateral distancing may wreck a marriage if it is perceived as unfair or ungenerous by the other spouse.

The main reward for Distancers is not having to compete with adult stepchildren for attention. Both spouses can focus exclusively on each other when they are together; no one else is allowed to enter their special space. Each spouse deals with his or her biological children as a separate matter in a separate time and space, which the other spouse may perceive as a welcome relief of an unwanted responsibility.

As sixty-five-year-old Marion told us:

Henry and I didn't want to get caught up in all those problems with each other's kids. Our decision to get married and enjoy our life was strictly between the two of us, and we like it that way. If he wants to see his kids, he goes to visit them, and the same with me. If they call him, I just say hello and hand the phone over.

Adult stepchildren who are Distancers want to keep themselves, their spouse, and biological family, including their siblings and siblings' families, as a separate unit. They have no interest in getting involved with a parent's spouse or the spouse's family. Generally, they are not enthusiastic about a parent's remarriage or are under the influence of and loyal to a sibling or divorced parent who has strong negative feelings about the remarriage.

For John, age forty, it was simple:

What my dad does is his affair. I don't need another mother, and my wife and I have enough brothers and sisters to have as much family in our lives as we want. I went to his wedding. I know he's being taken care of. We talk on the phone, and when I'm in St. Louis on business, we have lunch together.

Distancing may work for a while, but it has a tendency to become less effective over time. It may have to be modified or abandoned, at least temporarily, if a stepfamily member develops a serious illness. A crisis may force stepfamily members to deal with each other, whether they want to or not. For example, a biological child's illness may pull a Distancer parent back into his/her biological family. In traditional families, the female is expected to perform the nursing role. Sometimes, in fact, a stepmother may be drafted to nurse her stepchild. Life often forces members of a stepfamily to renegotiate all their roles.

Destabilizers

Finally, we have the Destabilizer. This is the family member who actively attempts to prevent the growth of a strong new stepfamily or one who tries to weaken the preexisting bonds between the new spouse and his/her children or other nuclear family members. Destabilizers usually fear the growth of any attachments that might diminish their own exclusive close relationship and/or control over a family member. Destabilizers are usually the most deeply dependent members of the family, even though they may appear outspoken or rebellious.

Destabilizers may want to see their parent's new marriage fail. Or, in the case of stepparents who are Destabilizers, they may try to weaken a preexisting parent-child relationship because they feel it competes with their marriage. In other families, an adult child may try to subvert a developing friendship between a sibling and stepsibling.

Destabilizing is different from, and more destructive than, Distancing. It means actively undermining and putting a negative spin on the behavior of someone in the other family. Destabilizers often feel threatened and assume they are in a competition for what they believe are scarce resources of love and support.

Here are examples of two kinds of Destabilizers. The first feels threatened by the strength of a newly developing relationship. The second feels threatened by a strong, durable biological tie.

In the first instance, Destabilizers may wish to punish their biological parent for what they perceive as disloyalty in light of the parent's commitment to a new spouse or the spouse's children. They often team up with a divorced parent or a disenchanted biological brother or sister, who is also feeling neglected.

Kathleen, age sixty, told us how her son, Jeff, became a Destabilizer:

My son, Jeff, was thirty-two when I remarried. Jeff was accustomed to being the center of my life because my marriage to his father was so empty that Jeff always came before my husband. The truth was, I got much more satisfaction from my son than I ever had from his father. I guess I had built up an expectation that I would always put Jeff first and continue to spend prime time with him, and when he married, with his wife and his children. Jeff's wife had lost her own parents, and she had become very dependent on me, too. We were a tight group.

Two years ago, I met Tom. Things moved fast. I had a real partner at last. Last year, we got married, and, of course, I want Tom to come first in my life. My son feels jilted by me, and he is very unpleasant to Tom. He and his wife have told me that they don't like Tom and never will. I'm heartbroken.

My son has become a timekeeper, nagging me about disappointing him and his children when I spend vacation time with my husband, and he is monitoring the hours I agree to be with him and his family. He makes me feel so guilty. His anger and jealousy make it impossible to bring my husband with me when I go to his home. The last time the four of us were together, we were discussing the situation in the Middle East, and Jeff told Tom that he didn't know what he was talking about. Now, Jeff is refusing to let his children, my grandchildren, visit me when my husband is around, because they don't want Tom's influence on them. Jeff's trying to break up my marriage.

Destabilizers, like Jeff, are under the influence of the Five Furies and have yet to recognize any of the Saving Graces, which we shall examine in the next chapter. Jeff has expressed at least four of the Five Furies: Fear of Abandonment and Isolation, Fidelity to Family, Favoritism, and Focus on Self.

Destabilizers are best handled by using Tact and Tacking skills. Protecting or defending yourself, without attacking the other person, is a real art. Once you go into frontal attack mode, you may make your point, but you may have lost your moral standing. In most cases, it is much better to try #1, Reframing; #4, Tenacity; and #5, Negotiating and Trading. Jeff's mother, Kathleen, has to find a way to stand up for her principles and refuse to enable Jeff's destructive behavior. Here is one scenario that could be useful.

Kathleen might *think:*

Fury #1: Fear of Abandonment and Isolation and Fury #5: Focus on Self

What does Jeff want from me? I've devoted my whole adult life to him and his family, until recently. Maybe that is one of the reasons we're having problems now. I've got to take responsibility for spoiling my son and his family because I needed them too much. I had no one else in my life to love.

Fury #2: Fidelity to Family and Fury #3: Favoritism

I'm finally happily married. I can't continue to give Jeff and his family as much of my time as they have become accustomed to in the past. I want to spend time alone with my husband. When we visit, they are rude to him. This hurts Tom and embarrasses me and makes me angry. They will have to adjust to see-ing me with Tom and learn to accept him if they want me in the picture. I've got to expect Jeff to be angry at me for pulling out, but not let him punish Tom, and I have to accept the fact that my standing up for Tom may make Jeff angry and even cause him to reject me.

What Kathleen might *say:*

Tact and Tacking #1: Reframe

You are my son. I love you very much and always will. The same goes for your wife and your children. If we didn't love each other so much, we wouldn't be having this problem.

Tact and Tacking #4: Tenacity

I've gotten remarried. I love my husband, and I want my marriage to work out well. I've learned through experience that in order to have a good marriage, my husband has to come first, just as I think your wife does for you.

Since Tom and I have been together, I have been introducing him to all of my old friends. Sometimes, my friends get along really well with him. Sometimes, they don't particularly like him. But if a friend of mine treated my husband the way you have, I would stop visiting that friend.

Tact and Tacking #5: Trade and Negotiate

When I bring my husband to your home, I expect that you will treat him with respect and try to build a decent relationship. This is what I did when you mar-ried your wife. I know it takes time to build a relationship. Meanwhile, what I expect from you is good manners and hospitality toward him, no matter what you are feeling inside. I do that with your family. It is only fair. He deserves it. And so do I.

In this way, Kathleen would spell out clear and reasonable expectations for herself, her son, and his family. She would show that she plans to stand by her husband and help him become a full participant in the new stepfamily. She would reiterate her love for Jeff, but make clear that she will not undermine her husband and jeopardize her marriage by allowing Jeff to reject and hurt Tom when the family gets together.

In a second example, a jealous stepfather became a Destabilizer by trying to break up a close, long-established relationship between his wife and her daughter. Sally, age sixty-three, was distressed that her new husband, Phil, seemed bent on weakening the love, intimacy, and trust that Sally and her daughter shared:

Phil takes every opportunity to say something negative about my daughter's behavior to get me to mistrust her or think less of her. If she brings us flowers when I invite her to dinner, he implies that she knows how to waste money on luxuries. If she's well dressed and her hair and nails are done, she is spending too much on her appearance. Lately, he puts a sour look on his face when I suggest getting together with her.

She's a stockbroker. She works for an investment house and is managing the bulk of my IRA. This arrangement began long before our marriage. When we are alone, Phil questions my daughter's motivation and tells me she is buying and selling stocks in my account unnecessarily fast to make higher commissions. He implies she is only interested in my money. He thinks she just pretends to be affectionate and knows how to flatter me with words, but then, he reminds me that she never shows up when one of us is ill, and we really need her to help us out. He says he's not surprised that she has no boyfriend. He's trying to make her look bad.

Destabilizers like Phil are beset by four of the Five Furies: Fidelity to Family, Favoritism, Finances, and Focus on Self.

Sally might *think*:

Fury #2: Fidelity to Family and Fury #3: Favoritism

Phil is jealous of my relationship with my daughter. He's always looking for the worst in her behavior. I don't like what he's doing. I haven't given him any reason to be insecure about my love for him, but I didn't expect that my love for my child would threaten him so much.

Sally might *say* to Phil:

Tact and Tacking #4: Tenacity

It may seem as though I am so close to my daughter that I can't see any of her shortcomings. You're my husband, and I love you very much. She's my child, and I have a different kind of love for her than what I feel for you. Our marriage is my number one priority. I'm sure I have enough love in me to be a good wife to you and continue to be a good mother.

Tact and Tacking #6: Tolerance and #7: Transformation Through Wisdom

You seem to be warning me that she can be insincere and manipulative. You wonder if she's too self-centered to find a husband. You think she is overly interested in my money and not particularly interested in helping us out when we need her. I get your message, I value your input, and I'll have to think about her behavior. I may or may not agree with you, but I don't want that to hurt our marriage. Does that make sense to you?

As hard as you try, you can't force family members to like each other. Nonetheless, you can show each person that you won't be a party to destructive and hurtful behavior on either side. You can act like a policeman and blow the whistle on fights. At the same time, try not to act like a judge in court who determines who is right and who is wrong. Your mantra can be, "You don't have to like each other, but you have to act respectfully toward each other."

When you draw the line and refuse to go along with cruel or destructive behavior, you take a risk that a person you love will become angry with you. Yet, risking another's ire is almost always better than "stuffing" your own anger when a spouse or adult child tries to seduce you into turning against another loved one.

Sometimes, when unexpected events allow a Destabilizer to stop demonizing a stepfamily member, the Destabilizer then can take advantage of the opportunity. This may happen as a result of a generous act by the wronged stepfamily member during the Destabilizer's illness or other life-changing event.

Sometimes, a new grandchild disarms a stepfamily Destabilizer, creating an opportunity for a previously rejected stepparent to develop an important relationship with that grandchild. A stepparent's ability to love and support a new stepgrandchild may win over even a longtime Destabilizer. The stepparent who obviously loves the Destabilizer's new child may suddenly be seen as bringing additional resources to the family, rather than competing with the stepchild for scarce resources.

Another life transition that may turn negative family members into Joiners or Guardian Angels occurs when stepchildren become stepparents themselves. Then, a new alliance may develop. We have been amazed at how quickly stepchildren who had little affection for their stepparents warmed to them when they became stepparents themselves.

HOW DO STEPFAMILIES CREATE MEANING? WHAT MAKES THE CUP HALF-FULL?

Becoming a member of a stepfamily when a parent remarries rarely means the same thing to everyone. Some adult children are overjoyed by the possibilities of a better life for their parent; some are fearful that they will lose that parent's love. Others are indifferent or unsure what their feelings are. Some remarrying spouses can't wait to become friends with adult stepchildren; some expect, and often get, only hostility from them. Marriage doesn't make a stepfamily. Each member creates his or her own meaning, and, collectively, those attitudes and behaviors make the stepfamily what it is.

As we said earlier, everyone brings his or her own genetic makeup, personality, and personal history to the new stepfamily. Some family members have more influence, and they will play a larger role in persuading the others as to whether the new stepfamily is a good or bad thing.

We interviewed two brothers who experienced the exact same event: being thrust into an adult stepfamily when their elderly father remarried. Each brother interpreted the event differently, and, as a result, each had a very different response to it. One became a Destabilizer, the other a Joiner. Each brother created his own, very different stepfamily from the same set of circumstances and individuals.

Steve was forty and single when his father remarried ten years ago, soon after his mother died in an accident. He had always been close to his father and the apple of his eye. His stepmother had long been a friend of both his biological parents. Steve, now age fifty, told us:

Mary Jo, that woman my father married, had always flirted with him, particularly after her own husband died. The two couples were part of the same social set. My mother resented her behavior. So, I wasn't surprised when Mary Jo threw herself at my dad when my mother died.

She's obviously the dominant force. He doesn't have the backbone to confront her. Married to her, he has the life of a whipped puppy. He can't face having me think he's made a stupid choice, but he has really lowered his standards. So, any time he comes to see any of us, with her or without her, he feels compelled to say how happy he is, how happy she makes him. Especially to me, because I had that horrifying scene with them last year when she told me that what was in my father's will was none of my business.

He won't admit that it would be better for him to divorce her, but I hope someday he will see the truth about her.

The other son, Allen, age forty-five, told us:

Mary Jo, my dad's wife, is a person who speaks her mind. She's different from my mom, who was someone who never let you know if she disagreed with you. With Mary Jo, you know where you stand, and she'll fight you tooth and nail to get her way. But if you stand your ground, she never keeps a grudge afterward. She's got a lot of passion, and I think my dad enjoys how sexy she is. He looks ten years younger now than he did ten years ago when my mother died.

What makes one brother *inclusive,* the other *exclusive?* In analyzing the stepfamilies we interviewed, we discovered that whether a person worked for his or her stepfamily or against it depended largely on whether he or she tended to be optimistic or pessimistic. We know that such a tendency is, in turn, determined by a complex interaction of genetic factors, personality, and life experiences.

Do you believe that having more people in the family increases the likelihood that everyone will gain? Or do you believe in a world of scarcity and finite resources, in which more family members translate into having less for yourself? The members of stepfamilies we spoke to tended to have long established patterns of interpreting whatever happened to them positively or negatively. They brought that same reflexive positivity or negativity to their new stepfamilies.

Social psychology tells us that people who are *inclusive* are more likely to believe in a world of *increasing and expanding resources.* They perceive a world of plenty and opportunity. The introduction of new people arouses interest and curiosity, rather than fear and apprehension. They also tend to be more extroverted and comfortable socially, as well as more optimistic.

Within stepfamilies, these characteristics may predispose certain family members to function as Joiners and Guardian Angels. They are more likely to look for and exploit the positive possibilities of any situation. They tend to regard even the Five Furies as problems that have solutions.

When older couples are starting out, they are filled, like new lovers of any other age, with hope and enthusiasm for the step they are taking. Their behavior may be more expansive than when they were alone. Even if they are not innately optimistic and inclusive, they will tend to feel and act that way at this happy time. In the new family, they are more likely to function as Joiners and

Unifiers. Still, if their overtures are not accepted, over time, they may reluc-tantly—or reflexively—become Distancers or Indifferents.

Those who are Distancers or Destabilizers from the start tend to be more *exclusive* and wary of other people's motivations. These two groups contain more *introverts,* or at least people without the easy social skills that help every-one feel comfortable. They tend to be more *pessimistic* about human nature and cautious about new ventures.

Distancers and Destabilizers may look at life through the prism of the Five Furies. Consequently, they are more likely to see the stepfamily as having lim-ited and *finite resources.* Of course, even introverts can be Joiners and Unifiers, but it usually takes an introvert more of an effort to pull people close.

TOWARD A MORE PERFECT STEP UNION

We have discussed the many forms of involvement you might choose to take in your new stepfamily. You have to figure what role is most comfortable for you. Your choice may not be easy. Choosing a certain role may threaten your other ties. What happens if all your siblings choose to be Distancers, and you want to be a Joiner? That choice could require real courage and independence on your part.

For the marrying couple, what if your spouse is by nature a Distancer and you are a Joiner? What can you expect of each other? Ideally, you'll be able to discuss these important step matters before the wedding or early in the marriage. Actu-ally, you may not be able to clarify the issue until years later. Then, you might want to put the question this way: What kind of relationship would you like me to have with your children? Better to find out late than never how your spouse feels, especially if he or she wants a different level of involvement than you do.

The hardest thing for most people to accept is their lack of control over how involved other members of the stepfamily choose to be. To be a successful Joiner, Guardian Angel, or Unifier implies reciprocity. You can't function in any of these roles for long without support from other family members. And some people break their hearts trying.

If you are rebuffed, you will have to choose less involvement, like it or not. And you should try to do it without pouting, whining, or being aggrieved. You can expect no credit for trying to push or pull members of the two families together, but you can credit yourself for trying to do the right thing. Some fam-ilies simply don't want new intimacies. In that case, you will have to learn to manage your own expectations. At the end of the day, that may mean accepting rejection by people you care about or would like to care about. At that point, declare a personal victory and move on.

It takes maturity to share your affection, and it takes maturity to walk away from those who don't want it. As the twelve-steppers of Alcoholics Anonymous say, it also takes wisdom to recognize the difference. A rebuffed Joiner may have to fight the impulse to become a kind of intrafamily stalker. The best a disappointed Joiner may be able to do is to become politely Indifferent until others reach out. And they may never do so.

Much of the pain in adult stepfamilies is due to excessively high expectations on the part of the older couple (especially the wife). She often hopes to satisfy everyone's needs and win everyone as a friend. The other source of pain is frequently recalcitrance on the part of adult children. The children didn't choose this new arrangement. Just as fasting is different from starving, there is a sharp difference between being a volunteer and being drafted. The older couple volunteered. The adult children were drafted, and often they are none too happy about it.

If adult stepchildren do develop trust and affection for the stepparent, it usually happens much more slowly than the stepparent wishes. Adult stepchildren, after all, *do not need* a relationship with the stepparent. Their primary wish is to maintain a strong relationship with their remarrying parent. They often consider the stepparent the price they must pay to maintain this continuity.

Stepparents who feel an *urgent need for the relationship* often want it in order to please the new spouse. Yet, the rush to friendship makes many stepchildren feel pressured and even used. They want to be liked for who they really are, and they are uneasy when a new stepparent acts as if he or she has instantly plumbed them.

Sometimes, there is a discrepancy between how family members *think* their relationships are developing and how they really are. This can be the source of ironic humor, as well as serious misunderstandings within the family.

We interviewed a stepfamily where each person saw the new unit in his or her own way. The stepmother and her children were convinced that the two families had been happily united. Her adult stepchildren, interviewed separately, thought she was acting like an "overly affectionate fool." As a result, they didn't take her seriously. In this case, the adult stepchildren were polite and respectful to her face. They never made their stepmother aware of their true feelings in her presence. Yet, when she was out of hearing range, they told us that they would regale each other with scathing imitations of her.

IT'S EASY TO BLACKMAIL STEPPARENTS, PARTICULARLY WHEN THEY COOPERATE

In stepfamilies, it is very important to learn how to avoid being emotionally blackmailed. You are susceptible to blackmail if you have high hopes of making everyone happy, despite signs of noncooperation, and if you feel that your marriage depends on your success. Those attitudes set a stepparent up for trouble.

Adult stepchildren often emotionally blackmail stepparents into silence about verbal abuse, from little barbs to vicious insults. They know the stepparent won't dare complain for fear of hurting the spouse by reporting the unattractive behavior of his or her children. Adult children often seem to sense when a new stepparent has to "make nice" to them because he or she knows that the children's approval is important to the new spouse.

Blackmail happens when a stepparent accepts the adult child's unsung refrain, "You need me more than I need you." If you need a good report card from your adult stepchildren to show your spouse, you've let them kidnap you emotionally. You'll have to pay your own ransom.

Sometimes, spouses also attempt emotional blackmail. Your spouse may ask you to tutor his or her unwilling adult children. "You'll help my children," the spouse says in effect. "You'll be the father or mother they never had. You'll help me to get it right finally with my kids."

Those are unrealistic expectations on the spouse's part, and you should refuse (*tactfully* and probably by *tacking*) to put yourself in that position. It patronizes and infantalizes your adult stepchildren. They've had their childhood. It's over, however successful or unsuccessful it was. You don't have the power to bring it back again.

On the other hand, you can offer to listen to any problems your spouse is currently having in dealing effectively with a son or daughter. Maybe the difficulty is due to your spouse's guilt over divorcing the child's parent or over having been preoccupied with other priorities when the children were growing up. You may be able to help your spouse come to terms with those past events, but you cannot magically undo what has already been done.

Bette Davis famously quipped that old age is no place for sissies. Neither are adult stepfamilies. Big babies of whatever age don't belong. Stepfamilies are places for mature people, whether they are stepparents or stepchildren. They are places that require good judgment, flexibility, generosity, and often a willingness to forgive things you can't forget.

Adult stepfamilies are also places where you can gain personal wisdom and skills, such as how to negotiate, that will help you in complex interactions with other people. They are places where you can learn how to defend and protect yourself without attacking others. Moreover, they are places where you can learn how to accept rejection without being destroyed, plus when to give in and when to stand firm.

DEALING WITH STEP MATTERS

Step matters are all about managing your expectations. Older couples tend to wish for too much affirmation, too soon, from their adult children and stepchildren.

Adult stepchildren, as a group, have more realistic expectations and a slower pace as they consider and assume new roles. They usually have more of a wait-and-see attitude than stepparents, who might find things to emulate in that more cautious approach.

Older couples feel the pressure of time. For them, *carpe diem,* seize the day, is the eleventh commandment. Their horizons are shorter. At first, they may be more influenced by passion and urgency than by reason and reflection. They need time to determine which role in the new stepfamily makes sense for them. If you are already in a stepfamily, and your present role isn't very satisfying, it is never too late to think about changing it.

You must decide how much involvement you want, but remember, you don't always get what you want. Some adult stepfamilies pull you closer when you show yourself to be a Joiner, while others don't want to take in strangers, even those brought into the family by marriage. Whatever role you assume, the only thing you are sure to have control over is your own expectations. Eventually, you may become so deft and wise in that role that you are able to help other family members manage *their* expectations.

Much of this chapter has dealt with the negative roles some members of stepfamilies play, mostly because those roles tend to cause the most trouble in stepfamilies. In the next chapter, we'll look more closely at the many opportunities that stepfamilies offer. We'll examine the Saving Graces of adult stepfamilies and see how to make the most of them.

---

*Vinick, Barbara, and Susan Lanspery. (2000). "Cinderella's Sequel: Stepmothers' Long-term Relationships with Adult Stepchildren." Guest Editors, R. Robin Miller and Sandra Lee Browning, *Journal of Comparative Family Studies,* special issue, "Ethnicity and Gender in Non-Traditional Family Forms: Studies of Families Pushing Normative Boundaries," vol. 31, number 3, summer, pp. 377–384.

CHAPTER 4

Opportunities or Dangers? Can the Graces Overcome the Furies?

Does becoming a member of an adult stepfamily offer mostly opportunities or dangers? Do stepfamilies offer new opportunities for fulfillment or are they quagmires of unhappiness and loss?

As we shall show in this chapter, your answers to these questions will depend on how well prepared you are to help shape the life of your new family and the role, or roles, you will play in it. If you have been in an adult stepfamily for a while, we'll discuss ways you might revise or enhance your role.

Constructing your role in your stepfamily is an active and never-ending process. When things go wrong, remember that it's the role—not you—that needs to be fixed. You are making choices all the time, even when you forget to tell your spouse that his or her daughter called. If you act wisely, you can create a role in which you will thrive, not merely survive.

You need tools to help you achieve that goal, and we shall discuss some of those tools in this chapter. One of your first tasks will be to get beyond negative stereotypes associated with stepfamilies and to figure out what's really happening in your own stepfamily. Then, you can begin creating the role you want to play. In this chapter, we'll lay out certain principles that will help you fashion a satisfying role for yourself in your stepfamily.

Here is a road map that will guide you through the issues we shall be exploring in this chapter. First, a big part of how you respond to your stepfamily depends on whether you are thrust into your role or choose it voluntarily. Are you the one who initiated the action or has your life been changed by another person's action? Are you the protagonist or the antagonist? Protagonists are doing something they desire. Antagonists are, by definition, reacting to the actions of others. These two conditions lead to very different reactions, reactions that we'll explore so that you anticipate them and manage them more effectively.

Second, whether you feel happy, fulfilled, and included has a lot to do with where you are in the stepfamily's life cycle. Every adult stepfamily has its own rhythm and timetable for accepting or rejecting the new family structure. Generally, however, parents tend to accept the idea early on, at the very time when the children are most resistant. Later, parents and children may change positions.

Third, you must remember that it is up to you to define and structure your role within your stepfamily. You have a choice. You will probably choose more than once, reinterpreting and redefining your role as you and your stepfamily change over time. We'll show you some of the possibilities.

Sociologists say that a role is a set of expectations. One set—the traditional one that surfaces in every B movie about stepfamilies—is loaded with negative stereotypes that can make you feel imprisoned and prevent your true self from shining through. As a new stepmother, are you being forced to play the role of the heavy? Negative archetypes cling to certain roles in stepfamiles and make them more imprisoning than they have to be. In fact, in our culture, most "step" roles are so embedded with negative expectations that we often do not see the real people who are caught in those roles.

Negative stereotypes don't have to control you, even though they are dangerous. They don't mean you can't have different expectations of yourself. You are free to shape your own role at any time, although it's easier to do so from the beginning. You are part of a family system. When you break out of a stereotype and create your own role, everything begins to change, including how other people perceive you. The way you behave will affect everyone else. These changes will ripple through the system.

Finally, so much of how you behave will depend on how you choose to interpret the meaning of the events in your life. The facts themselves do not have one fixed meaning. To a large extent, you determine the meaning of what happens to you.

Do you choose to see yourself in competition with others in the stepfamily for what you believe are fixed and finite emotional and financial resources? Or do you know there are ways to enlarge the pie, instead of simply cutting it into more, and thus smaller, slices? In stepfamilies, as in other areas of your life, you can design or redesign the psychological space in which you live.

In Chapter 1, we discussed the Five Furies, the negative emotions that a parent's decision to remarry often unleashes. Later in this chapter, we introduce the

Five Saving Graces, five potential pluses that exist in every adult stepfamily. Just as the Five Furies unleash powerful feelings of anger and hurt, the Five Saving Graces are positive forces that can transform stepfamilies into places where everyone benefits and grows.

While the Furies can be felt immediately, the Graces take time to develop. If they are allowed to emerge and unfold, they can ease the process that turns an unsettled new stepfamily into a genuinely cohesive and healthy new family. The Graces are not miracle workers—they can't turn any real-life stepfamily into the Brady Bunch. But they can help stepfamily members come to see that they are part of a worthwhile new whole. The Graces are key to the development within the stepfamily of the feeling that members now have more love, money, and other resources than they did before they knew each other. We conclude this chapter by showing how some of the successful stepfamilies we studied faced down the Furies and encouraged the Graces.

OPPORTUNITY OR DANGER: INITIATION "RIGHTS"

When an older couple decides to marry, both people tend to see opportunity everywhere.

Fifty-eight-year-old Gloria told us:

I had never expected to find the love of my life at my age. Bob was so attractive and brilliant and successful. Our courtship was magic! When he asked me to be his wife, I'd already spent time with each of his fabulous children and grandchildren, and I was eager to take them into our life together. Bob adores his children, as I do mine. I thought that the more people we had to love, the better off all of us would be. Never in my life did I have more to give. I was eager for Bob's children and my children to benefit from our marriage.

The adult children who are party to such a remarriage may see it very differently. Where the couple sees opportunity, the children may see only danger. They were drafted, after all; they didn't volunteer. The adult children, whose lives are being affected by an action beyond their own control, may feel put upon and, therefore, hostile.

Forty-year-old Paul told us:

My mother's new husband is the biggest threat we've ever experienced to weaken our family unity. Their marriage divides us from our own mother and makes us feel like outsiders. All she wants is to please him. Soon she'll be closer to his children than to us.

I realize that my mom needs to be happy and have a life of her own aside from being our mother. But she is acting like an adolescent. We've got a role reversal here. She's the teenager, and I'm the parent. She's so in love and on such an emotional high that she can't see that other people are affected. They are both trying to recapture their youth and don't particularly care about the fallout on others. Even his kids roll their eyes when they see them holding hands and trying to eat while they do. They are so self-absorbed. Like they invented love. When her new husband invited me and my son to go to a Red Sox game with him, I just didn't feel like accepting.

These stories illustrate how the initiators of change can spark difficulties between the two generations. The kids often don't want to accept "gifts" of affection and celebration at the very time that the parents most want to give. Recall Shakespeare's Hamlet, whose pain from the loss of his father was heightened by the sight of his mother celebrating a new love. Gertrude and Claudius tried to engage Hamlet in making a happy new family with them. They encouraged him to get married himself—a sound insight on Shakespeare's part that the stepchild might be more understanding of his mother and new stepfather if he were in their shoes. Nonetheless, the older couple's efforts fell flat, only making Hamlet angrier. Of course, Hamlet's suspicion that Claudius murdered his father weighs heavily on his mind. By the play's end, the stage is littered with corpses—a really sobering example of what the Furies can do to a stepfamily. Of course, *Hamlet* is a Shakespearean tragedy, an immortal fiction, and life does not have to imitate art. Ambivalence about a parent's remarriage is normal and predictable for adult stepchildren. Taking revenge is not.

Many real-life stepfamilies have elements right out of *Hamlet*. When the curtain goes up, the older couple expects a future full of happiness and pleasure. The new spouses see opportunity not only for themselves, but they generalize it to include the whole family. They have chosen to embark on a new life and are in a celebratory mode. They can't understand why everyone doesn't share their happiness.

At that point, however, the adult children often don't know what to feel. They are frequently ambivalent and show it. They may have positive feelings as well as negative ones, but the parents tend to be most sensitive at that point to any signs of negativity.

BAD TIMING

We found that one recurrent source of anguish in stepfamilies is that the marrying couple tends to reach out most strongly at the very time when the adult children are least likely and able to respond. By the time the adult children have worked through their negativity and recognized the positive aspects of the situation, the parental couple may be too worn out by the children's testing and rejection to care whether they share the couple's happiness or not.

If parents anticipate this disparate response in advance, they may feel less disappointment. This is an example in which managing your expectations includes recognizing that different stepfamily members may have different emotional timetables. Parents who don't expect this lack of synchrony and respond too strongly to their children's lack of enthusiasm may find it harder to establish a favorable relationship later on.

Adult children tend to run the gamut from very cynical to somewhat dubious about new stepparents. This is especially true when the new stepparent seems overeager to please. The younger generation may question enthusiastic compliments by the new stepparent. As we noted earlier, they may feel that the stepparent's overtures have nothing to do with them personally, but are simply a way of pleasing their spouse. That may be true. After all, love at first sight is rare among stepfamilies. In fact, too much affection on a new stepparent's part tends to be seen as phony, misleading, even dangerous. New stepparents who resist the temptation to try too hard usually come across as more genuine and authentic.

Thirty-seven-year-old Dan described his stepmother of ten years:

She's very open with her feelings and tells me directly when she disagrees with me. Sometimes she reminds me of, well, have you ever seen the TV show Roseanne? *She has a very wry sense of humor. I consider her a friend, and I don't think she's gone out of her way necessarily to make herself liked. In fact, maybe it will turn you off if somebody tries too hard. I don't think she overdoes it, which would be a real turn-off. I'm sure that's a big problem, which some new couples have . . . trying too hard. But I didn't really experience any of that.*

Given the very different timetables for acceptance that most marrying couples and their adult stepchildren have, the newlyweds should expect to experience some rejection early on. They will have to decide how much of a problem it is for them.

Sixty-five-year-old Charles told us:

I made so many attempts early in our marriage to be a friend to my wife's children, and it seemed like her middle daughter, who was twenty-eight, gave me the roughest time. She was like a dark cloud. When she came to dinner, she would not even look me in the eye, let alone ever ask how I was doing. She was extremely rude to me. It pained my wife very much to watch her daughter behave that way. It took her daughter two years to look at me when she spoke, and I never would have guessed that we would end up feeling so close to one another after three or four more years. The early years were mildly disagreeable, but fortunately it didn't matter that much to me. It ended up taking us a really long time to find out how many interests we had in common.

We found that those older couples who were low-key at first about establishing close relationships with their adult stepchildren had the easiest time. Those with somewhat lower expectations of a happy merger did the best. They tended to be less hurt by early rejection and were more open to the stepkids when they finally started to warm up.

The most successful stepparents didn't wear their hearts on their sleeves. They treated their adult stepchildren the way they would treat their peers in a work situation. They were open to making positive connections but had a wait-and-see attitude about how things would develop over time. These stepparents didn't indulge their stepchildren, but they were fair. And they made allowances for their stepchildren. They didn't get angry when stepchildren failed to thank them for gifts that, in many instances, the stepchildren hadn't requested. The parents were able to write off the children's lack of civility. Some even acknowledged that the kids probably didn't thank them for the gifts because they didn't really want them.

Stepparents who had greater expectations for mutual affection from the start were hurt more easily and often. They became angry when they generously reached out and no warm response bubbled up from their bewildered or aloof stepchildren.

The stepparent's need for validation of his or her good intentions early in the relationship with stepchildren may, in the long run, impede the development of a genuine, unforced, and uncontrived friendship. In other situations, we expect to learn about another person's trustworthiness or generosity in the course of many interactions over time. These individual experiences eventually coalesce into a composite picture of a person's character. Paradoxically, consciously trying to find numerous ways to promote and nurture trust from the outset tends to interfere with its development. That only delays the positive bonding that naturally develops with the passage of time.

YOU CAN'T RUSH TRUST

Clinicians know that the building of genuine trust has to meet all kinds of tests. Can you keep private information really private? Will you respond promptly and with empathy in a crisis? Will you hang in there despite rejection? Are you thinking of your own needs (checking your watch) or telling your own stories, or are you really focused on what the other person is saying? Will you respond to phone calls on the weekend?

When people marry later in life, they often have the sense that time is short, and they sometimes try to hurry things. If your spouse urges you to "connect" with his or her kids, you can agree that that is an important goal. At the same time, start talking to your spouse about what it takes to build trust and make enduring connections.

Geography is another key factor in relationship building. Families that are spread far apart may not have the same opportunities to build family history with every new member. Sometimes, a parent will move across the country as a result of remarriage, and those left behind blame the new spouse for taking away their parent.

Technology helps to offset problems of geography. E-mail, instant messaging, faxes, and phone calls help make and solidify personal connections even when people are physically far apart. Successful stepfamilies often develop the habit of keeping in touch via e-mails, Internet chats, and the exchange of digital photographs, as well as by old-fashioned telephone calls and hand-written notes and cards. All these approaches allow the family to maintain important relationships between reunions.

Culture can also influence the building of trust and the depth of a relationship. Some cultures demand immediate inclusion and loyalty as an automatic consequence of the marriage ceremony. Some "hotter" cultures expect new family members to do things they aren't familiar with or comfortable with because of their less demonstrative upbringing. For example, there are cultures where even the men greet new members with warm embraces. Such physical demonstrations of familial affection may seem intrusive, instead of welcoming, to someone from, say, a reserved New England background.

Some cultures tolerate people getting angry and showing it. People who come from such cultures know which ones we mean. For others, raised voices and heated disagreements signify a lack of civility. These cultural differences can have a profound effect on how quickly acceptance and trust develop among stepfamily members.

IT'S THE ROLE—NOT YOU—THAT NEEDS TO BE "FIXED"

In the course of our lives, we play many different social roles. We choose some of them. We usually select our professional roles, for examples. We decide that we want to be a teacher or social worker or entrepreneur, and we voluntarily undergo years of training and preparation so we can assume these roles.

Other roles, like that of neighbor or stepparent, are not entirely ours to choose. They often come with the territory as an addendum to other decisions we have made, like buying a particular house or falling in love with a certain person.

Sometimes, as we have seen, our roles are the result of other people's decisions, like becoming a stepchild or mother-in-law. However we acquire them, roles have enormous power.

All of us—good and bad, funny and boring, considerate and thoughtless, generous and selfish—are cast in multiple roles that dictate aspects of how we act in various situations. In fact, our roles help make sense of our behavior and that of others. For example, if your pre-teen son seems feverish, and you feel his forehead to check his temperature, you both understand that you are acting in the role of concerned parent. If your office-mate complains that he is not feeling well, and you lay your hand on his brow, he may wonder what is going on. Your concerned, intimate gesture may be viewed as inappropriate because it is not part of the standard behavioral repertoire for professional colleagues.

Roles offer us guidelines to the expectations, rights, and responsibilities that go along with our vast array of relationships. When we are in a specific role, we understand, more or less, what is expected of us. Those who interact with us also know what to expect and the appropriate responses available to them.

SOME ROLES CARRY CULTURAL BAGGAGE

Some roles come with better typical scenarios than others. That is, the cultural expectations that are built into them are more clear-cut, more positive, and easier to meet. For example, no matter how old children are, they will always be the offspring of their parents and, for the most part, can depend on their parents for love and protection. Mother, father, child, grandchild, sister, brother, wife, and husband—all these roles have positive connotations. Many of the roles in stepfamilies, however, come with negative connotations and offer more ambiguous guidelines for behavior.

Fairy tales and myths routinely describe evil stepmothers and weak step-fathers. Such stories appear in almost every culture, and yet they rarely jibe with our real-life experience. How is it that all the stepmothers of myth are the mean-est, greediest, most cunning women imaginable, and all the male dupes of the world stumble into the role of the stepfather? When an aged father takes a new wife, he is simply a foolish old man. When an aged woman takes a new spouse, she is portrayed, at least in the storybooks, as a lustful crone with an unquench-able appetite for sex and money. How can it be that only the nastiest, most self-ish children become adult stepchildren? Clearly, there is some disconnect between our mythology and reality.

Members of stepfamilies, like in-laws, are the victims of all sorts of cultural projection and scapegoating. When we create real stepfamilies, we take up roles that are prepackaged with expectations of bad things to come. Stepmother is an especially loaded role. The *Oxford Concise Dictionary* includes as one of its definitions of the stepmother "a harsh or neglectful mother."* New stepmothers may even develop a negative attitude toward themselves, so fraught is the role with ancient implications of cruelty and other vices. You hear of wonderful stepmothers even less often than you hear of marvelous mothers-in-law. At some level, we seem to buy into magical thinking whereby ordinary mothers are transformed into demons when they remarry (in the case of stepmothers) or when their children marry (in the case of mothers-in-law).

THE TOXIC ROLE: ARE STEPMOTHERS NATURAL-BORN KILLERS OR VICTIMS OF A MISOGYNIST TRADITION?

It is more than a little disturbing to discover how ancient and deep are the roots of the wicked stepmother myth. Bad stepmothers appear in ancient Greek and Roman literature and go back as far as there are written records. In Patricia Watson's fascinating book, *Ancient Stepmothers,* we find many examples.** In ancient myth, it was usually assumed that the stepmother would try to subvert and harm her stepchildren. Watson quotes Euripides in his play *Alcestis:* "For a stepmother comes as an enemy to the children of a former union and is no more gentle than a viper."

According to Watson, in Roman literature, the Latin word for stepmother, *noverca,* is derived from the word for new, *novus.* The *noverca* introduces a new and unwelcome regime into the household. A stock figure of the Roman theater was the *noverca venefica,* the stepmother as poisoner. The association of stepmother with murder was so common in the Roman world that *noverca* came to be a synonym for "murderess." After Hercules kills his children, he refers to his hands as *novercales manus* (stepmothers' hands). In Greek literature, a treacherous harbor is sometimes called a stepmother. In Roman military culture, a place too dangerous to pitch camp is called a *noverca*. And the vilification continues after the fall of Rome. In Scotland, a year of deprivation or calamity is called a stepmother year, her bad rap leaping cultural borders in a single bound.

The cross-cultural development of such a persistent and overwhelmingly negative stereotype raises questions: How much of this dark view of the stepmother is symbolic, stemming from misogynist views of all women long held in most societies? How much is due to conflicted feelings toward our natural mothers? (Freudians would say that the negative part of this universal conflict is projected onto the stepmother.) Is the stepmother a scapegoat for society's fear and conflict about women in general and mothers in particular? Or is it a mirror of a real social condition that flows from genuine problems related to the stepmother's replacement of the natural mother and the disputes about inheritance and favoritism caused by a second marriage? Probably all these factors contribute to the stereotype, but none explains why it is so persistently and universally negative.

In many ways, the word *stepmother* has become a catchall for the many negative traits associated with all females. Stepmothers are often depicted as self-centered, destructive, greedy, lacking in self-control, calculating, capable of violence, seductive, jealous, cunning, and treacherous. It isn't a pretty picture, but it is a potent reminder of the many negative stereotypes that have dogged women forever and continue to complicate their lives to this day.

STEPMOTHER AS THE SHADOW PART OF EVERYBODY'S PERFECT MOTHER

In contrast, the terms *wife* and *mother* have come to represent ideals of good behavior, love, nurturing, and caretaking. Mothers satisfy the hungers and ease the pains of infancy and childhood. Mothers are seen as good when they cater to their children's every need. They are viewed as bad when they frustrate the child by not responding instantly to the child's needs.

Psychoanalytic theory argues that these different experiences with our mother produce conflicting feelings toward her. They may cause us to split our idea of mother into good mother and bad mother. As a child, it is scary to feel negative things about our mother on whom we are so dependent. We fear that she might turn on us and harm us for such negative thoughts. So, most of the time, we "stuff" the bad feelings and try to push them out of mind.

These bad feelings are unpleasant and dangerous, and they can be relieved by unconsciously displacing them onto the stepmother. That may help explain the persistence of wicked stepmothers in fairy tales, where they give the young child a place to dump all those uncomfortable feelings about his or her real mother. When we grow up, and Dad remarries, our stepmother may become a convenient person on whom to dump the negative part of our normal ambivalence toward our biological mother. In this way, we can experience completely positive feelings toward our biological mother and still have an outlet for angry, infantile feelings. The Freudians argue that this unconscious process is often hard to resist.

A STEPFATHER IS NOT SO BAD

The role of stepfather has less emotional charge. This may stem in large part from the fact that the stepfather traditionally enjoys higher economic status than the stepmother. Consequently, he is likely to improve the finances of his stepfamily instead of draining them off, as mythic stepmothers always do.

In literature, the stepfather is rarely depicted as grasping, unless he is younger than his wife and, thus, likely to be dependent on her. In addition, since, in the past, there has been little cultural expectation of emotional nurturance from stepfathers, perhaps anything he brings to the situation is considered an asset. In a recent study of attitudes of stepchildren over the age of nineteen, White found that a new stepmother is generally viewed negatively, but a new stepfather is not viewed differently from the children's own father. She concludes that the remarrying stepmother steps into a more difficult relationship than the stepfather.[†] Her finding comes as no surprise to most stepmothers. As more men either become househusbands or share equal responsibility for nurturing their children, the role of stepfather may engender the same emotional distaste as stepmother.

There are certain areas in which stepfathers have been viewed as suspect. There is a persistent stereotype that involves stepfathers' possible sexual advances to or physical abuse of their vulnerable stepdaughters. In adult stepfamilies, by definition, the daughters are adults living independently of their parents. Of course, that is no guarantee, and mothers should worry if a stepfather seems inappropriately attentive to their daughters.

STEREOTYPES OF STEPCHILDREN

The role of the stepchild has a mildly negative implication. In fact, the word *stepchild* is defined as "something that does not receive appropriate care, respect or attention."[‡] The connotation is that of a victim or an inadequate being. From Cinderella to Sleeping Beauty, Snow White, and Hansel and Gretel, stepchildren are seen as honest and engaging young people. Yet, they all become victims who are abused and overpowered by strong, evil females (stepmothers or witches). They passively await deliverance by strong, good people—all heroic men. The only fairy tale stepchild who transcends victimhood to become a hero is Hansel, the male stepchild, who instigates shoving the witch into the oven.

The word *stepchild* is also applied to an organization neglected by a thriving parent body. It has been used to describe struggling Third World nations. And a piece of legislation that is set aside, never to become law, is often referred to as a "stepchild bill."

When we think of stepchildren, we think of needy youngsters, cups in hand, who are weak, neglected, and deprived. We often see them as jealous, incomplete people, who may long to destroy the parent's new marriage.

All these negative connotations help explain why it can feel uncomfortable to use the term *step* when introducing a son or daughter acquired through marriage on social occasions. Imagine the double whammy of being both an adult stepchild in one family and a stepparent in your nuclear family. There, you are dealing with just too many negatives!

STEPPARENTS AND THEIR ADULT CHILDREN: MIRROR OF A REAL SOCIAL CONDITION

Beyond the symbolic factors we have discussed, there is a social reality to stepfamily conflict. As a result of remarriage, disputes often simmer around real changes in distribution of resources, including inheritance, and changes in the degree and quality of parental involvement and caring.

Our research showed that all members of the stepfamily are likely to become hostile and resentful on occasion. Adult children believe they are losing parental love, attention, and property to their new rivals. When parents remarry, they often fear disapproval from and abandonment by their children. These are the universal fears and feelings inherent in stepfamilies that we described in Chapter 1 as the Five Furies. Virtually all stepfamily members report feeling at least some of these Furies some of the time.

Our data suggest that, in adult families, the biological children of the stepmother are usually more pleased about their mother's remarriage than the biological children of the stepfather. Is this due to economic or social reasons or both?

The adult children of the father may anticipate more frustration about finances. They may feel this way because of their perception, and the common reality, that the father has more economic resources than his new wife. They may worry that he will give her a large part of their inheritance or, at the least, that her presence will delay its distribution to them.

This disparity in satisfaction among adult children may also stem from the realization on the part of the mother's children that it is much harder for an older woman to find a husband than for an older man to find a wife. Men are able to marry women across a wider age range—and do. For whatever reasons, adult children often see remarriage as improving their mother's situation, both socially and financially. The children of newly married fathers often assume he is getting, at best, more companionship, sex, and a live-in caretaker.

Historically, children have been correct in assuming their mothers are more likely to gain financially from a later-life marriage. Typically, in a remarried older couple, the wife is younger than the husband. The increased likelihood that the older husband will die before the younger wife means that, statistically, she is more likely to inherit his property than he is to inherit hers, and, in most cases, he has more property to inherit.

The inequality in wealth between men and women is changing, however, and the financial position of women in the future may be better than it is now. One consequence of greater financial equity between the sexes might be to remove some of the sting now associated with the role of stepmother.

As more women participate in the labor force, their resources may approach, equal, or even surpass their new mates'. In remarried older couples, a retired husband with a wife still in the labor force may find that her income is a significant source of their money. In such cases, her stepchildren may feel less threatened economically.

The future possibility that significantly more well-to-do women will marry less affluent, younger men adds yet another dimension to the tangle of financial complications that dog so many stepfamilies. Right now, in those still relatively rare cases where affluent widows marry much younger men, the young stepfather is often viewed as an opportunist or a gigolo—a negative stereotype that parallels that of the female gold digger.

WHAT HAPPENS WHEN ONE ROLE HAS TO TAKE A BACKSEAT?

Another aspect of the social reality of stepparenting is that parents usually find themselves in two roles: both a step- and a biological parent, with responsibilities that may conflict. Sociologists and social biologists argue that it is unlikely that stepparents will love stepchildren the same way they love their natural children simply because bonding hasn't taken place. A slew of problems arises from the guilt many stepparents have about their understandable preference for their own children. Many stepparents are never able to acknowledge these feelings even to themselves.

Stepmothers, in particular, may make extraordinary efforts to prove that the evil stepmother myth doesn't apply to them. Stepfathers, too, can overcompensate in an effort to be fair to stepchildren. Stepparents may fail to set limits because of guilt. And when they do set limits, their adult children may be angry and vocal in their displeasure. If stepchildren like the stepparent, they may feel that their fondness is a form of disloyalty to their displaced biological father or mother, whether that parent is alive or deceased. Ironically, stepchildren who like their stepparent may find that it feels safer to reject him or her because of this perceived disloyalty. Nonetheless, we've seen genuine affection grow among stepfamily members.

I'M MY OWN GRANDPA

Almost everyone in an adult stepfamily is trying to juggle at least two roles and sometimes more. In addition to being a biological parent, the stepmother or stepfather may also be a stepchild in another family or have stepchildren from a previous marriage. The adult stepchildren are often biological parents themselves, and, in some cases, may be stepparents as well. This begins to sound like the old country song "I'm My Own Grandpa," but such are the facts of life in a culture that allows people of whatever age to follow their hearts.

Forty-eight-year-old Alice told us:

When my adult stepchildren give me a rough time, I have to laugh with tears in my eyes and wonder if it is only payback for the way I punished my stepmother when I was a teenager.

The experience of having lived in different roles in stepfamilies earlier in one's life can lead to increased tolerance, as well as compassion, for family members suddenly cast in those roles. Many of us find that we actually have been in the other person's shoes.

WHAT'S IN A NAME?

We know that the negative myths and stereotypes associated with stepfamilies taint the words we use to describe step relationships. That said, as soon as we become part of a stepfamily, we find ourselves in social situations in which we have to use certain terms to define these precarious social relationships. The word *step* is generally perceived as an unpleasant way to introduce anyone, and it may splash cold water in the face of many social interactions.

When adult women or men are introduced as "stepdaughters" or "stepsons," two things generally occur. First, they may feel resentful, because they don't consider themselves the daughters or sons of the person who is introducing them. Second, they may be repelled by the implication that they want or need another parent. "This is my stepmother/father" can feel equally injurious to a stepparent. The terms "my mother's husband" or "my father's wife" or "my husband's son," etc., may be preferred, but these words are experienced by many people as implying a distant relationship. It may be a good idea to ask what terms would make your stepfamily members feel most comfortable. Some may prefer an introduction without any relationship heading, such as "I'd like you to meet Andy."

If the relationships warm up over the years, the language of introduction often warms up as well. Whether they have entered the family following their spouses' divorce or widow(er)hood, most stepparents feel self-conscious about appearing to elbow their way into the new parental role. Particularly in families where the adult child's other biological parent is deceased, we find that the word "step" may be gradually dropped and "our son or daughter" or "my folks" or even "mom and dad" may be used. In stepfamilies that were preceded by a divorce, the stepparent is also concerned about encroaching on the absent biological parent's turf. In this context, however, language and labels play out somewhat differently. Consequently, we have devised the terms "borrowed daughter" and "borrowed son" to imply a warm parental feeling without challenging the relationship with the biological parent. "Borrowed" suggests that you don't own the relationship and therefore are not competing with members of the biological family for love. Ours is a culture that has learned the power of words to wound and distance others—racial and ethnic slurs, for example—and has wisely adopted new, kinder words to describe others. Why not find kinder better words to describe members of the growing number of adult stepfamilies in our culture?

THE FIVE SAVING GRACES

In Chapter 1, we discussed the dangers, the Five Furies, that virtually all of our stepfamilies experienced to some degree. The Furies often take up much of the new stepfamily's time and leave members roiled and exhausted by their efforts to cope. So much time is diverted to allaying the Furies that we fail to appreciate the opportunities that are equally real, but less obvious, and may take longer to recognize.

Just as unhappy stepfamilies had much in common, happy ones evidenced certain similarities. There were at least Five Saving Graces that these successful families discovered in their new roles. These are the upsides to adult stepfamilies that members should look for and cultivate. The Graces are:

- fulfilling remarriage

- facilitating objectivity, maturity, and wisdom

- friendship between stepparents and stepchildren

- fraternity of siblings and stepsiblings

- freedom from filial responsibility

HOW THE FIVE SAVING GRACES WORK

First Saving Grace: Fulfilling Remarriage and the consequent surge in parental happiness may enhance the ability of parents to nurture their children and grandchildren, biological and step. Often, the parent's happiness results in his or her parenting more appropriately, because the parent's needs to be loved and cared for are being met within the new marriage.

Forty-year-old Judy put it this way:

My dad and mom were divorced ten years ago. After that, my dad acted more like a younger brother than a father, asking me for advice, confiding in me about the women he was dating. Our phone calls were 90 percent about him. Since he's been married to Sue, there has really been a change. He stays focused on how I am doing, my kids, my job. It's amazing.

Thirty-eight-year-old Brad described changes in his remarried father:

Ultimately, I have gotten closer to him, and partially it's due to the woman that he married. She is very open, and I think she cares a lot about being open, and I think—I'm not saying she is necessarily better for him than my mother was—but I think she is very good for him. And also around the time of his getting divorced and remarried he was having some alcoholic problems. I guess he was more like a tippler than an alcoholic. Anyway, eventually five years ago, my dad went into AA. He used to be kind of short on the phone. He never liked the phone and said it was for communication, not conversation. Now, I can actually talk with him. He'll actually stay on the phone, and I think he's a lot more emotionally open than he used to be.

Second Saving Grace: Facilitating Objectivity, Maturity, and Wisdom. All members of the stepfamily have the opportunity to become wiser and more realistic about themselves and others. This capacity develops as members of the new stepfamily renegotiate family roles, adapt to a new group of players, and learn from the process of creating a new, adult stepfamily.

Visiting a foreign country can make you more aware of aspects of your own culture that you might not have appreciated previously. Observing your stepfamily up close can serve the same function. You may find that there are positive things about your biological family that you never before fully valued. Additionally, you may discover admirable aspects of your stepfamily that can be applied to your biological family, such as better ways to handle conflict.

Greater objectivity about your own children is another benefit of this second Saving Grace. Hearing the point of view of a new spouse can give a parent a more realistic view of his or her *own* children and valuable insights into how *he* or *she* behaves as a parent. This is more likely to happen if the new spouse offers counsel in a tactful and constructive way, without evoking guilt or shame.

For motivated parents, it's never too late to learn new things about themselves and to see how another concerned adult perceives their adult children and grandchildren. Nonetheless, these moments require enormous tact and do the most good when the spouse has had sufficient time and exposure to begin to know a stepchild. Impulsive, angry remarks about a spouse's children are never welcome and are rarely helpful.

Seventy-year-old Bob recalled:

It was painful when my wife Mary told me that my thirty-five-year-old son, Peter, though he was charming and intelligent, would probably never learn to keep a job if I kept giving him money every time he quit his job after some disagreement arose at work. She was right. I was just helping him avoid having to learn to deal with frustration except by walking out. I was letting my guilt about having divorced his mother outweigh my good common sense.

Greater objectivity about your parents is another advantage of this second Saving Grace. Generous, insightful stepsiblings can help an adult child see a parent more clearly and deal with him or her more effectively. Stepsiblings may simply validate what an adult child already knows. At other times, they help adult children see their parents in surprising and illuminating new ways.

We were told about such a conversation between two stepbrothers, in which David told Tony:

> *I've never seen my father so respectful and proud of a woman as he is with your mother. He did all the talking when he was married to my mom. He really listens now. With my mom, he never wanted to know what she thought.*

David told Tony his father's current marriage had drawn out aspects of his father's personality he had never seen before, including a number of positive traits. For David, seeing that his father could succeed in a marriage was a relief—one that gave David hope for himself. After listening to David, his thirty-six-year-old stepbrother began to see his own mother in a more positive way.

AN EDUCATION IN CONFLICT RESOLUTION AND SELF-AWARENESS

People in stepfamilies tend to talk more about their relationships with each other, both positive and negative, than the average nuclear family. In some stepfamilies, the biological siblings start out banding together and telling stories about the failings and deficiencies of their new stepparent and stepsiblings. While not especially attractive, such talk may give members of the other biological family opportunities to observe how other people communicate and handle everyday problems. Stepfamilies, by necessity, have to learn to be more flexible and adaptive. They are undergoing a learning process, like it or not, and, with time, may well become more self-aware than intact nuclear families, who don't have to make as many accommodations.

Our culture promotes the process of dealing openly with negative feelings in stepfamilies by telling us it's acceptable to dislike your stepfamily. As a result, members of stepfamilies tend to recognize and tolerate their ambivalence about each other and talk fairly easily about their negative feelings. They usually discover that these negative feelings can be managed over time and don't have to become permanent barriers to accommodation. Having been thrown together without prior consent, they usually adapt to differences they never expected to face. In the process, they often develop and hone new social skills and considerable wisdom.

Individuals in stepfamilies are typically forced to interact repeatedly with people who don't share their history or their habits. As a result, members of stepfamilies are often called upon to explain their beliefs and practices. Thus, they have many opportunities to clarify and advance their own thinking. By contrast, biological families may never question their ideas or practices and, thus, remain naïve by comparison.

Stepfamilies go through a kind of a psychological boot camp, where they must learn to negotiate and reach workable compromises. They discover that there are many more stakeholders in family life than they had imagined. This kind of experience can be grueling, but it can also be rewarding. It accelerates maturity. And we don't just mean getting gray hair. It can enrich the lives of every member of the new family.

Third Saving Grace: Friendships with a Stepparent or Adult Stepchild. For the adult stepchild, reaching out to the new stepparent—for example, by arranging for time alone to get to know each other—can gradually develop into a true friendship. You can educate your stepparent about yourself and learn from him or her. Offer information about your likes and dislikes, hopes and dreams, and ask them about theirs.

Use the stepparent as a surrogate parent or mentor. The parent whom you love and admire may well have chosen a fine spouse once again, maybe even a better one. Take advantage of that new person in your own life. The new stepparent can be especially valuable because he or she is probably more objective about you than your parent. It is worth trying to enroll a new stepparent to your personal advisory council.

Your stepparent may, of course, not be willing or able to become your mentor, but it is worth a try. A new, special adult friend can be a partial replacement for a deceased, mentally ill, or inadequate parent. And a stepparent can be drafted to become a valuable and valued extra grandparent for your children. Your children can never have too many adults who care about their development and happiness.

For a stepparent, the opportunity to develop a genuine friendship with a younger kindred spirit can be an extra dividend of a new marriage. Stepchildren, after all, don't carry the emotional baggage of your own biological offspring. Nor do you.

As sixty-one-year-old Hal told us:

The easiest issue has been my friendship with my stepdaughter. I really love her, and we warmed up to each other right away. I'm happy to indulge her in material things because she has been less indulged than my children by my other two marriages. And she's so appreciative. My natural children are a little more blasé about that. So, when I found out that there was a computer she wanted and she was going to save up for it, I said "Let's just go next door and buy it." And she was so delighted. Now, my other kids would say, "Oh yeah, that's nice, thanks."

Remarriage may, in some cases, be a chance for a stepparent to share an interest—like sports or movies or computers—with this new friend. For some, it is the opportunity to have something very like the grown son or daughter they do not have biologically, without the sometimes burdensome feelings of parental responsibility.

Stepchildren may accept you as a mentor and advisor much more readily than your own children do. But the mentor role, like so much else about stepfamilies, requires tact. You need considerable finesse to do it in a way that doesn't compete with or threaten the biological parent(s). Generally, the difference in age tends to blur the distinction between parenting and friendship in relationships between stepparents and stepchildren.

If, however, a stepparent is of the same generation as an adult stepchild, a friendship between equals may develop. This may happen when a parent marries someone young enough to be his (less often her) child, even though his biological children may initially resent it. There are wonderful possibilities for friendship in stepfamilies if one party takes the initiative and reaches out to another member.

Fourth Saving Grace: Fraternity of Siblings and Stepsiblings. For siblings, parental remarriage may bring you closer to your own siblings and end in your creating a tighter family unit. You can share being outsiders or observers at a certain stage in the development of the stepfamily. Sometimes, a parent's remarriage leads to the reconciliation of estranged siblings. It can provide a chance to resolve old conflicts or forgive old hurts and to find a new closeness with siblings and enhanced pleasure in doing things with them.

Twenty-six-year-old Anna told us:

My sister and I have very different lifestyles. I'm an artist, and, half the year, I have to sublet my apartment and live in my studio to meet expenses. She's a successful investment banker and never took my work seriously. She spends more on clothes each year than I make. We are from opposite ends of the spectrum. But since our dad died and our mother remarried, we have become really close in a way I never imagined could happen. We helped each other to get through Mom's wedding and to learn to accept Mom's husband. Together with my sister, I found the courage to ask Mom if our dad had earmarked any of the property he owned to go directly to the two of us. Mom thought it over and agreed that he had wanted that, and she transferred it to us.

Stepsiblings may find they have real affinities to new stepfamily members that overcome any potential conflicts. Get to know your stepsiblings. Give them a chance. Make them allies. Be inclusive. We interviewed two families in which stepsiblings not only became friends, they married each other.

Forty-two-year-old Alice told us:

When Jeff and I met at our parents' wedding, we both felt a big attraction and started talking to each other, and, well . . . we found we had so much in common. Our feelings for each other just kept growing, and we married the following year. We feel so lucky that our parents married. Then, when our children were born, it tied us all together in a very special way.

Stepsiblings can become resources for each other, offering everything from advice about childrearing to job contacts.

Thirty-four-year-old Andrea told us:

When my first child was an infant, we had a lot of trouble putting her to sleep at night. She would scream, and I would go back to her crib and pick her up. She would scream again when I put her down. I was exhausted. I decided to call my husband's stepsister, who had had a baby three months before mine. She had read a book on establishing bedtime routines for babies and was very helpful.

Contact with stepsiblings can often ease fears that they are getting a better deal out of the parents' marriage than you are. And if they turn out to be adversaries, so be it. It is still better to have reached out to them and taken their measure.

> **Fifth Saving Grace:** Freedom from Filial Responsibility. A parent's remarriage allows an adult child to feel less guilty about not spending enough time with an unmarried parent. Now, you don't have to worry about whether Mom or Dad has plans for the weekend. You don't have to feel it is your job to relieve your parent's loneliness or fill your parent's calendar with social activities. You no longer have to make daily calls to check up on your parent. Having a loving someone to care for an aging or sick parent is an enormous relief, especially if the child has long had a conflict with that parent.

For parents, one of the joys of remarriage is knowing that your adult children don't have to feel unduly responsible for you at a time when they are working hard and raising their own children. Remarriage relieves parents from the guilt of feeling they are a burden on their children.

Sixty-two-year-old Frances said:

I used to feel so badly when I'd be on the phone with my daughter and sensed the exhaustion in her voice and heard the kids calling her in the background. I remembered when I was raising a family myself, and the last thing I needed was to have a long telephone conversation with my mother. Now, I'm busy with Tom.

Being able to share concerns about children and grandchildren with a spouse can be very comforting. Now you have a best friend, a mate, and a secure place of your own where the two of you can meet each other's needs.

NEVER TOO LATE FOR THE GRACES

The Five Saving Graces can enhance the life of your stepfamily, whether it is just being formed or it is long established. If you have been feeling stuck in your stepfamily for a long time, thinking about these potential positives may give you a more hopeful, upbeat way of looking at things. To discover the Saving Graces of your stepfamily, you need to reframe the way you look at the changes taking place in your family structure. You need to make the effort to discover assets, advantages, and opportunities in the new arrangement.

The Saving Graces can help you develop a new folklore and family history with members of your stepfamily without destroying or weakening the existing biological bonds. So much of our happiness depends on how we view our situation and the meaning we make of events. Having more family can feel better and richer, instead of lesser and poorer.

SOME ADDITIONAL ADVICE

Don't become demoralized and give up if you accidentally detonate an explosion or two. It happens, and our advice is to let it go. Hurtful words and actions often come from people who are feeling hurt themselves. Stepfamilies can be demanding, and sometimes all that holds you together is the legal fact that you are a family. Sometimes, the best you can do is forgive yourself and others and trust that your next encounter with each other will be better.

If you're the parent, remember that the adult child is still your child, and, under these unusual circumstances, may be reverting involuntarily to unattractive behavior he or she demonstrated at an earlier time. We found that the most dependent children reacted the most intensely. Responding with anger will only escalate matters.

Try to remember, it's the roles and circumstances that are driving emotions and behaviors. And, however charged with emotion the atmosphere becomes, you are still you and not just your roles. As we said earlier, it's most likely the role, not you, that needs fixing. In fact, in dealing with stepfamilies, it often helps to think more about roles and less about personality, although personalities don't go away altogether.

There are obvious similarities between steprelations and in-law relations. At first glance, one might think that the stepmother and the mother-in-law roles offer the greatest parallel, given the abundance of negative folklore that clings to both. When we look more closely, however, the real parallel is between the roles of stepchildren and mother-in-law: both find themselves in their new roles as the result of other people's—not their own—choices. Both may feel entrapped and frustrated.

Actors in both roles may say they are pleased that their parent or child has found happiness with a spouse, but their real feelings are probably ambivalent at best. Both know they have to make room for the new spouse, who, even by ancient tradition, is supposed to take emotional precedence over all previous relationships. But there is no getting around the fact that neither the timing of the new relationship, nor the particular individual chosen was necessarily the one that the stepchildren or the mother-in-law would have selected.

Remember, roles will "getcha if you don't watch out." That is true for both the new couple and all their children. Still, the stepmother probably has the most complex, demanding role in the new family drama. After all, as we have seen, there is nary a myth that features a good stepmother. In fact *wicked* and *stepmother* have been conjoined linguistically, culturally, and emotionally for so long that many contemporary stepchildren humorously update the phrase as "wicked stepmonster."

Still, the stepchild role is not easy, either. As we noted earlier, *stepchild* denotes things that are neglected or badly treated, whether they are poor nations or marginalized public policies. That usage is not coincidental.

Stepping into a role fraught with eons of emotional and cultural cobwebs is no easy matter. For some, it proves to be impossible. We have dwelt more on the stepmother's and stepchildren's roles, because they tend to be more problematic. But, rest assured, the whitewater rapids of adult stepfamilies are tough for everyone—and we do mean *everyone*—to negotiate.

In stepfamilies, as in other situations that are both emotionally charged and of critical importance, it is always wise to think before you leap into action or say things that you can never take back. Stepfamilies are new, complicated worlds. Your words and actions are yours to choose. But remember, the stepfamily is a social system. Everything that each person does has an impact—for better or worse—on everyone else. You can make life better for everyone and set a good example by promoting the Five Saving Graces while keeping the Five Furies at bay. It's worth a try or two—or two dozen.

In the next two chapters, we shall discuss the consequences of important events that occurred prior to the remarriage. First, we'll consider the aftereffects of divorce on the stepfamily. Next, we'll deal with consequences for the stepfamily when a parent remarries after the death of a spouse.

* Persall, Judy (ed.). (2002). *Concise Oxford English Dictionary*. 10th Edition (Oxford: Oxford University Press).

** Watson, P.A. (1995). *Ancient Stepmothers: Myth, Misogyny and Reality* (New York, NY: Brill).

†White, Lynn. (2001). "Acquiring Stepparents in Adulthood." *Proceedings of National Conference on Family Relations Annual Conference,* Nov. 8, Rochester, NY.

**Editors of the American Heritage Dictionaries*. (2000). *The American Heritage Dictionary of the English Language*. 4th Edition (Boston, MA: Houghton Mifflin Co.).

PART II

Does History Matter?

CHAPTER 5

What If the Old Marriage Ended in Divorce?

HISTORY COUNTS

Does it really matter how the old marriage ended—in divorce or widow(er)hood? You bet it does. But not in any simple way. Both divorce and widowhood create their own complex backdrops for later-in-life marriages and domestic partnerships. And, of course, each new relationship produces its own special complications.

In short, each case is unique. As a result, in this chapter, we can only talk about the most common patterns that flow from these two precursors of the new adult stepfamily. In fact, these patterns do not fit very neatly into a typology. Still, we think you'll recognize bits and pieces of your own situation in the patterns we shall describe. In this chapter, we'll deal with divorce as the precursor; in the next, we'll examine widow(er)hood.

WHAT'S SPECIAL ABOUT DIVORCE?

Divorce, as a forerunner to a later-in-life love, has its own pluses and minuses. On the plus side, if you are the new love and the ex-spouse is still living, you will be compared with a real person, not a romanticized, idealized figure, as dead spouses tend to become. You and the former spouse will be viewed, more or less, as human, with strengths and imperfections that all can see. Moreover, except in unusual cases, for at least the first decade, and we do mean *de-*

cade, your spouse will have many opportunities to remember just why he or she split from the ex-spouse.

After a decade or so, even the most estranged ex-spouses may mellow toward one another. They often come to see their former life as something quite distant, like the rerun of an old movie (often an old horror film) that has lost its punch. This mellowing is especially likely if both ex-spouses have moved on to happier relationships and lives. Still, remember that achieving this comfortable distance from a past marriage can take a very long time indeed. Moreover, one ex-spouse may arrive at this desirable state much sooner than the other, often depending on who initiated the divorce.

THE EX LIVES ON AS WELL AS OFF THE SCENE

On the minus side, while the idealized ghost of a dead spouse can haunt a new marriage, a divorced ex-spouse is very much alive, a constant presence in the new stepfamily, if only in the background. Sometimes, divorced spouses inject themselves into the foreground with potentially explosive results. This is most often true if they are nourishing fantasies of reconciliation and/or have not yet established a fulfilling new relationship.

When the former spouse has not remarried, things can be turbulent, particularly if the ex-spouse didn't want the divorce. This common scenario calls for serious patience on the remarrieds' part. Often the best strategy is to focus on your own new life and realize that the ex-spouse is probably doing the best he or she can do at the moment—even when that "best" is pretty awful. Venting with a buddy who is "living the life" or has been in the same situation in the past also helps mightily!

To some extent, you can avoid situations that invite comparisons between yourself and your new love's former spouse, but you will never be able to avoid them altogether. In fact, comparisons are made not just by family members but by friends and neighbors, too. Our best advice: Be yourself. Don't try to demonstrate that you are better, different, etc. There's nothing to be gained, and that approach only keeps you from establishing relationships on an authentic basis.

EVERYONE IS TRYING TO MAKE THE BEST OF IT

Over time, just being yourself will be all the proof anyone needs that you are a worthy—or at least a reasonable—new stepparent. Besides, it's exhausting to try to be someone else for any length of time. So, concentrate on your spouse, your stepchildren, and yourself, and let your predecessor handle his or her relations with everyone else. A good mantra for difficult moments is: "It's her/his problem, not mine."

If you are the stepparent, you are in the middle between your spouse and his or her children's other biological parent. Remember, however, that the stepchildren are caught in the middle, too, trying to balance their loyalties and affections between their divorced parents and also between their other very much alive biological parent and you. Everyone's position is fraught with some degree of confusion, ambiguity, and ambivalence. If you are also divorced with children, that only adds additional players and ups the ante all the way around.

So, you will need great stores of patience and empathy. If you can't muster those virtuous emotions, at least try to choose your words carefully. Others will remember them, even if you don't.

WHEN THE STEPPARENT HAS NO BIOLOGICAL CHILDREN

Let's start with the simplest situation: Only one member of the new couple has children (this applies whether the ex-spouse is divorced or deceased). When the stepparent has no children of his or her own, this can mean one of three things: either the stepparent has never been able to have children and may now be looking forward to having a "ready-made" family; or he or she has deliberately avoided having children because of career pressures, lack of interest, or other issues, and now finds that he or she has children nonetheless; or, in the most tragic situation, the new stepparent may have had children, who are no longer living.

Stepparents who were never able to have or have lost biological children may be the most open to being a Joiner, as we saw in Chapter 3. They are also the ones who may have the greatest—often, too great—expectations for the creation of a new, loving family unit with parents and adult stepchildren all linked together. Nonetheless, when a divorced, lonely biological parent is hovering in the background, the stepchildren, despite the best intentions, may be unwilling or unable to accept the overtures of the new stepparent.

Leah was a fifty-one-year-old, never-married woman at the time that she and Al married. She was ecstatic about the idea of "having it all" at this stage in her life. She had been a career woman, completely focused on building her small business, not an easy task under any circumstances. Al understood and even admired her dedication to her work.

In some respects, Al was attracted to Leah because she *didn't* bring a complex family situation into the picture. Since his divorce, Al had found relationships with single mothers were more than he could handle. He loved his three grown kids, a girl and two boys, and he wasn't all that interested in other people's children.

THE STEPMOTHER THINKS HER PRAYERS ARE ANSWERED

Leah, for her part, thought having a family of grown kids was perfect. No fuss, no muss—kids without labor or laundry, all of whom had lives of their own. The daughter was married with children, and the two sons were away at school, one an undergraduate, the other an MBA student. On the few occasions when she had met them, Leah thought them interesting, intelligent, and polite. She liked them and looked forward to including them in her relationship with Al.

This is how Leah tells her story:

At first, the boys seemed willing to be part of our new little family. Whenever they came to visit us in Vermont, we were happy to see them. They seemed comfortable with us. John, Al's oldest boy, expressed an interest in my business, a small financial consulting firm, and I thought he might want to join me when he finished his MBA. In fact, we talked about it from time to time. Not in a detailed, serious way, but in a "possibility" way.

We saw less of Naomi (Al's daughter) and her family, mostly because they lived in Seattle. They were nice enough when we were together. Not very outgoing, but not rejecting, either.

Things could sometimes be very confusing and frustrating for me, particularly with John and his younger brother, Ed. Whenever I thought John and I were really beginning to connect, the next time we spoke on the phone or tried to plan a family event, he would seem more distant. Almost as if he felt he had gotten too close for comfort. As if he felt guilty for "joining the other side."

I always felt that it was Al's ex-wife, Sue, who was behind it all. Somehow, she couldn't stand the idea of the kids being close to me and their father. She and Al had had a very angry divorce, and there are still a lot of sparks between them.

Al thinks she is still furious that he was the one who wanted out. She feels he dumped her after so many years and that that wasn't fair. Al thinks she wants the kids to take her side and cut him out of their lives. I don't think the boys want to cut their father out, and I think that, left to themselves, they'd be happy to be with both of us. I don't mean to the exclusion of their mother. After all, I had nothing to do with the divorce. I didn't even meet Al until two years after his divorce. But Sue has hated me from the first. I think she would have hated anyone who married Al. She thinks that's her rightful role.

When John got engaged last summer, we offered to have an engagement party for him at our place, but Sue stepped in and said it should be at her place. She still lives in their old house, the house in which the kids grew up, so it has sentimental meaning to them. I was sort of hurt that, after we offered first, John turned around and let his mother throw the party. He never even tried to explain it to me.

We were invited to the party, but I really dreaded going. You can imagine going to the place where Al had lived all those years with Sue and his kids. I had never been there. I knew I'd feel out of place, like an outsider. I wanted to be a good sport and carry it off with aplomb, but I wasn't sure that I could.

When the day came, I was very uptight. So was Al, but he didn't want to admit it. He kept attributing his mood to dealing with John's transition into marriage and a family of his own. I suppose there was some of that, but I think he dreaded confronting Sue in that setting.

Well, as you can imagine, it turned out to be a disaster. I was treated as the invisible woman. The kids totally ignored me, even John, with whom I felt I had a pretty good relationship, said about two words to me. Sue kept acting as if she were still Al's wife, dragging him away to greet old friends and leaving me standing by myself. I tried hard to be sociable with the other guests, but it was a total nightmare.

Later, I learned that Sue told some of the other guests that we had socialized too much with their old friends. Can you believe that? Al was just trying to be a real "father of the groom" for John's sake. And I was only trying to avoid being mistaken for a potted plant.

That whole afternoon, I tried to keep my feelings in check and my mouth shut so that Al wouldn't feel torn between his kids and me. It was pretty grim, and I was very upset for the rest of the week. What made things even worse was that Al felt I should blow the whole thing off. But I couldn't.

Not a pleasant picture, but one that is quite common. Part of the problem stems from that old bugaboo, high expectations. In this case, the troublesome high expectations were those Leah had for her relationship with Al's adult children.

THE STEPMOTHER COMES DOWN TO EARTH

Leah entered the stepfamily scene prepared, even eager, to have a close relationship with Al's kids. The kids, clearly, were conflicted. Yes, John, at least, appeared to like Leah, but his feelings for his mother seem to have gotten in the way. His mother, feeling lonely and angry, may be unwilling to relinquish her fantasy of reestablishing her relationship with Al and may focus most of her anger on Leah. Here, we see at least two sets of unrealistic expectations on a collision course: Leah's expectations that the kids will join her and Al in a happy adult stepfamily; and Sue's unrealistic hope of turning back the clock.

How could Leah have handled this situation in a way that would have caused her less pain? First, let's be realistic. This was a classic adult stepfamily situation from which few escape totally unscathed. So, perhaps the first thing Leah needed was to have a serious consultation with a buddy who'd been there, done that. Leah might have been warned by her friend that those old Furies, Fear of Abandonment and Isolation, as well as concern about Fidelity to Family, are almost always present, to some degree. Armed with that knowledge, she might have been able to scale back her expectations about the ease and rapidity with which she and Al could establish a happy new family unit. Leah wanted to assume the roles of Joiner and Unifier, but, generally, it takes time—sometimes years—for other family members to let stepparents take on the roles of their choice.

MEANWHILE, THE STEPCHILDREN ARE WORKING OUT THEIR OWN LIVES

The emotions of the stepchildren, particularly the sons, were jerking them in several directions at once. The biological parents may have been jerking them around as well, whether they knew it or not. Further complicating the situation, these two unmarried sons were still in the process of making the first emotional break from their parents to become independent adults. John was further along than Ed on that score, but neither was truly independent, and that made Al's sons particularly vulnerable.

Naomi, Al's daughter, who was living three thousand miles away in Seattle, was geographically distanced. It isn't clear if she was also an emotional Distancer or simply Indifferent. Naomi had her own family, and she was focusing on that. She tried to comfort her mother, but she didn't see a big role for herself or her family with Leah and Al. Naomi's geographic distance also made her aloofness less of an issue for Leah.

The sons don't seem to have selected any particular role, but they seem to have been inclined to be Joiners. At least, that was true for John. Perhaps, if and when his mother develops a happier postdivorce life, John will feel less guilty about reaching out to Leah.

STEP INTO THE ROLE OF REPORTER

The actual engagement party was also full of painfully familiar pitfalls. As we have said, seeking the counsel of an experienced friend might have helped Leah—and it might have helped Sue, as well. Another Tact and Tacking strategy for coping with an emotionally tense command performance is to take the role of a detached observer. Step back from the situation a bit and try to assume the role of an objective observer. Try to forget that you are emotionally involved in the family psychodrama and act as if you were reporting on it for CNN or *The Washington Post*. Yes, you can see how nervous the future bridegroom and his fiancée are. Yes, you notice how the remarried parent is ill at ease and how this makes him act in ways that you wouldn't have predicted. Yes, the former spouse is also in a difficult spot, perhaps the toughest one of all. So, try cutting your predecessor a little slack, even if you know her well enough to have angry feelings of your own.

Try to "stay in role" as the observer, not as a family member. Of course, you can't get so caught up in playing the observer that you fail to respond appropriately to other guests and family members. After all, you're the stepmother at a family party, not Christiane Amanpour reporting from a war zone.

WHEN THE EX-SPOUSE WON'T ACCEPT THE "EX"

Sometimes an ex-spouse acts as if the divorce never occurred. The next vignette demonstrates how a former spouse can be an irritating flesh-and-blood presence.

This is the story of Florence, age sixty-five, married to Chuck, whose previous wife, Annabelle, manages to make her presence seen, heard, and felt. Chuck and Annabelle have four grown children, three married daughters and one unmarried son. All four grown children live nearby.

Florence was a widow, whose daughter was killed in a car accident five years before her marriage to Chuck. Florence and Chuck have been married for almost eight years.

This is how Florence told her story:

I don't really know what to do about Annabelle. She is there all the time, at every holiday and every birthday. She just won't go away. She and

Chuck have been divorced more than fifteen years, but that doesn't seem to make much difference.

Annabelle lives in the next town, so she is quite close by. She acts as if she is entitled to be considered part of our new family. Of course, I realize she is my stepchildren's mother, but she intrudes into our lives whenever she can.

There isn't a single holiday or birthday at which she doesn't appear. I can understand how it came about, almost naturally, from the way Chuck and Annabelle lived after their divorce. During those years before Chuck and I got together, Annabelle always invited everyone to her house for the holidays. Chuck would go back to her house for the children's sake. So, if you look at their photos from holidays and birthdays before and after the divorce, you can't tell the difference. All the same faces, at least among the adults. A few new grandchildren appear in the later photos, but that's the only change.

When Chuck and I got married, I was sort of surprised that Annabelle was still so much a part of the family scene. The first Thanksgiving, we invited all the children and their families (only Chuck's son isn't married) to our home for dinner. Since my own daughter died, I was looking forward to having children again around the Thanksgiving table, in this case, stepchildren. I felt I could be a loving stepmother, and I couldn't wait for the chance.

Chuck was in a bind. I guess he didn't quite know how to tell me that we'd have to invite Annabelle, too. I was still a newlywed, and I felt uncomfortable starting a fuss about this. Besides, I couldn't believe that Annabelle would come. I just thought it was a pro forma invitation, and that she would understand and decline. I couldn't believe she would be comfortable, any more than I would be.

Perhaps, I should have gotten the clue when Chuck invited her to our wedding. He said he wanted to do it for the children's sake. Since she was one of fifty-something guests, I didn't pay much mind to it then. I thought that was quite big of Chuck to invite her. Besides, I didn't particularly notice her at the wedding.

Annabelle acts as if she is the Queen Mother, entitled and in charge. If I say dinner will be served at six, she somehow manages to change it to five. I try to be calm and polite when she is around, but I seethe underneath. Chuck doesn't seem to get it. He just sees a family that has "adapted" wonderfully to the divorce and remarriage. He doesn't see that I feel like an outsider, an interloper, when I should feel that I'm his wife, without the constant presence of his former wife.

Annabelle is always pleasant and charming on the surface. But it's very weird. She treats me as if I'm a guest in my own home and that she is really the wife and mother. She's even told me that her divorce from

Chuck "doesn't seem real" to her. I think she's telling me she's really still his wife.

I've tried talking to Chuck about this, but he never wants to discuss it, except to say that he can't see any difficulty with how we do things. He thinks we'd be buying trouble, creating a hornet's nest, if we tried to change anything now. He thinks this way we are being "very civilized." I want to be civilized, too. I don't want to be petty. But this whole thing just gets to me.

Annabelle is off the charts, compared to most ex-spouses, who usually exert their presence as a voice on the telephone or more indirectly through their children's actions. What is Florence's best strategy for coping with Annabelle's presence at every family get-together?

ONCE YOU ACCEPT A TRADITION, HOW DO YOU CHANGE IT?

First, Florence needs to weigh the costs and benefits of trying to change a pattern that she has seemed to accept for more than eight years. Up to this point, Florence has taken the Joiner role on all of these occasions. She needs to think seriously about how she will be perceived if she suddenly changes roles and how she will explain it to those members of her stepfamily who are old enough to require an explanation. Florence must be certain restructuring this arrangement is worth the tension and unhappiness it is likely to cause. If she decides it is, some Tact and Tacking, particularly *negotiating,* would be useful here. If Florence decides the effort is worth the potential turbulence, she should approach Chuck once again—he, too, may be weary of the scene by now.

Dilute

If Florence wants to avoid the head-on approach, or if she finds Chuck too resolute, then there are ways to dilute the impact of Annabelle's presence at holiday meals. First, Florence might engage in a familiar Tact and Tacking strategy: She could *reframe* the situation by inviting additional guests, particularly friends and acquaintances who otherwise might be spending the day alone. This restructing of the event would give everyone a fresh opportunity to regroup. At birthday celebrations, too, Florence might consider a slightly enlarged guest list, this time to include special friends of the birthday person. The presence of more people, including some whom the birthday person is especially fond of, might make Annabelle's presence less intrusive. If so, the modicum of extra work involved in adding a few more guests when one already has invited a crowd would be more than worth the effort.

Redesign

Alternatively, if the celebration involves a sit-down meal, how about seating people at tables for four? Then, Florence and Chuck could sit with the grandchildren or adult children without having to interact directly with Annabelle. If the meal is buffet style, it would be quite easy for the couple to select dinner partners and seating far away from Annabelle without its being painfully obvious. That way, Florence and Annabelle probably only need to greet one another as the guests arrive and leave. Minimizing their interaction should diminish the emotional pain on both sides.

Reprocess

Arranging for a predinner psych session and a postdinner catharsis with a friend in the same boat can work wonders here, too. You need not spend all your time comparing notes, but both of you will get a sympathetic ear from someone who understands your feelings and your situation. In addition, a friend with similar stepfamily problems probably has a vested interest in keeping your chat strictly confidential.

Observe

Remember, one way to deal with emotionally difficult scenes with stepchildren or stepparents is to think about how you would report this to a journalism class or a therapy group. Forcing yourself into the *observer* role gives you some emotional distance from the fireworks that may go off in such situations.

The *reporter*'s or *observer*'s role also helps you to see both the humor and the pathos in the situation—even the humor and pathos in your own reactions when the Furies are nipping at your heels. Think how you would present your report if you were appearing on the *Oprah* show. Laughing at ourselves often is the best medicine.

Generosity—another reliable Tact and Tacking strategy—helps here, too. We aren't Pollyannas, and we know how hard it can be to act with grace and generosity when you are hurting. Yet, it is almost always worth a try. If nothing else, it allows you to claim the moral high ground—even if no one knows it but you and your spouse.

Alternate

Florence might also consider alternating the Chuck *en famille* scene with visits to members of her own family—siblings, cousins, or aunts, for example. Annabelle and her children could then spend the holiday together on their own, an opportunity for uncomplicated intimacy that they might enjoy occasionally. That way, at holiday time, Florence would only have to deal with Annabelle half as often. Changing a long-established pattern requires some *negotiating,* especially when the drill has been set for so long. Still, Chuck would probably see the equity in this new arrangement: half the time with his children and former spouse, half the time with Florence's extended family.

Reward

Florence might also think about planning a weekend getaway with Chuck to offset the tense togetherness of stepfamily encounters. Having next week's minivacation to think about, while preparing for Annabelle's presence, could put Florence in a happier, more tolerant mood. After all, 98 percent of the time, Florence and Chuck are together without Annabelle. The remaining two percent can be made more tolerable—just as visits to the dentist are—by imagining yourself on some tropical island.

STEPPARENTS WITH KIDS OF THEIR OWN

Stepparents who have their own biological children may be less interested in or more wary of creating "one big happy family," as we saw earlier. They understand that having kids means hard work, even when the kids are adults, with complicated, demanding lives of their own.

When both newlyweds have biological children, one or both members of the remarried couple may feel they'd like to keep their distance, not in a mean or nasty way, only in a wary but civil way. But, like many other stepfamily roles, the newlyweds may have little choice. Often, the exigencies of the new stepfamily draw even the most wary stepparents into the currents, despite their initial misgivings.

BEEN THERE, DONE THAT

Stepparents may be weary from bringing up their own kids, particularly in the shadow of divorce or death. They've been through their own kids' adolescence, that emotional rodeo in which just hanging on for dear life can seem like too much to handle. In fact, biological parents who faced harrowing experiences with their adolescent children may have occasionally wished their own kids were stepchildren. Then, they could have sent them back home to somebody else. So, taking on a new set of adult children, whom they may not know very well, may take more resilience than they can muster at the moment.

BEEN THERE, LEARNED A LOT

On the other hand, stepparents who bring a fund of parenting wisdom and experience to the table often find they can play a constructive role in helping rebuild families traumatized by divorce and death. Many of the stepparents we interviewed, particularly the women, looked forward to creating new family structures, even though they knew doing so would not be easy. The most successful stepparents we interviewed were old hands at balancing the good and bad that make up the warp and woof of all family life.

When children are grieving for a parent who has passed away, that is usually abundantly clear, as we shall see in the next chapter. It is natural to sympathize with their pain. When children, even adult children, find themselves in the midst of a divorce, they, too, feel that their lives have been torn apart without their consent. They, too, need time and space to grieve for their lost nuclear family. Their grief may not be as apparent as that of the stepchild whose parent has died, but the grieving stepchildren of divorce also need help.

The new stepparent, however, may not be the ideal person to provide that help—at least in the child's eyes. So, don't feel too upset if your efforts to approach your new stepchildren in the midst of their mourning meet with rejection.

The adult stepfamily is foreign territory for everyone, including the stepparent. Stepparents are usually the most fortunate explorers, since they are typically swept up in the joy and euphoria of new love. The remarrying couple must keep in mind that they actively and happily chose their new life. The children, however, didn't plan this trip. Rather, the new stepfamily was imposed upon them. It is useful, as a new stepparent, to be mindful that your choice to remarry, though it was not meant to hurt anyone, may nonetheless be a source of real misery for the children, who now realize that any chance of the nuclear family being restored is probably lost forever.

The opening act of the adult stepfamily drama sets the stage for much, though not necessarily all, that follows. Sometimes, adult stepchildren do and say things that are hard to forgive and forget. They may feel they can prevent the whole thing by their resistance. Biological children may be resistant as well, but the biological parent is usually more tolerant of their behavior. Stepchildren are easier to demonize than our biological children. Sometimes, stepparents demonize stepchildren because they act badly, sometimes because the stepparents themselves are in a bad place. When a stepparent has a negative response to stepchildren who are themselves acting badly, the stepparent should take some time alone to sort out those feelings. Are you angry about their response because it triggers some old feelings in you, feelings that come from another time and place? Is it easier to project this familiar anger onto the stepchildren rather than digging into your own past traumas?

WHAT IF YOU ARE THE ADULT STEPCHILD?

The divorce of your parents is never an easy experience—not for you and not for them. Because you are an adult, perhaps with a spouse and children of your own, your parents may sometimes forget that you are hurting, too. They may have been "waiting until the children were grown" to take this step. If so, you've probably lived for some time with considerable tensions between your folks. When parents have had a volatile relationship for years, their children often feel, *That's just the way they are.* The children come to accept the cycle of feuding and making up, feuding and making up, feuding and making up. As tumultuous as the marriage has been, the children may be genuinely surprised when the parents decide to end it.

If your parents' divorce was unexpected, you may still be in shock or in a state of hoping against hope for a reconciliation, especially if no third party was the "cause." Nonetheless, if one or both parents decide to remarry, putting your parents' chance for happiness above your own unhappiness is the golden rule of adult stepfamilies. This is never easy, but it is absolutely necessary if the stepfamily is to succeed.

WHEN DIVORCE WAS UNEXPECTED

Priscilla, age fifty-two, told us her story:

My mom and dad had always argued, ever since I can remember. My sisters and I thought they would just keep fighting and living together till their dying day. We never thought they would split. That blindsided us!

When my mother called to tell me they were getting a divorce, I just couldn't believe it. I think it was a shock to my mother, too. She didn't want it, but my father did. I don't know if you'd call it a midlife crisis or what, but it soon became clear that Dad wasn't going back.

Mom took it very hard. At first, she thought my dad would get over it.

But he didn't. Pretty soon, he started to date. We all thought he was going through a midlife crisis and would come home eventually. Unfortunately, that didn't happen. Both Joanne, my sister, and I tried to console Mom. We both spent a lot of time on the phone with her, since we are both married and live out of state.

All three of us were pretty angry at Dad for just walking out like that. He took care of Mom financially, but that didn't make up for the emotional damage he caused. My mom is attractive, has a nice figure, a good personality, is well-educated, and has devoted herself to us and to his career. She played the traditional wife, while many of her friends were out carving professional careers for themselves. We all thought he was downright selfish to do this to her at that point in their lives.

Dad dated several women over the next few years, probably more than he ever let on to us. We thought he'd just keep playing the field. But that's not how it worked out. Instead, one day he called me to say he'd like me to meet a friend of his, a woman friend. They would fly down to meet me. That didn't sound too good to me. I still wasn't ready to see him with someone else. I also felt he was trying to woo me to "his side."

At first, I begged off. But after he called several times, I felt I really had to accept. Besides, he'd always been a good father to me, and I really love him. I don't want him to be miserable the rest of his life, but I don't think he has any idea of the heartache he's caused all of us, not just my mother.

When I met him and Stephanie for lunch, I was pretty nervous. I didn't know what to say. Mostly, I felt tongue-tied. They were holding hands during lunch, which really turned me off. It was clear that this was not just a casual relationship. I've never had a more uncomfortable lunch in my entire life. I kept wishing the lunch would end, but they seemed to be dragging it out. Finally, just as I thought lunch was over, Dad said he and Stephanie had some great news they wanted to share with me. My heart sank. I just knew what was coming. They were going to get married in three months. My heart sank even more. It wasn't that I still expected him to go back to Mom at this point, but I wasn't ready to see him remarried.

Stephanie was okay, nothing special, nothing terrible. Not someone I would have picked for a friend. She seemed oblivious to what I was feeling. Maybe, I just did a good job of hiding it, although I was so miserable I don't think I was doing much to cover how I felt. I tried to be polite. I wished them happiness, but my heart wasn't in it. I think Dad could tell, but he just kept up this happy exterior. When Joanne met Stephanie, she felt the same way, although I think she was more resigned than I was.

They've been married about four years now. They've come to visit us several times on holidays. I'm okay about it now, but not thrilled. I can see that they love each other and get along much better than Mom and

Dad ever did. And I guess he's entitled to have a happy relationship. On the other hand, he was never that sweet with my mother.

Stephanie tries to reach out from time to time, but there isn't much enthusiasm on either side, hers or mine. Maybe, if we lived closer and saw each other more we'd find some common ground, maybe learn to like each other. Maybe, it's better this way. No sparks really fly. I don't feel she's my stepmother. She's just my dad's second wife. I don't need a stepmother. I have a mother. Stephanie has a grown son. I only met him once, at the wedding. So, Stephanie isn't really looking for someone else to mother. I think we are both okay with this arm's-length relationship. I think Dad would like us to be closer, but he doesn't know how to make it happen.

In this case, geography serves as both a plus and a minus. On the plus side, the geographical distance between Priscilla and her father and stepmother keeps the emotional lid on the pot. On the minus side, since both stepmother and step-daughter seem to have opted for the Distancer role, the geographic distance reduces the kinds of interaction that could nourish a better relationship between the two. Stephanie's son isn't a significant part of the new stepfamily, from Priscilla's perspective. He's Stephanie's son, nothing more. This adult stepfamily operates with little friction and little familiarity. Stephanie and Priscilla may both be in protective mode, each protecting herself from the possibility of hurt.

VETERANS OF REMARRIAGE

Helen, a thirty-two-year-old woman, had a different story to tell. This was her mother's third marriage. So, she'd been through this once before. When Helen was twelve, her father died after a lingering illness. Soon after, her mother began to date. In a very short time, she married a widowed neighbor, who had just moved in next door. Helen never really connected with her mother's new husband. He seemed cool and aloof. That marriage lasted two years, followed by a divorce. Her mother remained single for the next nine years. When Helen was twenty-four, her mother married John, an artist, who worked out of his own studio.

This is Helen's story:

John is a great guy! My mother really lucked out with him. He is warm and kindhearted. He also has a great sense of humor. John has two sons of his own, but he never had a daughter. We just clicked from the outset. He's been a real father to me. I didn't realize how much I missed having a father. For the last few years of his life, my own dad was too sick to be much of one.

John likes to have his sons around, and they drop in very often. So do I. My mother likes John's sons. I guess they're the sons she never had. They're also the older brothers I never had. None of us is married, so we sometimes hang out together. Their mother is remarried and lives in another state, so, when holidays come around, they usually come to my mother's and John's house.

John's first wife left him for another man. Can't see why she would, actually. I think John's sons felt a lot of sympathy for their father, so they were happy to see him link up with my mother. It's clear that they get along very well.

When the five of us are together, we laugh a great deal! John is an artist. He's really cool, very unlike my mother's last husband. John tries to nourish what little artistic talent I have, but he also listens to the problems I have at work and with men. His studio is at the house, so he is always around. Bill and Jack, his sons, are good listeners, too.

Last month, my mother gave John a birthday party at the house. They invited about forty people. After the birthday cake was cut, people just got up and spoke about John. It was very touching. Everyone loves him. You can tell by what they said. I wrote out what I wanted to say because I was afraid I would be too emotional to speak without notes. I thanked him for being such a good father to me. Some of John's friends later commented to me that they were surprised (in a nice way) that someone my age would find another father, but they thought John was just that kind of person.

I can't believe that we have this little family. Maybe, because we have all had harder lives before this, we really appreciate what we have here and try to protect it. I would never want to hurt John or my stepbrothers. I don't want to lose what I have.

Helen's story is far from the norm, yet we include it as evidence that adult stepfamilies can work, particularly when all—or most—of the members appreciate that they have a second chance at happiness and try to grab it.

WHEN A LOVE AFFAIR RESULTS IN REMARRIAGE

Eric's story introduces another familiar theme: the remarriage of a parent, following an affair. This is how Eric, age forty-three, told us about his parents' divorce when he was thirty:

I always thought that my mother and dad got along fine. I never noticed any tension or anything. So, the news that my dad wanted out hit me like a ton of bricks. When I learned he was in love with another woman, I was furious. How could he do that to us? Particularly to my mother!

From the outset, it was clear that he was determined to marry this other woman. She was about fifteen years younger than my mother and only about ten years older than me. He married her, all right, and I stopped talking to him. What right did he have to act this way?

As far as his girlfriend was concerned, I didn't have any use for her. She's an airhead. She was pretty, all right, and sexy. Maybe, a bit too sexy. She wore tight sweaters and short skirts that really didn't belong on someone her age. But I guess that's what got my old man.

As if that weren't enough, she wanted a baby. She'd been married and divorced, but she didn't have any kids. About eight months after they got married, they had a baby. That was another blow. I couldn't stand the thought of my father having another kid. I couldn't call it any-thing but "It" for at least the first three years. My wife got on my case for calling him "It," but somehow I had a hard time seeing that kid as my half-brother, even if we did have the same father. Besides, he's the same age as one of my kids. So, my father's having his own grandchild, so to speak.

Eventually, I began to talk with my father again. He just kept calling. He wouldn't give up. I've even gotten to know his kid, who's not so bad. After all, it's not his fault. But I must say, my father never spent that much time with me when I was a kid. He was always too busy.

As for Harriet, my father's wife, I'll never get used to her. In my heart, I hold her to blame for my parents' breakup. My mother never remarried. She says she doesn't want to take the chance of getting hurt again. She doesn't date, but she has her girlfriends. So, she keeps busy, but I don't think she's truly happy.

We always spend the holidays with my mother. After all, she needs us. My father and Harriet invite us for the holidays, but we never go. I wish they'd stop that annoying ritual of inviting us when they know we're never going to accept.

Eric is pretty unrelenting, a Distancer with a vengeance. Despite the passage of thirteen years, he still refuses to let go of his anger both at his father and his father's new family. He is beset with Furies: Fear of Abandonment and Isola-tion, Fidelity to Family, Favoritism, and Focus on the Self. He seems to have softened only toward his half-brother, and then not much.

Eric's nursing his anger toward his father doesn't help Eric's mother very much, either. It only locks her more tightly into her cocoon of hurt and fear. Families are systems of interconnected parts. If Eric would let go of his anger, it might help his mother to let go of hers. Maybe, then both of them could get on with their own lives.

If Eric's mother gives up the anger toward his father that bonds them, she is, in a sense, abandoning Eric—hanging him and his anger out to dry. After thirteen years, his anger has become a way of life, one that drains time and energy away from healthier, more productive ways of living, both for Eric and his mother.

Eric has violated one of the most basic rules of dealing with people who are getting divorced, be they your parents or people outside of the intimate family circle: Try not to take sides. Try to support both parties. They usually know what they want and what they are doing, even if you don't agree with them. It's their choice, not yours. When they are your parents, you can't avoid the consequences of their behavior.

You may be understandably angry at being forced to deal with a situation that you neither chose nor made. Still, you don't have to articulate that anger to your parents. Find someone in whom you can safely confide. This is a situation in which complete candor serves no one. Act supportively, even if you don't feel like it. And there is a reward for being restrained and unselfish in your response. Putting your parents' needs above your own marks you as someone of character and maturity.

Fran's experience after her parents' divorce and her mother's remarriage offers us another adult stepchild's viewpoint. Fran, age forty-seven, explained:

My mother left my father for Ray when I was thirty-five. I couldn't believe that my mother would ever cheat on my father or vice versa. I don't think my parents were ecstatic together, but I didn't think their relationship was unbearable, either. Obviously, my mother did. It's true that my father was someone who was angry most of the time. Not just at my mother but at the world. He wasn't very easy to live with, but I figured that's just what marriage is like. For better, for worse, for richer, for poorer. He was a loner, so it was hard for my mother to develop friendships with other couples. I think she was pretty lonely, particularly after my brother and I grew up and moved out.

I was pretty unhappy about the whole thing, since I felt Dad had been a decent husband and father. We were a very religious family, so the idea that she had been having an affair with Ray was extremely offensive, as well.

Because of the way their relationship began, I kept my distance from

Ray. He tried to relate to me, but I wanted nothing to do with him. Over the years, things softened a little bit, but I still felt they both had done my father a serious wrong. My father has developed all kinds of physical illnesses, none serious, but they keep him from having a full life. He's depressed, overweight, and angry. I worry about him.

It wasn't until last year, when my best friend left her husband for another man, that I began to see things somewhat differently. Carrie, my best friend, was in a dead marriage, but she had kids, so she stayed. We've been friends for a very long time, and I could see how the life was really going out of her. We talked about her problems all the time. I think that was the only relief she had. Our conversations were a safety valve for her over the years.

A while ago, she met Ed at work. I know for certain that she wasn't looking for an affair, but it just happened. Looking at it from Carrie's point of view, I could see that she didn't set out to have an affair, but I guess her misery at home made her vulnerable. For the first time since I've known her, Carrie was alive. She was a different person. That doesn't mean she didn't feel guilty about her kids and even Michael, her husband. She was so happy that at times, I confess, I felt a little jealous.

Watching this play out with Carrie has given me more sympathy for my mother and Ray. I've begun to understand that my mother was really in a dead marriage, too, and she had a right to some happiness. After all, she waited until we were adults before she left my father. She's changed tremendously. In fact, she's a different person now, too.

This experience with Carrie also helped me to see Ray in a new light. He's actually a decent guy, and he and my mother get along very well. They have a good life together. Ray is far more upbeat than my father, and he and my mother are best friends. It's so easy to see that now.

It has taken Fran almost twelve years to develop some empathy for her mother and Ray. She had held on to her anger and righteous indignation for all that time. Seeing a similar scenario played out by someone her own age gave Fran a different slant on her mother's relationship. Although there is no evidence that Fran had tried to destabilize her mother's remarriage, she clearly had distanced herself from Ray.

THE STEPPARENT IS A "SAFE" TARGET FOR ANGER

Not infrequently, adult stepchildren of divorce project all their angry, negative feelings on the stepparent. They may be unaware that they are doing this out of fear that they will lose the love of the biological parent. It's an instinctive, unconscious mechanism that leaves the biological parent relatively, if not completely, blameless. In this case, Fran had disapproved of her mother's behavior, but still maintained a relationship with her. Religion had played a part, but the Furies undoubtedly were hard at work here: Fear of Abandonment and Isolation and Fidelity to Family, in particular. Seeing a parent's behavior through another lens—that of a friend—may give an angry adult stepchild some objectivity. The Furies are a little less furious when the people involved are not our parents.

In some ways, whether the remarriage was preceded by a parent's divorce or death becomes less relevant as time goes by. Still, in the early years, the ever-present former spouse or the ghost of a deceased parent/spouse, as we shall see in the next chapter, can cast an aura over the new stepfamily that is hard to dispel.

SOME ADVICE FOR STEPPARENTS

Remember, you hope to be in this new family for the long haul. Here, the same advice applies, whether the new marriage was preceded by a divorce or a death. The long-term strategies of tolerance and forgiveness, transformation through wisdom, and emotional, spiritual, and financial generosity usually pay off in the long run.

As you become more familiar with everybody's hot buttons, you can learn to avoid them and prevent explosions whose debris will inevitably have to be swept up later. In stepfamilies, as in other situations requiring crisis management, avoidance is always the best strategy.* Everything else is damage control and mop up.

As stepparents, it is important to remember that, although the stepchildren are adults, they are still the children, and you are still the parent. Setting a good example—by using all the relevant Tact and Tacking strategies—offers the best hope of changing the entire family for the better. If your behavior remains adult and admirable, it eventually will have an effect on the adult stepchildren—although "eventually" can be a painfully long time.

Finally, some advice you may not like, but which proved effective in all the successful adult stepfamilies we studied: patience, patience, and more patience. Sometimes *years* of patience may be required. This same advice, hard as it is to carry out, applies to stepchildren, as well.

SOME ADVICE FOR ADULT STEPCHILDREN

Although you may feel comfortable in your Indifferent or Distancer role at the outset, over time, you may find that you want to join that new family after all. In the best scenario, your parent's remarriage will work. So, we recommend that adult stepchildren think long and hard before becoming Destabilizers. Playing that role may limit your future options, in addition to generating unhappiness all around.

For stepchildren, too, talking with a friend in the same boat can offer release and comfort. You may even have a few good laughs along the way. Choose a confidant who has experienced the same familial choppy seas. Although people who have never been in an adult stepfamily may be sympathetic to your pain and confusion, their well-meaning advice is much less likely to be helpful. Besides, there are plenty of adult stepchildren who can and even need to play the buddy role.

Talking to someone else's stepparent (or stepchild, if you're the stepparent) may also help you to see the situation through your own stepparent's (or stepchild's) eyes. If no appropriate buddy is available, time spent with a wise counselor or therapist can help you deal with the present tumult and may even help you put old dogs to rest.

The issues faced by adult stepfamilies that follow divorce could fill a volume of their own. In fact, E. Mavis Hetherington's landmark study has demonstrated the wide range of possibilities after divorce and reconstruction.** In our study, age differences between a parent and the stepparent, history of extramarital affairs, loyalty to a divorced parent, midlife crises, religious concerns, and step- and half-sibling relationships were all important factors in the adjustment of the subsequently formed stepfamily. These and other issues make stepfamilies that develop following divorce among the most complex. Still, adult stepfamilies that grow in the shadow of widow(er)hood have challenges of their own, as we shall see in the next chapter.

---

*Fink, Steven. (1986/2000). *Crisis Management: Planning for the Inevitable.* (Lincoln, NE: iUniverse.com, Inc.)

**Hetherington, E. Mavis, and John Kelly. (2002). *For Better or For Worse: Divorce Reconsidered.* (New York, NY: W. W. Norton & Company, Ltd.).

CHAPTER 6

What Happens When Widow(er)hood Precedes Remarriage?

NO MERRY WIDOW(ER)S OR ADULT CHILDREN HERE

Contrary to Franz Lehar's charming operetta, *The Merry Widow,* the remarried widows and widowers and their adult children whom we studied were anything but merry. Widow(er)hood, in fact, brings much grief, even when the relationship with the departed spouse was less than ideal. For children, no matter how old, losing a parent is one of life's most profound and resonant events.

The circumstances surrounding the death of the parent generate enormous differences in how the children react to both the new marriage and the stepparent. How long ago did that parent/spouse die? Did that person die young? Did he or she die unexpectedly or after a lingering illness? Was the late parent or partner so diminished by a long illness that he or she had already "left" the family long before the death? The answers to these questions influence how adult children perceive the surviving parent's new life.

THE SURVIVING SPOUSE AND THE ADULT CHILDREN: TWO SETS OF NEEDS

While both the surviving spouse and children may grieve, their future needs and coping strategies may be quite different. The surviving spouse may have been the longtime caretaker of the late parent and the person who bore all the responsibility for medical and legal choices. In such cases, both remarried widows and widowers spoke about their gradual adjustment to a painful reality. They recalled both their sadness over their loss and their eventual realization that they needed to repair and rebuild their own lives after their spouse had died.

Winston, a remarried widower, age seventy-five, described his situation:

Francesca was sick a very long time, years, in fact. During that time, I grieved. After she died, I continued to grieve. It seemed like I had been sad my whole life. I never thought I'd be happy again. It took a long time. When I met Peggy, that terrible feeling of sadness and isolation began to lift. She brought happiness back into my life. I think it was hard for my children to think of me married to anyone other than their mother, but I feel Francesca would understand and not want me to remain miserable. I hope my children gradually will begin to accept our relationship. I don't want to hurt them. I love them, but I love Peggy, too, and I feel I'm entitled to a little happiness, particularly after all those years of misery.

Winston alludes to the Fury of Fidelity to Family that he recognizes in his adult children's response to his remarriage. Wisely, Winston used several familiar Tact and Tacking strategies—sticking to his guns and letting time do its work—because he recognized the legitimacy of his own needs. He also understands they are different from those of his grown children.

Adult children, on the other hand, often feel that their deceased parent never can, or should, be replaced. That feeling makes it difficult for them to empathize with their surviving parent's need to pick up the shards of his or her life and move forward.

Maryellen, thirty-five years old, recalled that her mother died at fifty-three, when Maryellen was only twenty-three.

It all happened so fast. It seemed like one day she was healthy, and the next day the doctors told her she was dying. She died eight months later, still young and beautiful with so much to live for. It was so hard to believe. Even now, I can barely believe she is gone.

My parents had a strange relationship, or maybe that's how all marriages are. They fought a lot, but I think they really loved each other, too. They had been together since they were teenagers, and they had grown up together over the years. They did everything together. My dad is a lawyer, and he traveled a lot to conferences and meetings. She went with him all the time, even though it meant twisting her own schedule into a pretzel. She didn't seem to mind. In fact, she loved traveling with him. She looked forward to their trips and did all the planning.

When my mom died, I was still living at home. My brother and sister were both married and living with their families. When my dad began to date, which was not too many months after Mom died, I couldn't stand watching it. He tried to hide it from me, but I knew he was seeing several women. I decided it was time for me to move out, too. Better not to have to watch what was happening. So, when I had the chance, I moved to London for a job that I really love.

After about a year, my dad began to settle into a relationship with a woman he met through a friend. He really fell hard for her, which was tough for me to hear about through my sister. When I met her, I could see it, too. He was like a silly teenager, totally "gaga" over her. If Mom had acted that ditzy, he would have had a fit. But with Michelle, he was just mush. That really annoyed my sister and me. I'm not sure how my brother felt. He didn't say much about Michelle.

My mom always took care of everything so my father could be free to do his work. Michelle acted like a self-centered hippie teenager, and my dad just lapped it up. When I was with them, it really made me sick. She wanted his undivided attention, but when he really needed her, she usually was too busy with her own kids or her own activities. My sister was the one who had to step in and help Dad when he needed it. Michelle was like an irresponsible adolescent when it came to Dad. Eventually, he caught on, after a few serious episodes. But that took a few years. That relationship eventually fell apart. I'm not sure of the details. But my sister and I were relieved.

About a year later, Dad met Janine. Although she is about the same age as Michelle, she acts much more grown up. She is there for Dad, and I think they really love each other. She has no children, so perhaps that makes some of the difference. She isn't pulled in other directions. I don't know, maybe I wouldn't have liked her, either, if she had been Dad's first serious relationship. I don't know.

I'm not mad about Janine, but I can see the difference between her and Michelle, and I really appreciate how much better Janine is for Dad. Still, when they announced that they were getting married, that was a bitter pill to swallow.

I'm still living in London, so I don't get to see them that much. I mostly hear reports from my sister about what's going on with them. Doris (my sister) seems to think Janine's okay but, again, I think that's because she seems so much more acceptable than Michelle.

It's still very hard for me to see my dad with someone else. My mom *was too young to die. She was cheated out of all the good times they could have had together. After all, she lived through all the lean years, when he was going to law school, and we were all little kids. Now that we were grown and I was the only one left at home, they could really have lived a terrific life. But it's not Janine's fault. And, of course, I don't want my dad to be lonely or sad.*

Maryellen's ambivalence is obvious. The Furies are flexing their muscles, with the Fury of Fidelity to Family leading the way. The fact that Maryellen's mother died in her prime made it particularly difficult for Maryellen, who felt fate had dealt her mother an unfair hand.

Sensitive to the unfulfilled promise of her mother's life, Maryellen found it hard *not* to see both Michelle and Janine as usurpers, unintentional usurpers perhaps, but usurpers nonetheless. The passage of time and the "tryout" experience with Michelle seem to have made Maryellen somewhat more open to Janine, but she still has strong, unresolved feelings about her father's new life.

Maryellen has chosen the role of Distancer. She stays in London, where her job is the focus of her life. She doesn't have any plans to return to the United States at this time. She is still dealing with one major Fury, Fidelity to Family. Seeing her dad with someone new is difficult for her. She misses her mother, and seeing someone else in her mother's role is a constant painful reminder of what she has lost. That may lessen over time. Maryellen is still single. When and if she marries, her intense focus on her father and his new wife may well shift to her own new family.

WHEN DEATH COMES SLOWLY

Sometimes, when the parent died after a long illness things look different to adult children. This is particularly so if the sick parent faded slowly and painfully into a shadow of his or her best self.

Often adult children worry that long-term caretaking and loneliness are taking a toll on the well parent. By the time illness finally claims the sick parent, much of the grieving may have already taken place, both by the children and the surviving spouse.

Here is the story of sixty-two-year-old John, an adult stepchild:

About twelve years ago, my mom had a stroke that left her quite disabled. She couldn't speak, and she was paralyzed on one side. So, she couldn't feed or dress herself. My dad hired a full-time nurse to take care of her. It was so heart wrenching to watch the two of them. He would sit with her every day for hours. He was retired by that time, but he still had his golfing buddies at the club. That helped some.

At first, my mother struggled to speak and move, but after a while she just seemed to give up. At least, that's how it seemed to me.

My parents were a very loving couple. We never saw them argue. My mother was tall and beautiful, always elegant. You could see that my dad really thought she was beautiful, even after the stroke. And my dad is quite dapper himself, always meticulously turned out. They lived a very civilized, happy life together. For years, they went to the club with friends, and they liked to travel once my brother and I were grown. So, when she had the stroke, everything turned upside down. More correctly, everything came to a dead halt. No pun intended.

The next few years were a nightmare. Dad was in a daze, too. His life became so robotic. Every day, he'd sit and read to my mother. I think, at the beginning, she understood, but gradually she seemed to fade away. At first, I think he thought he could pull her out of it by talking to her and keeping her engaged. It was hard for him to put that much effort into what became a futile task.

As time went by, he seemed to grow weary. He aged a great deal during that time. Then, she had another stroke. This time, she was paralyzed on the other side. I think that was the last straw for Dad. He realized that she needed far more care than he and Michael (the caregiver) could handle. Very, very reluctantly, and with incredible guilt, my dad put Mother in a nursing home. He still visited her every day, but you could see that chapter of his life drawing—very sadly—to a close. He was letting go, slowly, guiltily, but definitely letting go. I don't see that he had any choice. The person he had known and loved wasn't there anymore. Yes, she was there physically, but not in any other way. He could barely stand to watch how she was dwindling away. I felt the same way. So did my brother, Tom.

Things went on that way for several years. Then my dad started to go to social events with Emily, who, with her husband, had been part of my parents' circle of friends. Emily's husband had died several years before my mom's stroke. They all belonged to the same club, so it seemed perfectly natural for Emily and Dad to go to those things together, instead of each going alone.

I didn't think of it as "dating." I just saw it as keeping each other company. Emily is a very elegant and attractive woman, too. Much like my mother. So, I could see that Dad was comfortable with her, an old and trusted friend, someone from his own circle of friends, someone very much like my mother. As time went by, I could also see a twinkle in Dad's eye. Maybe, it was there from the start, and I didn't notice.

My mother died about two years later. That is, two years after she entered the nursing home. We were all very sad to let go, but, in a way, we already had. And it was merciful for her to be released from that nonlife that was her existence.

I don't think they'll get married. Too much money and property involved. Too many kids. Emily has five grown children, and I have a brother. That makes seven children, and there are eighteen or twenty grandchildren. As you can see, it gets very complicated. But Emily sold her home to be closer to Dad. Dad stayed in our old home. He's lived there for sixty or so years. My dad's in his late eighties, but he's pretty spry. Dad and Emily do everything together. They're married in every way except legally. I think that everyone's comfortable with the arrangement. At least, that's how I see it.

John seems to be dealing pretty well with his father's new relationship. His mother's illness, difficult as it was, gave John and his brother time to deal with the gradual loss of their mother. Still, it's worth noting John seems rather relieved that his father and Emily have not made their relationship legally binding. There is a hint of Fury #4, Finances, in John's attitude. Remember, he alludes to Tom's and his inheritance, which he seems to feel is safe because his father has not remarried.

WHEN A FAMILY FRIEND BECOMES MORE THAN THAT

The long illness of a parent that results in death causes the whole family to suffer—the spouse, the children, the dying parent's siblings and parents (if they are still living), even the grandchildren. In such cases, we noticed that many older widows and widowers tended to enter relationships with someone long known: a family friend or a person from an earlier period in their lives. This was often the surviving spouse of a couple with whom they had once been a foursome. Some of those we interviewed said it was extraordinarily comforting to be able to talk about their late spouse with someone who had also known and cared about that person.

While that may make for a relatively easy transition for the marrying couple, it doesn't necessarily make things easier for the adult children. Several adult children we interviewed had a difficult time seeing an old family friend, whom they had loved in that role, step into their dead parent's shoes (or house, as we shall see in Chapter 7). This often came as a shock to the surviving parent, who thought the children would be as happy as he or she was.

You may recall Mary, from Chapter 1, who married an old family friend, Arthur, fourteen years after she was widowed. Arthur and his wife, Jan, had been virtual family members even before either couple had children. When Jan died, Mary and her first husband, Roger, had brought Arthur even closer into their family circle. Then, after Roger's death, Mary and Arthur just naturally gravitated to one another. They shared their worries about their grown children, gave each other advice, and shared many of the same interests. They felt safe and comfortable together. And yet, when, after fourteen years of being together, Mary announced to her adult children that she planned to marry Arthur, her son, Jim, thought the decision was "impetuous."

Mary told us:

I couldn't believe my kids' reaction. I thought they would be thrilled for us. After all, we each knew what we were getting. We'd been friends for more than forty years. I loved his kids, and he loved mine. And I thought the kids felt the same way. Well, I was in for a big surprise. When my son, Jim, called our decision "impetuous," I couldn't believe my ears. Forty years of friendship and fourteen years of "keeping company," that's "impetuous"? Then Jim wanted to be sure that the tiny cottage in the country that my father had left me would be kept safe for him. Can you imagine? I've known my kids a long time, but I never would have predicted they'd react this way.

My daughter, Kathleen, asked if I would still keep my baby-sitting days, because those were her "days out with the girls." My other daughter, Catherine, asked why we couldn't simply live together if we just wanted sex. I told her that Arthur was impotent since he had to take medication for his high blood pressure. She seemed more relieved after that, but now I'm mad at myself for even telling her. Why should I have to explain or apologize to them for wanting to marry again? When they got married, I was so happy for them. I'm beginning to see my kids as sort of selfish, and that makes me very sad.

Here, we see several Furies at work on the adult stepchildren: Fear of Abandonment and Isolation, Finances, and Focus on the Self. Mary had been a wonderful, loving, and cheap baby-sitter. Mary's upcoming marriage meant that Arthur would have a legitimate claim on her time. Arthur had frequently helped Mary baby-sit, but Kathleen was still worried that her mother wouldn't be as readily available.

Kathleen is beset by Fury #1, Fear of Abandonment and Isolation, and Fury

#5, Focus on Self. She was used to having her mother drop everything and come running whenever Kathleen or the grandchildren needed her. Now, things might change.

Mary's son, Jim, lived two thousand miles away in Chicago, so he didn't have any expectations about loss of his mother's time and assistance. Yet, he had his own *bête noire*: Fury #4, Finances. This is an interesting case, because it reminds us that the amount of money a family has is not what matters. Money, as we shall see in Chapter 11, is often a symbol for other things that the children fear losing. Very little actual wealth is on the line in Mary's family, but the children's potential inheritance is an important symbol of their mother's caring and love.

Never underestimate the power of symbols. They can pack a huge wallop. Mary and Roger had always managed to make ends meet, but not much more than that. The country cottage was tiny and dilapidated, according to Mary. Still, Jim saw it as something of value that he didn't want to lose.

Mary needed to understand that the cottage was a symbol of her love for Jim, not just a piece of property of limited financial value. She needed to reassure Jim that she still loved him and that her love for him would not diminish or be usurped by Arthur. It's also important to remember that other people's symbols aren't always easy to understand, even when you're the parent or the child of the person who holds the symbol dear.

WHEN AN OLD LOVE ENTERS THE SCENE

In several instances, we interviewed members of adult stepfamilies in which the widowed parent had sought out a long-lost love. In some cases, the parent reestablished a relationship with someone he or she had cared about before marrying the now-deceased spouse. In several cases, the new mate was someone with whom the surviving parent had had an extramarital relationship. Not surprisingly, in those families, the adult children tended to be uncomfortable with the parent's new relationship.

Somehow, seeing a parent return to a premarital love or one who had been there during the parents' marriage can unleash Fury #2, Fidelity to Family. The adult children often question both the surviving parent's loyalty to them and his or her past fidelity to the deceased spouse.

Frank, fifty-three years old, had lost his mother twenty years ago after a long bout with breast cancer. Some months after her death, Frank learned that his dad was seeing Anita, his old high school sweetheart. When Anita had fallen in love with and married someone else, Frank's dad had been distraught. In fact, Anita's breaking his dad's heart had become part of the family lore, along with several premarital boyfriends of his mother. This is the way that Frank told us about his family situation:

Mum had always teased my dad about Anita. She would say, "Are you sure you didn't just marry me on the rebound?" Dad would blush when she said that and assure her that she, my mother, was the only true love of his life. We always believed him and saw that as a game they both liked to play. It all seemed like affectionate kidding around.

But after Mum died, when I heard that Dad was calling on Anita, I was stunned. I had never met her, only heard about her up til then. I didn't even know if she was still living. Dad said that Anita saw the obituary in the newspaper and had written him a condolence note. And that was what started it all up again.

Anita had long since divorced her first husband, and husband number two had died a few years before Mum. According to Dad, he called Anita to say, "Thanks," and they decided to meet for old time's sake. It just took off from there, the way he tells it.

Still, it makes me wonder if Dad was always secretly in love with Anita the whole time he was married to Mum. Anita keeps saying she made a huge mistake dumping Dad for her first husband, but Dad was married by the time she and her first husband split.

And I'm not sure how to think about Dad's feelings in all this. Had he really loved Anita all along, the whole time he was married to Mum? They are so cozy together, it gives me a pang. Did he marry Mum simply because she came along at the right time to heal his wounds? Or was Mum truly the love of his life, as he used to tell her?

I really don't know, and, in truth, it probably doesn't matter, given that my mother is gone, anyway. The way they act now, I think Anita wants to believe they were always meant for each other and that all of their other marriages—her two and Dad's one—were just make-do until they could reunite. Most of the time, I think that is romantic hogwash, but, at other times, I begin to wonder. If I let myself begin to think Dad was always in love with Anita, my blood begins to boil. But they're married, so what's the difference?

Frank is suffering from Fury #2, that old favorite, Fidelity to Family. Frank has suspicions about his father's real feelings toward Frank's mother that are hard to put to rest. It is possible, of course, for Frank to ask his father what really happened and how he really feels. We strongly recommend against that approach. What is to be gained? If Frank's father really *had* kept a hidden flame alive for Anita during his marriage, he's going to feel guilty and uncomfortable with Frank's effort to uncover his secret. If he "confesses," that only further complicates the father/son relationship, because the "fact" of his father's disloyalty will be even more difficult to accept than Frank's suspicion of it. The only result will probably be to undermine fatally Frank's relationship with his new stepmother, even if his father's torch carrying wasn't her fault.

If there is no genuine basis for Frank's suspicion, he risks impugning his father's honesty—to Frank's mother, Frank, and the rest of family over the many years of his parents' marriage. That affront to his father might undermine their relationship—and Anita might easily be drawn into the vortex to defend her new husband.

One effective way of dealing with a situation where you'll never learn what really happened is Tact and Tacking approach #9, Turn Away from It. The truth is ancient history, whatever it was. Let it be.

Even if his father secretly harbored an unrequited love for Anita all those years, it may not have had any negative effect on his parents' marriage. In fact, his mother seemed willing and able to laugh about his father's feelings for Anita. Even if those feelings did harm his parents' marriage, it is of no real consequence now. The affronted party is gone, and there is no way to turn back the clock. For all concerned, Frank's best course of action is to put the past behind him and move on.

Tact and Tacking Strategy #6, Generosity, is relevant here, too. At this point, Frank's mother can't be hurt. So, whether his father and Anita were always in love or that is simply a romantic revision of history, why not let the newlyweds create whatever mythical landscape for their relationship that best supports their happiness? After all, most of us cherish the romantic story about how we met and fell in love. Over time, most of those stories mutate and imperceptibly take on embellishments that may diverge from the literal truth. Generosity is always a gift, and, if Frank can muster it, both his father and he will benefit.

A REKINDLED EXTRAMARITAL LOVE AFFAIR

When the old love is someone with whom the surviving parent has had an extramarital affair, things can become more complicated. In most of the cases we learned about, the extramarital relationship had caused considerable *sturm und drang* within the parents' marriage. Sometimes, the children had not actually known about the affair, but many suspected. In such cases, the old lover is usually seen—at least initially—as Dracula or the Wicked Witch of the West, depending on his or her gender.

Harriet, a forty-one-year-old mother of two, was quite upset to learn that her widowed mother had reestablished a relationship with Don, a man for whom Harriet's mother had almost left her father about ten years before he died. A Vesuvian confrontation had erupted between Harriet's parents at that time. Although Harriet didn't know all the intimate details, her mother's relationship with Don had ended, and her parents reconciled.

All Harriet really knew were the simple outlines of her mother's romance: Harriet's mother, an operating room nurse, had scrubbed with Don on most of his surgical cases at the hospital where they both worked. She often talked about him admiringly—what a great surgeon he was, how intelligent and skill-ful, how his daring surgical maneuvers saved desperately ill patients. Harriet's mother saw him as a mythical figure, and her rapturous reports eventually began to wear on everyone's nerves.

No one—not Harriet's father, nor Harriet or her sister—ever thought "any-thing was going on" between Harriet's mother and the dashing surgeon. And there probably wasn't much going on during the period when her mother so openly sang Don's praises to the family. Still, Harriet's father began to get irritated whenever Don's name came up. In fact, he began to call him "your mother's boyfriend," much to Harriet's mother's annoyance. Since Don was divorced, it was easier to joke about him that way than if he had been a married man with a passel of kids.

Harriet knew that her parents' marriage was not a thing of great beauty. Like most marriages, it had its scars and warts. Still, her parents had been married a long time, and everyone assumed that their relationship was pretty solid—at least Harriet and her sister did. When the relationship with Don turned out to be real, the family faced some rocky times, according to Harriet.

As she told it:

We were shocked. That is, my sister and I were shocked. It's hard to know just how surprised my father was. He didn't talk much to us about it. We couldn't believe that this "boyfriend" stuff had anything to it. How could my mother consider leaving my father and us? Of course, she kept telling my sister, Jane, and me that she would never abandon us, but we were still pretty upset.

This went on for what seemed like forever, but actually it was probably no more than a month later when my parents told us they were staying together. That was a great relief to me. To my sister, too. Even though I didn't know him, I really hated Don for threatening to ruin our family. I was glad to hear the end of him. His name was never mentioned in front of us again.

So, you can imagine how astonished I was to learn about six months after my dad's death in a car accident that my mother and Don were in touch again. I felt that that was a real betrayal of my dad. I couldn't under-stand how she could violate his memory that way, and so soon, besides.

I told her how I felt, and so did my sister. But that didn't seem to make any difference to her. She just hung in there. She said they really loved each other and that was what counted. After all, she argued, we two were grown-ups with our own lives, in fact, with husbands and children. She said she felt she was entitled to her own happiness now that Dad was gone. Once, she even intimated that it was selfish of us to deny her happiness a second time. She made it sound as if she had never been happy with Dad, even though she didn't say it in so many words.

My mother and Don got married about a year and a half after my Dad died. I was mortified. I didn't want to go to the wedding, but my sister convinced me it would only make things worse if I didn't go. So, I went, and I was really miserable. It was the worst day of my life.

I have to admit that I think Don really loves my mother. And they seem very happy. Probably happier than my mother and father were together. But it's been very hard to get used to Don as my stepfather, although he has tried nonstop to win me over. I'll give him that much. He keeps trying, even when I rebuff him again and again.

Things can get very rough for the entire family when a parent's former love enters the scene. Sometimes, the fireworks continue for a very long time. Even when the parent decided to remain in the original marriage, despite a strong desire to start over with a new love, family members rarely welcome the parent's old love with open arms. If that person becomes the new stepparent, you can be sure that much Tact and Tacking will be required on everyone's part.

Louise, age sixty-six, described the family situation in which she had been living for almost ten years:

I was widowed young and brought up my two sons on my own. When my boys were young, I was particularly anxious not to subject them to any more trauma, since they'd already been through enough. My first husband, Tim, had committed suicide, and things got very very bad for all of us after that.

Losing a husband and a father under ordinary circumstances is tough enough, but, when you add suicide, everything gets so much more difficult and murky. It's bad enough to deal with the immense guilt and the anger. We also had to deal with the huge financial muddle Tim left behind. That's how I met Zack. He's a financial planner, who helped me sort through some very thorny financial issues. Without Zack, I don't know what would have happened to us.

Zack was in a very bad marriage, but he hung in there because of his kids. Neither of us was actively looking to fall in love. It just happened.

Gradually, over a few years. We were on the same wavelength in many ways. The fact that we had both been unhappy, for somewhat different reasons, probably made us vulnerable to the empathy we each had for one another. I don't know. How do you explain how or why you fall in love with someone?

We just knew we belonged together, but neither of us liked the prospect of Zack's going through a divorce. Zack felt too guilty about upsetting his kids. He's a good father. And I wasn't looking to get married. The thing I hated about it was not that we couldn't get married but that we had to lie about our lives to everyone—our kids, our friends, our family. It made something wonderful feel sleazy and dishonest. Eventually, there was a big blowup. Zack told Peggy about us, and she told the kids. It was a mess. There was a lot of going back and forth, but Zack decided to stay with Peggy.

It's a long story, but after Peggy died, Zack and I got together. Zack was getting out and dating one or two women. I think he was taking a deep breath of freedom. Although I was reluctant to enter the picture again, Zack kept after me. I guess we both knew we couldn't stay apart. About a year and a half after Peggy died, we started to live together. I wasn't in any rush to get married. I could see all the complications. His kids didn't seem too keen on our getting together, either. In fact, they told him outright that they hoped he wouldn't go back to me.

I couldn't tell exactly how my kids would react if we got married. They didn't say much, and they seemed to like Zack. Besides, it was a long time since their father had died.

I didn't have any clue as to just how hard it would be. Zack's five kids ranged in age from their midthirties to their midtwenties. On the surface, most of them were polite. Mostly, they ignored me as if I weren't there. But his oldest daughter, Rose, really made things tough for me from the outset. She made it clear I was persona non grata. She was particularly angry that we were living in "her mother's" house.

At one time, Rose and her husband stayed with us for a month. Once, during that time, when we were out for the evening, Rose and Rod (her husband) invited some friends to come for a barbecue. After dinner, they rearranged all the furniture in the living room for dancing. The next morning, Rose asked our housekeeper to straighten up the living room and put back all the furniture. She said Zack and I had had friends in for dancing and had been too tired to put things back. I found out because the housekeeper asked if Zack and I had enjoyed dancing, because she liked to dance, too. When I casually mentioned it to Rose, she admitted she had done it to keep the housekeeper from feeling she was causing extra work. I felt I was being booby-trapped all the time.

Over the years, Rose and I have grown a little closer. Maybe, it's just that we've both grown up or grown wiser.

THE HALLOWED GHOST

One of the most difficult aspects of a late marriage is the way deceased spouses turn into hallowed ghosts. Once the deceased spouse has been transformed into a saint, he or she may hover continuously in the background. No living, breathing, imperfect human being can hope to compete with a saint.

That metamorphosis of the departed one into a virtual saint is understandable. Speaking ill of the dead is a deeply ingrained taboo in our culture, whether we realize it or not. That process usually begins at the funeral, where eulogies often sound more like hagiographies than the lives of the flawed humans we actually knew and loved.

Moreover, obliterating the former spouse's or biological parent's imperfections is a convenient way of putting to rest any guilt or unresolved conflict we had with that person. Beatifying the deceased spouse or parent also allows you to maintain the fiction that you are permanently faithful to that spouse or parent and that fate alone, not your own needs or desires, has pushed you into new relationships.

Many problems arise for the new spouse because the infinite virtues of the now saintly departed spouse are unchangeably frozen in time. There is no way to argue with a stepchild's declaration that "My mom would never have done that!"; or your new spouse's faulty recollection that "Susan was an impeccable housekeeper (or gourmet chef, social hostess, or sex partner)"; or your own insistence that "John never lost his temper and was always financially responsible, generous, warm, and open." Anyone who tries to prove otherwise inevitably looks like a petty, jealous misanthrope.

Consider this story:

Suzanne, a thirty-seven-year-old divorcée, married Jeff, a fifty-five-year-old widower, after a courtship that makes "whirlwind" seem lethargic. They met at a Fourth of July clambake in New England at the home of a mutual friend and were married by Labor Day. Many of Suzanne's friends were quite skeptical of the whole process, since they worried about Suzanne's fragile emotional state. Within the previous five years, she had struggled through a difficult divorce and was hospitalized for a nervous breakdown. Only recently, had she put her life back together, or, at least, so it seemed.

Although Jeff lived in New York and Suzanne in Boston, he pursued her with hours-long telephone calls, wired her flowers, and flew her to New York for the evening to attend gala benefits studded with the "rich and famous." Suzanne didn't know what to think, given her own recent marital history and the fact that Jeff's wife had died only three months before they met. Yet, Jeff's persistence and panache overwhelmed Suzanne and quieted the inner voice that urged her to go slowly.

Suzanne worried about her sixteen-year-old son, Michael, an only child, bright, hyperactive, and dyslexic. Jeff had two older children, a son, eighteen, and a daughter, twenty-three. Suzanne liked the idea of a ready-made family for Michael, who didn't have many friends.

Jeff's son, Toby, was a rock musician; his daughter, Ann, was in graduate school. Toby was on the road much of the time with his group. The rest of the time, according to Jeff, he lived in his own rather funky pad.

After they married, the newlyweds lived in Jeff's Manhattan condo. For Suzanne, who had grown up in a Boston suburb, the pace of city life was almost overwhelming. Every night, Jeff had them scheduled for a different social event.

This is how Suzanne described their life together:

When I first moved to New York, I didn't actually know anyone there besides Jeff. Oh, I had an old college friend, but I hadn't seen her in years. So, I had to rely pretty much on Jeff for direction and advice.

Jeff really liked to take charge. He sent me to Melanie's (his former wife) hairdresser. He took me shopping in all the stores she had liked. Melanie had been a beautiful fashion plate. (Her portrait was still hanging in our living room. Jeff said the kids would be hurt if we took it down.) I don't mean that disrespectfully, but I was much more a New England type, more understated.

I remember the first time I had a dinner party. I was terrified. These were all Jeff's and Melanie's friends, and I was really on display. I've always been uncomfortable with being in the spotlight, but there was no escape. Jeff kept telling me not to worry. He and Melanie had done these things as a team, and he could direct me. That only made me feel worse, but I couldn't say that to him. At least, not then.

I was a nervous wreck the whole week before the dinner party and during the entire evening. I couldn't wait for it to end. Our guests were very nice. They tried to put me at ease, but every now and then someone would make a well-intentioned remark that made me feel I was in a race with Melanie. I was miserable. Jeff was quite nervous, monitoring everyone and everything to see that things were perfect. When his friends said, "This is a great party! Just like the ones you always throw," I wanted to curl up in a corner. I felt like I was simply a stand-in, a plainer cardboard cutout of Melanie.

Over the next few years, our relationship became very strained, largely over the Melanie issue. I couldn't help feeling insanely jealous. I knew that was stupid, but I couldn't help it. When Jeff was annoyed at me, he always managed to make it plain that Melanie wouldn't have acted that way. I felt there was no way that I could ever reach her level of perfection. And after a while, I just wanted out.

Oddly enough, it was Ann, Jeff's daughter, who clued me in to what was happening. I was shocked when she told me her parents had been on the verge of divorce when Melanie was diagnosed with a brain tumor. She died within six months. This model of perfection that I was trying to outdo had been human after all. But that knowledge came too late to make much difference in our marriage. Maybe, if I had known earlier, I wouldn't have been so intimidated. By the time Ann told me, our marriage was on the rocks. Even though I worried about pulling Michael away from his new older "sister" and "brother," there really wasn't any other way.

Readers who are old enough will see in this story parallels with the Hitchcock thriller *Rebecca,* in which the new, rather innocent wife is locked in competition, if only in her own mind, with a dead spouse who is too good to be true. In that film, as in Suzanne's experience, the ghost is not really a paragon at all, but a woman with all-too-human flaws. Our advice to a new spouse faced with a larger-than-life predecessor is to try Tact and Tacking strategy #9: Just Don't Go There. The flawed living can never win a competition with the perfect dead. Try to avoid situations where comparisons can be made, because you will always be trying to read them to see if you or the dead spouse is ahead. A respectful attitude toward the deceased that does not invite recitations of the ghost's virtues or your weaknesses probably serves everyone's best interests.

Our counsel to the spouse who has canonized his or her late partner: It is not surprising that you have chosen to transform your former spouse into a saint. It may help you deal with your guilt about remembering the imperfections of someone now gone, as well as your own imperfect responses when he or she was alive. We all feel that way to some extent. Still, pretending that the dead had no flaws is ultimately unrealistic and unhealthy for you and those around you, especially your new spouse. It doesn't help the person who is gone; it doesn't help you; and it certainly doesn't help your new relationship.

Better for you to think quietly (if you can't discuss the issue with your new spouse, a buddy, or a therapist) about the times when your former spouse annoyed or infuriated you and your own less-than-perfect response. Then, deal head-on with those difficult memories. Work on confronting those guilt-provoking memories rather than converting them into impervious, ongoing guilt that will permanently poison your outlook and any new relationship you might attempt. It may be difficult, but not nearly as difficult as carrying that burden of guilt around for the rest of your life.

Spouses are not the only ones who idealize a dead family member. Children are, perhaps, even more prone to erase a dead parent's flaws. After all, as children, most of us saw our parents as paragons of perfection (except when they didn't let us have our way). For adolescents, living parents tend to be seen as square, uncool, unsympathetic, and downright stupid during those tumultuous years (which, as we know, may not end until one enters one's forties).

Only when we emerge from the long, dark tunnel of adolescence do we begin to see our parents in a more charitable light. Was it Mark Twain who said that the older he got, the more intelligent his parents became? It is clear that idealizing the same parent who was seen as uncool or annoying in life helps to ease the adult child's guilt toward a dead mom or dad.

Grown children who see their widowed parent involved with a new love will probably have trouble with their own feelings about this new person—both as their parent's new spouse and as their "new" parent. Guilt plays no favorites in this scenario. Adult children's guilt toward a dead parent is often a powerful wedge between the children and the new stepparent.

Jonathan, age thirty-three, had a difficult time with his mother's death and the subsequent remarriage of his father. This is how he described the situation to us:

My mother was an unusual woman. She was strong, intelligent, down-to-earth, beautiful, and kind. I know that sounds too good to be true, but she really was all those things. That doesn't mean she didn't have her moments occasionally, but then, who doesn't? When Maryjane and I got married, she was a true mother to Maryjane, whose own mother had deserted their family when she was quite young. My mother really mothered Maryjane, to the point where my sister, Louise, was rather jealous. Maryjane was just as devastated as I was when my mother died. How could God be so cruel? After all, my mother was only in her midfifties. And Maryjane had just found another mother after so many years of misery.

We were still dealing with our grief when Dad announced he was moving in with Barbara. We were bowled over. That seemed so callous. I really love my dad, but he seemed to be moving ahead with his life on a very fast track. Too fast for us. Maryjane and I were devastated. First, my mother dies, and, now, my dad was replacing her before she was even cold in her grave. It infuriated us, too.

We didn't know Barbara, and we didn't want to, either. When we finally met her, about eight months later, we couldn't stand her. How could my dad pick someone like that? My mother had exquisite taste in everything she did. Barbara didn't know what the word "taste" was all about. She wasn't very educated or sophisticated, and my mother was both. It was hard to see what Dad saw in her. She tried very hard to please us, but she and my mother weren't in the same universe.

When they married, about a year after that, Maryjane and I couldn't bring ourselves to go to the wedding. They've been married for about four years now, and we are glad that we live too far away for us to have to be with Barbara too often. She keeps trying to do things like my mother did, and that just turns us off. Sometimes, I feel guilty about how we feel about Barbara, but we just can't help it. She's so different from my mother that I have a hard time connecting to her.

CAN A STEPPARENT EVER FILL A GAP?

Paradoxically, the death of a parent, particularly when a child is quite young, can create an opportunity for a stepparent who comes along much later to fill in gaps that the child's biological parent never had the opportunity to close. Young women who lost their maternal role model early in life often miss out on all the things that mothers can teach daughters about being a grown-up woman. The same holds true for dads and sons.

Nan was only ten years old when her mother died. Her brother was thirteen. Her physicist father buried himself and his grief in his work at the university. Nan was brought up by the live-in housekeeper, Geraldine, who was kind and loving. Nan's brother began to hang out with a group of hippie types, who smoked pot and dreamed of great adventures. That only further isolated Nan.

Nan, who had always been a good student, threw herself into her school-work. By the time she finished high school, she was valedictorian of her class. She felt her father loved her, but he seemed to be "all thumbs" at raising a girl. Consequently, he mostly left Nan to Geraldine's care. It was not until fifteen years after his wife died that Nan's father remarried. This is Nan's story:

I was twenty-eight and in graduate school when my dad remarried. Carol was a nice woman, gentle and sort of quiet, but competent, too. I could see that she knew how to take charge in a good way, not pushy. When she moved into my dad's house, she started sprucing it up. Although I hated to see some of the old stuff go, that place really needed some attention. Nothing had changed since my mother died. We were still living with the avocado color scheme of fifteen years ago. I didn't know the first thing about redecorating.

I was worried that I wouldn't have a place in my dad's life anymore. After all, he had closed himself off after my mom had died. I felt he loved me, but he was quite distant. I felt Carol would have a big influence on whether or not I would be included in his new life.

Carol had been married before, and her husband had died about five years before she met Dad. She was about Dad's age, and she had a daughter close to my age. I worried about her, too. Would she and Carol let me in? After all, they were pretty close.

Well, I guess I lucked out. Carol and Robin (her daughter) took me into their lives. I felt like someone who'd been living out in the rain until they came along. Carol taught me things that you might think I would have known, like how to set a table for a dinner party, how to shop for clothes, even how to deal with Dad when he got grumpy. Can you believe she showed me how to do my eyes much better, too? Maybe, Mom would have taught me those things had she lived long enough. Geraldine (the housekeeper) loved me, but she didn't know these things, either.

I always felt drawn to older women, not sexually but emotionally. I think I was looking for a mother since my own mother died. Carol didn't come on strong, but she opened her heart to me in a gentle way, and I walked right in. And Robin is the sister I always wished I'd had.

Not all adult stepfamilies work that well or come together that easily. In this case, however, and several others we studied, when the death of the parent occurred long before the establishment of the living parent's new relationship, a wise and open stepparent was able to form a strong, loving bond with the grown stepchildren. This was particularly true when the adult stepchildren still felt the need for some affectionate, gentle parenting.

Yet, here too, it takes a lot of goodwill and openness on the part of many of the new family members to make it work. If Robin had felt resistant to Nan or worried that her mother was giving too much attention and affection to Nan, things could have been much more difficult. In both of the families that came together to form this adult stepfamily, time had worked its healing balm. Both families had had enough time to grieve and set guilt to rest. Healing had occurred, and everyone was ready to move forward.

Luckily, Carol and Robin were comfortable being Joiners. Carol was particularly gifted in the role of Guardian Angel and Unifier. Nan, too, was a Joiner, who basked in the warmth that Carol and Robin brought to the family. Even Nan's dad seemed to shed his emotional shell in the welcoming, affectionate ambience created by Carol. Carol and Robin welcomed Nan and her brother and felt nourished, themselves, by the new family bonds they were able to establish. Nan's brother, who lived in another state, was less involved, but was welcome whenever he came to town.

Still, not all widowed partners want to wait for the years to heal their grief. For some, moving forward and establishing a new life help them to mend. They may be moving faster than their adult children can handle, and that can cause tumult at the outset that surfaces again from time to time.

For a new stepchild, remember that opening acts count. They are long remembered. So, think before you act and try to remember that acts of peace, rather than acts of war, go a long way toward establishing you as someone of character. We are not suggesting that phony or hypocritical niceness is an appropriate strategy. Simply try hard to think about your parent's right to be happy. Over the years, your parent has probably put your happiness before his or her own thousands of times. This might be a time for a little reciprocation.

For the parent and stepparent embarking on a new journey, if you are convinced that you know what you're doing, our advice would be Tact and Tacking skill #4, Tenacity. Stick up for what you believe, and remember, you have a right to a full life, just as your adult children do. Another piece of advice from our list of Tact and Tacking Skills is #3: Get Some Emotional Distance, talk to a buddy, someone who has lived through this same difficult scenario. Be sure, however, that your buddy has real wisdom—not boiling anger—to share.

For stepparents, it is worth remembering that patience and sensitivity go a long way toward setting a positive stage for the new adult stepfamily drama. You could attempt the FEAT of Tack and Tacking #6, Forgiveness, Empathy, Apology, and Tolerance (if appropriate). One key question you might ask yourself is, "If I were the one who had died, how would I want my children's new stepparent to treat them?" Wouldn't you want that stepparent to have the mature wisdom to ignore off-putting behavior on your children's part? (This doesn't mean becoming a permanent doormat for abusive stepchildren, of course!) In the mirror of hindsight, your new stepchildren will probably see the image of the decent, understanding stepparent you chose to be. Even if they don't, at least when you look in your own mirror, you'll be proud of what you see.

One last recommendation for stepparents and stepchildren alike, regardless of whether the adult stepfamily took root in the shadow of death or divorce: Give your new family member a chance. Give change a chance. Give love and understanding a chance. And don't forget to give yourself a chance, too.

That advice, "give yourself a chance," will never be more needed than when you confront the decision about where to live as a new married couple. This is particularly true when you have to decide about what to do with the houses in which one or each of you lived with your previous spouse. That is the subject we shall tackle in the next chapter.

PART III

Critical Landmarks Along the Way

CHAPTER 7

Whose House Is This Anyway?

Polly Adler once wrote a book (in a very different context) titled *A House Is Not a Home*. That title does not apply to the adult stepfamilies we studied. For them, a house *is* a home, whether it's a mansion or a shack, whether it's been in the family for hundred years or was bought when the kids were young. Whether it's a mansion or a modest apartment, it's still home—an emotionally loaded place, full of nostalgic meanings and memories for everyone who's lived in it.

The family residence is usually home sweet home even to adult children, who haven't slept there for fifteen years. Often, it is home for the remarrying parent who lived in it, with another spouse and their growing children, through good times and bad. And, of course, there's another home, the home that the new spouse gave up when he or she moved in—a home full of memories of its own, forever lost to the new spouse and his or her children.

Here's a story told to us by one adult daughter about her widowed father's remarriage fifteen years earlier. We include it because it describes so many of the problems that stepfamilies encounter as they try to work through problems of house and home.

Constance, age fifty-one, told us the following story:

I have two younger sisters. We lived with Mother and Dad in an old house we all loved. There were woods and a pond in back. We each had our own rooms. It was in a nice quiet neighborhood, a great place to grow up.

Then, I went off to college and eventually got married, and my sister Joan did, too. Dorothy, the youngest, was still at home and in high school when Mother died.

Dad and Dorothy stayed in the house until Dot went off to the university. Then, Dad was left in the house by himself. He was still working, so he kept busy, and we all tried to help because we knew it was difficult for him. Of course, the house got more and more tatty and run-down because he didn't take care of it the way Mother would have.

Then Dad met Marian, and they hit it off, and he perked up. A year later, they got married. She sold her small house and moved into our house with Dad. We were pleased at first, because Dad seemed so much happier now that he had someone.

Marian, of course, wanted to fix up the house, but her taste was very different than Mother's. Dad went along with about everything she wanted, but he did put his foot down about changing one or two things.

Anyway, Marian wanted to expand their bedroom into a big master suite with walk-in closets and a fancy bathroom. To do it, they had to take out the wall between their room and Dot's room. That simply eliminated Dot's beautiful room, the room she loved, that looked out over the pond and the trees. Marian didn't even tell Dot she was going to do it.

Dot had a hard time digesting that one! Thank heavens, they didn't touch my room! She redid almost everything else in the whole house, and in a really tacky way!

Then, one day, something curious happened. Marian had left her purse in the kitchen, and someone came in through the screen door and stole it. Marian's reaction was very strange. She got very upset and said the house wasn't safe, that they might be robbed any time, and she just couldn't live in that house any more! It was quite silly. We knew who had stolen her purse. It was a neighbor's wild kid, who got into trouble a lot. But he wasn't dangerous, and, shortly after that, his family sent him to some special school.

But Marian went on and on about it. So, very reluctantly, Dad went along. They sold the house. It was very sad. It was a great place to bring the grandchildren, with the woods and the pond. But Marian didn't like the children running around anyway.

They moved into a huge apartment on the tenth floor of a big new apartment building. Marian felt it was safe up there, and, of course, she decorated it in her own way. But I think Dad was miserable there. He loved gardening and working in the yard, and now all he could do was look out the window.

When one of us came with our kids to visit, Marian would get upset because the kids messed up the apartment. So, more and more we got together outside, at restaurants or on picnics or at one of our homes.

I think that's when Dad began to dwindle, and it wasn't very long after all that that he died.

Dad had told us three girls that the money from the house was to go to us. He had other investments and things for Marian. Eventually, we got our money, but I think Marian tried her best to block it.

Marian stayed in that monster apartment paying that enormous rent with Dad's money. Then, her health began to slip. She developed Alzheimer's and had to be put in a nursing home.

Marian had two daughters of her own. We had tried hard to be friendly with them. One of them was very nice, but that was the one who moved to Brazil. The other, Alice, never liked us and vice versa, but she took care of Marian until she finally had to put her into the nursing home. She resented that whole burden, I think. Maybe, we should have helped Alice more, but she was so nasty and unpleasant!

She had to put all the stuff from that big apartment into storage, and that started something that isn't finished even now, fifteen years after Dad's death. Dad had been in the war, and he had helped liberate a little village in Belgium. When we were teenagers, he took us all to visit that village. Some of the people there remembered him, and they treated us wonderfully. Anyway, at the inn where we stayed, there was this big poster in the lobby, a print from a painting of the village, the church and some nearby buildings. We all loved it, especially Dad, and they offered to give it to us, but he wouldn't accept it, but he finally bought it.

Marian had it framed and hung in their apartment. Dad, when he was sick, had told me that he wanted me, specifically, to have that picture, so when Alice was putting everything into storage, I called her and asked her for it. She got very angry and said absolutely not and that she had never heard of anything so rude!

She's been treating my sisters the same way, refusing even to talk to them. I don't understand what's going on, but I think it's really about money. I think there's some money that Dad left for Marian, but what was left was to go to us when Marian died. I'm not sure, but my sisters and I are getting together next week. We'll talk it over. It's been fifteen years since Dad died, but not all the problems have been solved, even yet.

That story underscores many of the emotional booby traps that lie hidden in "practical" questions regarding houses and other physical things. Whatever those questions seem to be about, they are really about new spouses' rights and obligations and children's expectations. They also are about the relationships between the two sets of adult children, who become intertwined when older couples remarry.

Stories like that one taught us that you can *never* underestimate the many deep symbolic meanings of the place we call home. All Five Furies can be unleashed by it.

YOUR PLACE OR MINE?

The rest of this chapter is written mostly from the perspective of a new wife now living in her new husband's house. But if you're a man who has moved into your new spouse's place, simply change all the *she*'s to *he*'s. That will usually work, although there are a few real differences between men and women when it comes to matters of hearth and home that we shall explore. Those differences are especially evident among older folks who grew up in more traditional ways.

Taking care of the home was, and still is, much more women's territory than men's, particularly for the older couples in our study. The decor, the furniture, the kitchen, those have traditionally been *her* power centers rather than his. Let the husband have the garage and the workbench. Let him worry about the car, let him go out and earn their living, but the interior of the house is hers! So, when the new wife moves into his house, she will probably expect that territory to be ceded to her.

Consider, for example, this discussion between a soon-to-be-bride and groom. It took place after the decision to marry, but some time before the wedding:

She: How shall we arrange things? You have a house, and I have one, too. Shall I move into your place or you into mine?

He: I have that big empty house, and yours is much smaller. And mine is much more convenient to my office. So, if it's okay with you, I think it makes more sense for you to move in with me.

She: I suppose you're right. Let me think about it for a few days. I love my house, and my sons love it. But if we sell it, we can use the money to remodel your kitchen and master bedroom. They really need it. They haven't been touched in years.

He: [frowning just a little]: Well, we'll see. But let's figure that we'll live in my place.

Would that it were so easy! There are sure to be a host of practical problems, problems like these—and these will turn out to be the easy ones:

> What about all the furniture? We'll have two of almost everything. I think my dining room set is really the one we should use. What about my beloved collection of Native American rugs? Where can we put those?

True, these problems can stir up a couple of the Furies, including Fury #3, Favoritism; #4, Fidelity to Family; and #5, Focus on Self. Nevertheless, we repeat, these will be the easy problems. If two grown-up lovers can't work through these minor issues, you might want to split up right now, because you're probably not ready to tackle the really serious house-related issues—the ones that are deeply felt and too often left unspoken, the ones that touch our hearts and our egos.

Consider just a couple of these more complex problems:

> **She:** [to herself]: Does he really expect me to sleep (with him) in the same bed he and his former wife slept in for thirty years? With her pillows? Am I to use her dressing table? He even keeps her picture on the piano. How can he be so insensitive? Am I just a visitor in another family's home?

> **He:** Doesn't she realize how much this place means to me? My kids grew up here. Helen and I built our lives here, through good times and bad, in sickness and in health. Now, she wants to put her furniture into the living room and change the carpets and completely redo the bedroom! I thought she would be more understanding than that.

But she *is* more understanding than that, and this is the way she probably understands it:

> **She:** This is his home and his children's home and their mother's home. It's not my home. I feel like an outsider, an interloper, and a lonely one at that. So, what should I do? Should I leave things exactly as they are so he can feel comfortable? Then, when the children visit, they will see that nothing's changed and may be they'll feel better, too? That would be saintly of me, but I'm not sure I'm ready to be canonized.
>
> Or shall I try to turn it into our home? Change things, fix things, remodel things, so I can feel it's also my home, at least partially reflecting my tastes and interests? After all, this is our new beginning, the start of a whole new life for both of us. We should take a fresh view of how we're going to spend the rest of our lives together. The children are all adults. They can manage perfectly well. We shouldn't be tied down by the past.

This is a time when we should be changing things! Or is that kind of thinking really too selfish of me?

Be careful! This time is *not* like that other time, that first time, when you were both young and setting forth on a long adventure together. Back then you, the young bride, were probably the one who mostly ran the new household while your young husband ventured forth to earn you both a living. This time, you're not starting from scratch. You're moving in on someone else's territory and probably damaging, however unintentionally, a powerful sentimental legacy.

Sometimes, housing problems can become even more complex. Suppose, for example, that she lived in Boston and he in Los Angeles, each for many years. That's not just three thousand miles of separation. It's two cultures, with two very different sets of attitudes and values.

Or what if he met her in Warsaw, where she had lived all her life. He brought her back to live in his home in America's heartland, in Springfield, Illinois. Those aren't just great physical distances; they're great, difficult-to-bridge differences in culture. In these days of jet travel, distance has become almost trivial, but culture certainly has not.

Your initial response might be: Oh, forget culture and stop lecturing at us. We love one another, and that's all that really counts. As a mature adult, however, you know better than that. The wiser course is to treat cultural differences seriously, to think hard about them, and to discuss them fully.

You might ask yourself:

Am I ready to give up my home, in my familiar community, to move into a strange house, in a strange new part of the world? If I do that, I will—for a while at least—have to depend entirely on my new spouse to connect me to new people and new surroundings. At home, I felt independent. I knew who I was and where I belonged. I had a clear place in my community. If I move to his world, I'll be alone except for him. I'll have to build my identity all over again! That might have seemed like a great adventure when I was twenty-one, but now I'm not so sure. Like Blanche, in Streetcar, *I shall have to depend on "the kindness of strangers."*

We've considered the consequences of cultural differences in more detail in other chapters, but here we just want to point out how serious and complicated the seemingly simple question of "your place or mine?" can become—particularly in new partnerships between older adults.

"Come on-a My House, My-y House, I'm Gonna Give You Everything!"

Okay, so she moves into his house (or he into hers), and they both survive the stresses and strains of relocating and getting settled. They sell one of the sofas and give some of the duplicate furniture to the kids and the rest to charity, and they get all those practical matters resolved. Now, they can really begin their loving new life together, just the two of them. It's really all quite wonderful, a reinvigorating new beginning!

Stop! We haven't considered the children yet!

But we don't have to worry about the children. After all, our children aren't really children. They're grown-ups. They have their own lives, their own places, their own families. We don't have to worry about them!

Oh, but you do have to worry about them. You don't have to worry about diapering them or getting them off to school every day, but, unfortunately, you have to worry about them, nonetheless. To illustrate how fraught with Furies the situation can be for both spouses and adult children, here's the first act of an imaginary play:

The Cast:

(In order of appearance)

Helen, in her late fifties, recently remarried to **Joe**.
Susan (a voice on the telephone), **Joe**'s twentysomething daughter, married, without children. She and her husband, **Sam**, live in a small apartment nearby.
Joe, in his late sixties, **Helen**'s new and second husband, and **Susan**'s father.

The Scene:

Joe's *spacious house, where the new couple has now lived for about four months. It is about 5:00 P.M. on a lovely spring afternoon.* **Helen** *is home alone, preparing dinner. The phone rings. It's stepdaughter* **Susan**.

Susan: Helen? It's me, Susan. How's everything? Great! I called to tell you that Sam and I are planning a big barbecue in our backyard this coming Friday night. It's going to be a surprise birthday bash for Sam's brother, Charlie. You and Dad are invited!

Helen: Fine. But Susan, you don't have a backyard at your apartment building, do you?

Susan [laughing]: I mean our backyard. The one at our house—at my father's house, where you live!

Halen [taken somewhat aback]: Our backyard? Oh, Susan, please, not this Friday! We're both exhausted. We've planned an absolutely quiet, uninterrupted weekend.

Susan: Don't worry. We won't disturb you at all. We'll bring all the food and stuff, and we'll clean up afterward. We've even hired a little jazz combo. The back porch and the yard are perfect for it! You won't have to do anything unless you want to. See you Friday. 'Bye.

[*Enter Joe, looking haggard after a long day at the office.*]

Helen [kissing him lightly]: Joe, you look exhausted. I'll fix you a snack.

[*Joe stretches out on the sofa, while Helen fusses with the snack, etc. She returns carrying a bowl of fruit.*]

Helen: Joe, I know you're tired, but there's something I have to talk to you about. Susan called a few minutes ago. She's planning to have a big party here this coming Friday night. That means there'll be a whole gang here all day Friday, getting ready. The house will be a wreck. She says they'll be quiet, and they'll clean up, but you know Susan!

Joe [wearily]: Oh, what the hell. Let them do it. It might even be fun! Their apartment is too small to do anything there. And you know how kids are. They grew up here, so they still feel that this is their house!

End of Act I

Now, dear reader, you write Act II. Does it begin with a mounting quarrel between Helen and Joe, perhaps something like this?

Helen: Joe, it's not their house anymore, it's our house. They've got their own homes, their own lives. They can't just take over this house any time they want to.

Joe: Oh, Helen, don't get so upset. It's only one night. We'll have the rest of the weekend. I'll help make sure they don't wreck the place, and I'll make sure they clean everything up.

Helen [more upset than ever]: Joe, you always side with the kids. I thought when we decided to live here it was going to be my house, too. I want to be nice to your kids, but Susan didn't even ask our permission. She just announced it! If Mary were alive she would certainly have said no, and in no uncertain terms. Why shouldn't I?

Joe: You know why. Because Mary was Susan's real mother. You're her stepmother, and that's different.

Now let's write another possible opening for Act II:

Helen [telephoning back to **Susan**]: I'm sorry, Susan, but absolutely not! We just can't let you have a barbecue here this Friday night. I've talked it over with Joe. You can have your party a week from Friday, but not this Friday. We have other plans.

Susan [angrily]: But we've planned it. We've invited people. Is Daddy home? Let me talk to him!

Now let's try yet another beginning for Act II:

Helen [capitulating, on the phone to Susan]: Hello, Susan? Okay. Have your party here. What time will you and your gang come on Friday? What dishes and glasses will you need? Not paper plates! Let's do it right!

Are there any other options for Act II? What do *you* think is the best thing for Helen to do? What will the consequences be for her relationships with Joe and Susan? What will the consequences be for her own self-esteem?

Here's what we suggest:

WHAT'S EASY IS DIFFICULT OR WHAT LOOKS EASY IS HARD

Remarrying adults who decide to move into their spouse's old family home too often see only half of what they are doing. They frequently don't recognize that they are moving into their adult stepchildren's family home at the same time. In so doing, they have asked for trouble and better be prepared to be tested.

Helen chose what must have appeared to her (and appears to many others in the same situation) to be an easy solution to their housing dilemma. She agreed to move into Joe's spacious home, perhaps thinking that it would spare Joe the effort of making a major move. She probably thought she was doing Joe a favor by doing all of the accommodating. But Joe's home was no bachelor pad. Helen didn't reflect on what her moving in would mean for Joe's children, who had grown up in that house. Given the many different claims on the home, it was inevitable that the question would arise: "Whose house is this, anyway?"

Susan acted on what she assumed was her *right* to use her old home on special occasions. Helen didn't understand that her choice of living arrangements would have an effect on her own *right* of privacy. She should tell Joe that what seemed like an easy solution to their housing problem was shortsighted.

Helen needs to accept responsibility for the problem with Susan about the party and to apologize to Joe for putting him in the middle. Helen should deal with Susan directly, but let Joe know in advance what she plans to say. Helen should communicate to Susan that she was not being sensitive enough to Susan on this occasion and didn't take into account how deeply Susan might feel that this is still her home. Tact and Tacking #6 is the FEAT (Forgiveness, Empathy, Apology, and Tolerance) Helen should aim to achieve. When she acts courageously, Joe is likely to admire her and follow her lead.

It's okay for Helen to say she is still learning about her new family and is bound to make mistakes. Helen doesn't have to lie down and roll over. She should definitely ask Susan to give her notice in the future when she wants to use the house, so she and Susan can take each other's needs into account.

After that conversation, Helen and Joe need to start talking about selling both their homes and moving to a third place that is definitely theirs. Otherwise, Helen and Joe will have to accept that variations on this scene will be played out *ad nauseam*.

Of course, children almost always feel that the place they grew up in is still their real home—even ten years after they've left and started families of their own. That's just as true in non-stepfamilies as in stepfamilies. Kids want their childhood room left intact, just like it was, even though they seldom even visit it. They resent—often very deeply—having their backyard swings taken down or their old mementos boxed up and sent to the attic. Adult children may never forgive their parents for throwing out their baseball cards or Barbie dolls.

Sure, that kind of behavior is irrational, but one's emotional "home" is not a very rational place. Home is a symbol as much as a physical reality. It's a psychological anchor that helps keep us from drifting away into too much frightening independence. It's a lifeline that lets us cling to the security of childhood—or at least the illusion of childhood security.

In adult stepfamilies, such issues become dangerously explosive. And, from the children's perspective, it's not too hard to see why.

This is what one of those "adult children," Emma, age forty-two, had to say about her childhood home:

All during my young life, this house has been "our house." Not just Mom's and Dad's, but "ours." I'm part of that "ours." I know Dad paid for it and all that, but it's my house, too. Just because Mom died, does that make it any less ours? Why should Dad's new wife act like it's hers? She hasn't lived in it like we have! She didn't grow up in it! She has no right to act as though she owns it!

This is where I grew up. I know every inch of it, every bit of the yard, the house, my room—yes, my room. I'm not living in it right now, but it's still my room. How dare that woman try to turn my room into a den?

Should the parent reply this way?

Oh, come on! You're forty-two years old. You have a spouse, kids, a place of your own. You're not a child anymore. Coming back to your old home may be nice, but things change. Children grow up. This house isn't really yours anymore. Get over it! Get a life!

Do you think that speech would help? Even if spoken by the child's real dad—with his new wife standing at his side? No way! The adult child might go on, almost pleading:

I got married in our garden. That means a lot to John and me. And I want my children to know their roots, to realize that this is where their mummy came from. Lots of my old friends and my old schoolmates are still here. I know I don't live here anymore, but I'm still connected to that house and that community. I feel I still have rights to it.

Then comes the zinger:

If Mom were with us, she would keep the house the way it was. She wouldn't go changing everything!

Children—biological children, as well as stepchildren—don't like to cut their ties to home, even though hanging on to those ties may be quite unrealistic. But don't dismiss that attitude as mere foolishness.

The feelings that underlie such behaviors, while mostly unconscious, are real. They also run deep. They're like the almost invisible threads of a spiderweb. They may seem thin and easily destructible, but try jarring them, even slightly. You will find that the itty-bitty spider is magically transformed into the furious twin Furies: Fear of Abandonment and Isolation (is the wicked stepmother trying to drive us out of our own home?) and Favoritism (Dad, do you really care more about *her* than you do about us?).

And that's not all. That old house had pets, as well as children! There were beloved cats, dogs, horses, and birds. They're all part of home, too. The kids may have grown up and left, but the dogs and cats haven't. They still live here with you. The children visit them, of course, but now those animals are the new couple's responsibility.

Here's one father's view of the nontrivial question of pets, after he remarried and his new wife came to live with him, in his house, with his (or rather his children's) two old dogs:

I loved our dogs as much as the children did. But by the time Ann and I got married and she came to live here, many things had changed. My wife was gone. Both kids had married and left. I had retired. Ann and I had a little extra money, so we wanted to go places and do things. But we couldn't just jump in the car and go. We had to worry about the dogs.

Ann was sympathetic enough, but she'd never had animals before. She wasn't afraid of them or anything like that. They just weren't her thing. Finally, we decided we had to find the dogs a new home. I called each of the kids, but they weren't in any position to take both of them, and nobody wanted to separate them. So, I took them to the city animal shelter. They guaranteed they'd find a home for them, together. I was sad about it, but times change!

When the kids found out what I'd done, they got really mad! Their beloved friends sent off to a common animal shelter! How could we do such a terrible thing? "Why didn't you tell us? One of us would have taken them!" Nonsense! I had already told them. They had conveniently forgotten all that.

And, of course, they really blame it on Ann. She's the convenient scapegoat!

THE HOUSE AS THE FAMILY'S HEADQUARTERS

One helpful way to think about house-and-home issues is to remember that a house is a family's headquarters. It's home base, the container that holds the family together.

In all families, headquarters eventually crumble—not always physically, but psychologically. Then, either a new headquarters is established by members of a new generation, or the family more or less breaks up. When there are children, the headquarters shifts—gradually or suddenly—from the parents' household to one of the children's households.

As parents grow older, for example, holiday gatherings may transfer from the parents' house to one of the children's homes. This year, son Mike and his wife will host the family Thanksgiving dinner, and then we'll have Christmas at sister Sue's. But that shift is more than just a shift from one house to another. It's a psychological shift, a role reversal. Parents often become more and more dependent on their children, some eventually going, albeit reluctantly, to live with them.

That meltdown of the family's longtime headquarters is painful for both parents and children, in some ways even more wrenching for adult children than for their remarried older parents. The parents have found each other and see themselves as beginning anew. The children, however, lose their emotional anchor (and they rarely expect that to happen). They must recognize that their own homes, not their parents' old family homesteads, must now become the family centers. Otherwise, eventually, there will be no family center at all.

Of course, many adults visit their childhood home, even long after it's been sold and occupied by strangers. Most of us get an emotional charge from seeing that nostalgic shrine again. We show it to our children, and we tell them tales of the old days. That's part of the family transition process. In adult stepfamilies, that process just tends to happen faster and perhaps more unexpectedly.

SEX IN OUR OLD HOME?

Parental sex also complicates the family home. This time, it's not the *fact* of sex between the newly marrieds. They can take care of that part very well by themselves, thank you. This time, it's the *location* of sex.

Of course, children—both step and biological—seldom openly acknowledge the existence of parental sex. They seem to feel their parents did it once or twice, just to create them, but then that whole business went away. Now, when the new wife or new husband moves into the old homestead, sex again becomes an issue—a shadowy, off-screen issue—especially for adult stepchildren.

To themselves, certainly, and perhaps to one another, they ask: "Has *she* really moved into Mama's room? Is she using Mama's closet, her dressing table? Is Dad really sleeping with her in Mama's bed? Are they really 'doing it'?"

Such questions, or versions of them, inevitably arise when a new spouse moves into the old family home. It doesn't matter much whether she moves in with him or he with her. Nor does it matter much whether the ritual of marriage has sanctified the new partnership or the couple is just living together. Either way, the new steppartner has moved into the displaced partner's intimate, private sanctum. That reality will generate discomfort—for both the new partner and especially for the children of the replaced partner.

The notion of Dad or Mom having sex with another person is bad enough—bad enough so children often manage not to let it even rise to consciousness—but in Mama's *house,* in her *room,* in her *bed?* The child's sense of some spiritual violation of Mother, of her memory (if she has died) or of her "rights" (if she is divorced), is brought into unavoidably sharp relief by the physical reality of "home." For "home" always means *our* little clan, *our* dad, *our* mom, *our* dog, *our* house. Everyone else is an outsider. A stranger having sex with our dad (or mom) in our house is very hard to take!

How should new spouses deal with this issue, if they have moved into the other's house? Separate bedrooms or other such foolishness? Denial? Abstinence?

Or is this yet another reason to make some radical changes? Remodel the house, especially the master bedroom? Or move out, to a new, ghost-free neutral place!

THAT HOUSE IS WORTH A LOT OF MONEY THAT SHOULD COME TO ME!

Our home is a symbol, a special place loaded with deep personal meanings and nostalgic memories. But it is also a physical reality—a structure made of lumber, brick, and mortar—a structure full of real property: dishes, silverware, furniture, clothing, paintings, appliances, and lots more. When questions about the ownership of real property come to the fore, you can be quite sure that the Furies will be lurking nearby.

The adult child's inner conversation may go like this:

That house has been in my family for three generations. I'm not selfish, but I've always felt our house was part of my inheritance, that when Dad and Mom were gone, I would move my family into it. Now, is she going to get it?

Or like this:

In today's market, that house is worth a mint! Dad's much older than Doris. When he passes on, does she keep the house? She might just decide to sell it and walk away with the cash! Sure, Doris will need a place to live, but she's young. She might even live in our house for another thirty years. Then, we children would never get it. That's not fair!

Even if the house has only been in the family for five or ten years, these crass but painful, and often unspoken, issues lie just beneath the surface. Who will get what when the old folks are gone? That question spells trouble in almost every family. In stepfamilies, as you might imagine, it spells more trouble than usual.

Maybe, just a few objects are involved, like the family piano or Mom's collection of antique candlesticks. Some of these things the children really didn't think about (consciously) until Dad decided to remarry and bring his new wife to live in the family home. But now, they feel they're in competition with their stepmother for these prized possessions and that they deserve them—not today, of course—but after Dad passes on.

Even if *she* (and you know who *she* is) indicates loudly and clearly that she has no interest in his family's things—that she prefers her own things—her pronouncement is unlikely to be believed. Suspicions about her will linger. "After all, should Dad pass on, she might just decide to go on living in the house, or she might sell our things one at a time, and we wouldn't even know it."

A SPECIAL ISSUE: DADS AND DAUGHTERS

We know we've said you can replace *he* with *she* and vice versa, whichever happens to fit your situation better, but there are a few exceptions. The symmetry between the sexes doesn't always apply.

Relationships between fathers and daughters, for example, tend to be somewhat different from relationships between mothers and sons—particularly, when it comes to who takes care of Dad and the house after Mother's gone. Psychologically and traditionally, running the household and caring for its men has been, at least in the past, women's "duty" (or her "right" or "prerogative" or "obligation"—pick your own descriptor) more than men's.

These days, you can argue that assigning the caretaker and homemaker role to women is inappropriate and sexist, and it is. Still, it's also widely accepted and expected, especially in traditional families. So, even today, young women often feel (even though their feelings can be quite mixed) that somehow they have a special responsibility for taking care of Daddy after Mother's gone.

Here, for example, is the memory Joe, a younger brother, has of his older sister's behavior after their mother passed on:

Even when she was alive, whenever Mom went away, my sister Eve used to act just like Mom. One time, Mom had to go away for a week to help get Grandma settled. Eve just took over. She cooked breakfast and dinner and pushed Dad and me around like a dictator. She made me wash my neck and make my bed even more than Mom did. And she took special care of Dad. She made sure he ate right and took his pills on schedule. I tried to help, too, but she would just shoo me away. She acted more like a queen than a mother!

Then, after Mom died, she behaved the same way. By then, she was married and had her own place, but she still came around all the time to make sure the house was clean and Dad was okay. I had left by then, too, and I was glad she did all that. But she was awfully bossy!

I don't think Eve liked it at all when Dad got into his relationship with Christine. Eve just didn't want to be pushed out of her job!

To the extent that such special relationships continue to exist between fathers and grown-up daughters, incoming wives need to beware. Daughters are often in unacknowledged, but real, competition with their stepmothers for Daddy's affection.

Once their biological mother is gone, such daughters will not welcome a new person stepping in as Dad's primary caregiver. They covet that role for themselves. Dad's loving helpmate is a role some daughters—quite unconsciously, perhaps—have been waiting to occupy for a long time. In such cases, the new stepmother needs to be particularly cautious and diplomatic.

SOME SUGGESTIONS FOR STEPPARENTS

We want to remind the reader, once again, that the size, shape, and location of the place we call home is of no consequence. For the family who lives in it, it is home. A house is like a nation's flag or a new bride's wedding ring. Its value lies in its meaning.

So, when we, as stepparents, remodel the family home or when we sell it, we are not just dealing with matters of taste or finance. We're also dealing with matters of the spirit and emotional well-being. We have stepped into the land of the Five Furies.

Here, then, are some practical suggestions for stepparents dealing with home matters:

Once again, feel free to change the genders at will. Where we have written *he* or *his,* switch to *she* or *hers,* if that's more appropriate to your situation.

- *Slow down!* If you're the newcomer, and it's his longtime home, be patient and go slowly. Don't immediately start changing things, even if he seems willing to have you do so. Don't put your pictures on his walls and new carpets on his (and his children's) floors. He wants to make you comfortable, but, in truth, he's probably feeling more than a bit nervous about how his kids will feel. And, like them, he may be remembering the special past meanings of some of the things you want to toss into the trash bin.

   If you're the longtime occupant and he's the newcomer, be understanding. Empathize. This change isn't easy for him. Yours is a new and different culture, and the house you live in is the center of that new universe. Think how you would feel if you suddenly found yourself dropped into an unfamiliar world. Apply the Golden Rule. Be patient and very sensitive.

- *Don't expect smooth sailing.* This may be moon-in-June time for the two of you: a loving, exciting, romantic new beginning. Unfortunately, it's also reality time. Expect stresses, strains, even quarrels. There are lots of sensitive buttons in your newly enlarged family that you may be pushing accidentally. If you *both* realize that you will inevitably encounter bumps and glitches, you'll get past them!

- *Whatever happens, keep talking.* The worst thing you can do is *not* talk about it—no matter what "it" happens to be.

- *Make a special space that the newcomer can feel is his or her own.* Is she a gardener? How about the two of you building (or buying) a little greenhouse to set up next to the garage? Perhaps, adding a needed nook to the kitchen or a small workshop out back somewhere will make the new occupant feel a little more at home.

- *Use some other bedroom.* Don't sleep in the bedroom he and his former spouse slept in for years and years. He'll be uncomfortable about it (and it may even have some sexual impact), and the children will probably be even more uncomfortable. At a minimum, if changing rooms isn't feasible, get another bed!

- *For the time being, assume there is a Keep Out sign on the door and don't invade the sanctity of the children's rooms.* Turning that space into a home office or making other changes is rarely worth the tumult that inevitably follows. Down the road, if you need the space, you and your spouse might revisit this issue.

- *If possible, move to neutral ground.* No solution is perfect. Every option has costs, as well as benefits. Nevertheless, we have noticed that moving is one solution that generally provides the most benefits at the lowest psychological or emotional cost. Find a new place, a place without ghosts. A place that's neutral territory for everybody can dilute many tensions. A place where no other man or woman has gone before! Take some of your things to the new place, and some of his. Give the children whatever they treasure from their old homesteads, and start afresh! The children will still feel bad about the loss of their old homesteads, but they will not be reminded of their grief every time they come to dinner. You, too, will probably have some lingering regrets; however, you also will have created a fresh place, without ghosts, in which to build your new relationship.

    On the practical side, moving to a new place may strain your budget. Still, check out the tax laws. They may protect much of the profit from the sale of a home, making it easier to purchase a new one.

    Moving is a radical step, but so is a new marriage. Don't risk it by remaining entangled in the past. You may decide to move down the street, or to an apartment intentionally too small for many guests, or to another part of the country with a better climate and lower costs. Now is the time to focus on yourselves.

WHAT HAPPENS WHEN AN ADULT STEPCHILD ASKS TO MOVE IN TEMPORARILY?

Regardless of where you decide to live, children may ask to move back in for a while.

Dorothy, age sixty, tells a familiar story,

I'm a remarried widow with a married son. My husband is a widower with two married daughters with their own children. Recently, my oldest stepdaughter's husband left her and wants a divorce. She is a working mother but can't afford to keep up the house payments on her own, so they will have to sell their home. She has two boys, six and ten years old. She asked my husband if she could move in with us temporarily until she finds a new smaller place. I don't know what to say. We live in a comfortable, quiet home that my husband and I bought together when we married five years ago. I'd like to help her, but I don't want to end up raising her children.

Situations like this one, in which an adult stepchild becomes separated, divorced, unemployed, or disabled, create a difficult dilemma for the older couple. It's important to be fair. Would you be inclined to allow your own biological child to live in your home under the same circumstance? Would your first step be to offer suggestions and assistance in finding a different solution? If that didn't work, would you then offer your own home? If so, what kind of commitment would you make in terms of length of stay and your own financial and physical assistance?

These are some of the questions that you and your spouse need to think and talk about until you reach consensus. This process could test your marital commitment. Would you feel like moving out if a stepchild, or even your own biological child, and family moved in? On the other hand, perhaps, you and your spouse come from a family that welcomes adult children to move in for as long as they need and assumes they know how to share household responsibilities. Adult children will want to think about these issues, as well. The same concerns may come up when an older couple asks to move in with them.

Here are some suggestions for you to consider:

SET THE HOUSE RULES

- The guidelines you develop should apply to all your adult stepchildren and biological children. Everyone should be informed if you decide to set a precedent with one child. In this way, everyone can see that you are being fair. Additionally, setting up standards that apply to all the children will ensure that you are being realistic about your offer.

- Before anyone moves in, have a written agreement with that adult child. The agreement should state the ground rules for living in your home for a specified period of time, with provision for renewal if both spouses agree. This agreement should specify the conditions, such as responsibility for rent, food, household chores, telephone, utilities, and noise level. The fewer surprises the better. Periodic review of the agreement will allow you to renegotiate after you have lived together for a short time.

- When anyone moves in, there has to be an exit plan. That is particularly important if the reason is job loss, divorce, or widowhood, all of which could evolve into an indefinite stay. The children moving back in are asking for temporary help. They should be able to give you a realistic plan of how and when they can become independent again.

SOME SUGGESTIONS FOR ADULT STEPCHILDREN

- *Give Mother or Dad a chance.* You may not be entranced by the person who has come into Mom's or Dad's life. But think back. Are you sure your parents adored the partner you picked? Of course, you have some responsibility here. You need to do some due diligence to make sure that Mom—if you believe she is really naïve—isn't about to marry a criminal or a con man. On the other hand, you must also show your parent some respect. He or she has managed thus far and has made mostly good decisions, as well as corrected his or her own mistakes. In general, try to support more and criticize less—exactly how you would like your parent and stepparent to treat you.

- *Accept reality.* The old home just isn't yours anymore. It's gone. Your home or your sibling's place may have to become the new family head-quarters. If you have kids, show them photo albums and maybe your dolls or baseball mitts. Tell them stories about your childhood, stories about Mom and Dad, and how the dog had a confrontation with a skunk, and about those lovely long summer days of childhood. Let the spirit of your childhood carry on, even though the physical setting has passed into other hands.

- *You don't have to dwell on it, but accept the fact that those parents you perceive as "old folks" do continue to have sex.* Back off, and let them enjoy it!

- *It's okay to think about your inheritance, but don't build your life around it.* Treat your potential inheritance the way you treat the lottery. You could win millions, but you probably won't, at least not for a very long time. So, get on with building your own life, your own career, your own family, even your own wealth.

- *Expect change.* If your parent and new mate choose to stay in the old house, bear with it. They will make changes. You wouldn't put up with a sink that got clogged up once a week. So, when your dad and his new partner replace it, and they redo the rest of the bathroom, remember, that's *not* an attack on your mother's memory. It's just a remodeled bathroom. The old bathroom is gone, except in your memory, and at this point in everyone's lives, that's where it belongs.

We began this chapter by saying that a house really is a home and that homes are made of more than bricks and plaster. They're also made of meanings and memories. Both kinds of materials play their parts in adult stepfamilies. If one partner has lived in that house for a long time, the new partner will have to cope with much more than broken lamps and stained carpeting. He or she will also have to deal with the ghosts of other people's pasts—unpredictable, potentially dangerous ghosts who live in those old lamps and carpets. So, newcomers, beware! Go slowly! And know that, no matter how careful you are, there are bound to be a few unpleasant surprises along the way.

We have offered, in this chapter, suggestions for coping with some of the sticky stepmatters that cluster around the home. There is only one that we want to reiterate as we close. Our research tells us that one strategy is most effective in relieving the stress that new stepfamilies feel vis-à-vis the family home. That is: Move! If you possibly can, move into a home that is new to both of you. Find neutral, ghost-free ground. Find a place that's neither yours nor mine, nor the children's. Find a place that's *ours*.

Such a move may bother the children for a while. It may bother one or both of the newlyweds for a while. Nonetheless, moving to a neutral place chosen by the new couple seems to work pretty well for all concerned. And when it comes to step matters, "pretty well" is often as good as it gets.

In the next chapter, we shall consider a question that unsettles virtually every stepfamily: Whom do you love the most? It is a question that is bound to be asked, if only indirectly.

CHAPTER 8

Whom Do You Love Best? Your Lover or Your Other Loved Ones?

Whom do you love best of all? Your spouse or your children? When the late comedian Jack Benny faced an impossible question like this one, he would be silent for a long, long time, and then would say, very slowly, "I'm thinking . . . I'm thinking. . . ."

THERE'S NO HIDING

Most of the time, we avoid giving a direct answer to this question. We duck it with words like, "I love all of you equally . . . just in different ways." Or, "You can't compare loving a wife or husband with loving a child. I don't think of it as loving one person more and the other one less. It's not a zero sum game." Nice try. You can "love" everybody, but who comes first is still the elephant in the bedroom.

Even after decades of remarriage, the question of whom you love the most may keep coming up. This chapter deals with Fury #3 of the Five Furies that afflict adult stepfamilies: Favoritism. It is a Fury that affects virtually every stepfamily, even the celebrated ones. Frank Sinatra's three children, then ages forty-nine through fifty-seven, were said to be furious when Capitol Records released his *Live in Concert* album because the eighty-year-old singer had dedicated it to their stepmother, Barbara, "the love of my life."

Family members almost always manage to sniff out the order of your preferences; who comes first, who comes second, who comes last. You can try to put them off with carefully chosen words. Nonetheless, everyone in a newly merged family will try to find out precisely whose feelings are considered first when important family decisions are being made. As we said earlier, even fame doesn't keep this Fury at bay. Paul McCartney discovered that when his children balked at his marriage to Heather Mills following the death of their mother, Linda Eastman.

If you try too hard to make it appear that you have no preference, strange things can happen. We interviewed a couple who invited all their adult children along on their honeymoon. Between them, they had four unmarried children in their twenties and thirties. Their plan was to demonstrate that everyone in the family could come first and that no one had to be demoted as a result of their marriage. They rented a three-bedroom, oceanfront condo in Hawaii. You can guess what happened. For starters, there was no sex between the newlyweds on their honeymoon. Furthermore, the adult children confided to one another that having to witness their parent's honeymoon was a very strange thing. They wondered what they were doing there.

COME CLEAN AT THE START

It is better to come clean from the start and be clear about how you plan to operate. You *will* have to decide under which circumstances your spouse comes first. Everyone in the family will be watching carefully. If you don't have a method in mind, figure one out. Then, everyone can settle down and breathe normally.

In any stable family, just ask the husband, wife, adult children, and grandchildren who comes first. Everybody in a functional, predictable family environment knows who's on top because the process by which decisions are made is consistent. In adult stepfamilies, children quickly get to know whether their parent regularly consults his/her new spouse in making decisions before announcing them to the family. The children are the first to observe the shocked look on the face of an uninformed spouse upon hearing, "We are all going to Disneyland for the children's spring vacation," or "Honey, Jill and the children are staying over at our place tonight."

If you are not just starting out, but have been married for years, now may be a good time to reconsider this issue. You might want to discuss the subject with your spouse and modify your behavior as a result. Even ten years into a marriage, you will probably find your spouse is interested in hearing the ground rules you use in making decisions.

FIRST TO KNOW IS DIFFERENT FROM ALWAYS COMING FIRST

In order to create a secure marital union, the couple has to let each other be the first to know how they stand on most issues. This doesn't necessarily mean they have to agree.

Being first to know is different from coming first 100 percent of the time. As an example, let's take the case of a parent giving a significant monetary gift to an adult child. The spouse might not agree on the necessity for it or the amount. Still, your spouse is much more likely to back your decision if the two of you have discussed the issue and your spouse has had a chance to express his/her opinion.

Even when the gift comes out of money that one spouse had long before the marriage, informing your spouse is a good idea. In our experience, keeping major gifts a secret in an attempt to avoid conflict rarely succeeds. The result is usually more conflict, not less. In fact, secrecy among family members tends to encourage a destructive pattern of suspicion and the testing of loyalties.

Forty-year-old Malcolm told us:

My wife and I couldn't have bought our new home without Dad's generous gift. We are so grateful. But I don't know why he was such a wimp and insisted we not tell his wife about it. The check he wrote was from his personal account. Now, I'm starting to wonder if Dad is keeping it a secret because his wife would think that he should give the same amount to her kids. That doesn't seem fair to me. He earned that money.

Sixty-five-year-old Henry confessed:

My wife is so secretive about giving her children birthday and Christmas gifts that I have to admit I looked around for her checkbook. I was shocked that she had given her son so much money, after telling me that we should be more careful of what we spend on our vacations. But, because I sneaked, I can't tell her how angry I am. It's been hard to be affectionate with her.

In both examples, secrecy is undermining marital and intrafamilial stability. This kind of covert behavior is likely to cause additional problems of trust down the line.

AVOID SURPRISES

The ideal time to discuss your philosophy of making decisions is before you are married, so that your lover doesn't have to guess. The fewer surprises the better. If that time has passed and there are obvious problems, create a second chance for yourself.

This process requires determining your own priorities and then having the courage to put them on the table. Does the biblical injunction about the primacy of the marital union apply only to the first, but not to second or later marriages?* Does "putting your spouse first" mean making every decision in your spouse's favor? Or does it mean agreeing on all decisions about whose needs take precedence, whether those needs have to do with finances or holiday visits? Or does it mean making a commitment to discuss decisions with your spouse first?

These are three very different contracts. The first calls for the fortitude to withstand your children's complaints—particularly, when they are justified. The second requires perfect attunement, something few, if any, couples attain. The third contract—which is a much more realistic goal—demands cultivating tolerance and the ability to live with differences of opinion. It also means accepting your spouse's right to behave independently, when necessary. Any two people who plan to marry, at any age, need to talk about these issues. If nothing else, you will learn valuable things about each other. As French filmmaker Jean Renoir tells us in *La Règle du Jeu* (*The Rules of the Game*): "The trouble with life is, everyone has his reasons." Having our reasons, however, doesn't mean we always will or should get our way.

Life requires striking a balance. To achieve balance, you need to understand your own thinking. The process of telling another person what you plan to do helps you do just that. The discussion also allows your partner to have some input. If you can't risk stating your point of view, it may be a decision you should reconsider.

You may be in a marriage where your spouse is someone who won't talk about a particular subject. How do you handle a spouse who won't engage? Very often, people who don't wish to reveal their thoughts are still able to listen to and even learn from a spouse willing to articulate his/her position.

If you explain your stance and your spouse chooses not to respond, you have done your best to avoid surprises. You have also set a good example for the future by explaining what you would like to do before you do it. Your spouse may be an active participant next time.

HOW DO YOU BELIEVE YOUR FAMILY WILL FUNCTION BEST?

Some couples develop rules of thumb and a system for making decisions that affect others.

Peter told us:

My wife and I have put a lot of thought into this. In making important decisions we agree that, first, you have to think out what is best for you as an individual. Then, the two of you decide what is best for your marriage. Talk it through for as long as it takes. The children are the third priority.

On the other hand, some people resist the notion of authority in family life, even their own. Instead of establishing procedures, they prefer a one-person-one-vote approach.

Nancy says:

My husband and I are easy about decisions. When choices come up, we find out what everyone in the family wants and go with the majority. We never know in advance how it will turn out. The best idea may come from my ten-year-old stepgrandson. No big deal.

HOW DID YOU DEVELOP YOUR DECISION-MAKING STYLE?

Usually, the way your parents operated when you were a child was the first determinant of the parenting style you adopted with your own children. Did your mom and dad come first for each other? Let's say your parents had a close and powerful partnership in which you, as a child, had little or no say. Whether you want to repeat that style or not, it probably had a major impact on how you make decisions. Perhaps, you followed in your parents' footsteps, and you and your spouse make the rules.

On the other hand, you may have resented your parent's authority. Maybe, you promised yourself as a child that you would give your own children greater choice when you were a parent.

Perhaps, you grew up in an atmosphere of parental disorganization and chaos. You might, as a reaction, have created more structure and discipline in raising your children. Your message to your children might have been, "While you are growing up in this family, we make the rules. When you are grown and able to take care of yourself, you can make your own rules."

Whatever your history, your parental style or philosophy evolves in the course of raising your children. It may be a fluid and intuitive style, which is spontaneous and lacks precisely defined rules. It may be influenced by whomever you talked to last or whoever is screaming the loudest. Or it may be based on reaching consensus, no matter how long it takes.

On the other hand, your child-rearing philosophy may be based on the principle that having the responsibility for raising children gives you the authority to make family decisions. When you remarry, you have an ideal opportunity to rethink your decision-making style and decide which aspects of it worked well and which didn't. Such reconsideration can prevent a lot of fuzzy thinking and bad decision making in the future. Besides, making family decisions that involve adult children is not the same as making them about young children.

When you remarry later in life, the way you deal with your children is often not discussed because there are no more children at home. Still, the way you have dealt with your children in the past is likely to shape how you interact with them and your stepchildren in the future. You might think that, after writing a prenuptial agreement protecting the financial assets you had before the marriage, there would be no cross-generational conflicts. Wouldn't that be nice?

If you and your new spouse had different family styles with regard to family activities, you will have some adjusting to do.

Cary, age thirty-two, told us:

When my mother was alive, we did a lot of things together on the spur of the moment. For holidays, we didn't plan months in advance. But now, with Dad's new wife, she wants to know where we will have Thanksgiving dinner the next year before we finish eating the pumpkin pie this year.

Discussing your differences until you reach a decision both spouses can live with takes emotional strength, but it pays off handsomely. The precedents you set in a new marriage are crucial. Deal with those issues on which you disagree as soon as possible. Putting off such discussions only makes problems fester. Besides, there's a wonderful plus in teaching your adult children how mature people should handle family issues.

Let's face it. Everyone in the family knows when a decision was made thoughtfully and both husband and wife are "together" on it. Being together means having discussed, or thrashed out, the differences to the point where both parties can accept the outcome (sometimes just barely). It does not mean that one person got his or her way and the other quietly capitulated. Demonstrating the value of negotiating decisions is an invaluable inheritance you can give your adult children, even if they don't know it at the time!

It's reasonable to assume that responsibility creates authority. If you are the one who is responsible for preparing Christmas dinner, you have the right to decide the menu and the time. That still requires taking other people's needs into consideration. If you are the one who is responsible for the care of an ill spouse, you must be ready to assert your authority. This means decisions about how and where your spouse is cared for, even when your stepchildren question that authority. We saw too many families come to grief on this matter. That was particularly the case when children demanded certain health care arrangements for their parent, but then refused to help make them happen.

OLDER COUPLES DEPEND MORE AND MORE ON EACH OTHER

Sixty-year-old Michael, father of four adult children, told us:

As far as I'm concerned, you've got to have ruthless preference for the wife. My wife has thrown her lot in with me, and I put her first. It's the only way the whole thing can work.

In later life, married couples are more interdependent than at any other time of life for two main reasons. First, they typically spend much more time together than at any earlier stage of life. This usually happens because one or both are retired, and there are no children at home to dilute their focus on each other.

Second, because aging often brings health problems, older spouses rely on each other for physical and emotional support of the most intense kind. Their adult children simply tend not to be there when a decision must be made about whether or not to call an ambulance. Life and death issues associated with health crises come more and more frequently. When an older person vows to take his or her spouse "for better or for worse, in sickness and in health," the new couple is much more likely than their younger counterparts to encounter both "sickness" and "worse."

IF YOU THINK CHILDREN SHOULD COME FIRST . . .
SAY IT CLEARLY

Putting the spouse first is only one of the legitimate ways to think about who's on top. Here's another point of view about a new marital contract.

Dorothy, age seventy, told her husband:

My relationship with my children started long before our marriage. I'm looking forward to a wonderful loving marriage with you, but because my children and I have a deep and long relationship and history together, I want you to know up front that I will be taking their interests into account first when there is an important decision.

It's probably better to clarify this before the marriage, not after you've tied the knot.

You can think it, but we recommend that you don't actually say, "Blood is thicker than water." Such a position may threaten your new marriage, but if it is the way you really feel, better to tell your spouse now rather than surprise him or her with it later. That can only lead to disaster. It could very well be that your new spouse feels the same way about his/her children, and then no one has to play games. The children come first.

We are not suggesting that you undermine your future marriage by acting as if your future spouse is the last person whose needs and feelings you will take into consideration. If you feel that way, you may want to reconsider whether the relationship should involve marriage. Still, if you plan to give priority to your children's wishes when important financial decisions or holiday schedules are made, you should say so up front. If your future spouse can't accept that, maybe you should try living together without the complication of marriage.

Of course, your ideas about who comes first may change over time, especially as you grow older and the kids become more and more preoccupied with their own lives. Whether it started out that way or not, your spouse may become the primary person in your life as the years go by. If your spouse has become more important to you than you ever imagined possible, you shouldn't be embarrassed to say so. That doesn't mean, however, that you have to announce the change in the family pecking order over a communal loudspeaker.

PAY ATTENTION TO EARLY WARNING SIGNS

If you and your beloved have set the date to get married but your spouse-to-be hasn't informed his or her children for fear of their disapproval, no need to wonder who will come first in your marriage. It won't be you.

If you find yourself in this situation, it's important to recognize that your spouse-to-be is either someone who wants to please everybody or who feels guilty about remarriage, or both. This pattern of avoiding conflict at any cost impedes the development of trust and should alert you to the likelihood of future problems.

Joan, age thirty-eight, had never been married. In fact, she had almost given up hope of ever finding a partner when she met her future husband:

Tony and I met when we were both working on the same project at a dotcom company six years ago. The hours were long, and the work was intense, and we were together all the time. He was an inspiring boss and a great mentor. I knew he was married and had grown kids. But, as time went by and we talked about our personal lives, I gradually found out from him that his marriage had been unhappy for a long time and that he had been thinking about a separation. Shortly after that, we started having an affair.

We were extremely compatible, and the work and our relationship were making us happier than either of us had ever been. Well, it took three years for him to tell his wife he wanted a separation and another year for him to move out. His kids were angry at him for leaving their mother, and he never got around to telling them about me, even after he got divorced.

We decided to buy a house together and set a wedding date. Things were very good between us. After we moved into our home, he still hadn't told his kids that he was getting married. When he finally did tell them, they said that they would never see him again if he got remarried. Tony went into a deep depression and wanted to postpone our wedding. We got married, but it was only after I set a deadline after which I said I would move out.

About six months later, his son called him to ask for a loan to buy a house. Tony agreed to lend him the money and right after that, he told me he was going help his daughter to pay her mortgage "to be fair." He never asked me for my opinion. I didn't know we were going to support his grown children.

It requires courage for parents to tell their children that they are remarrying. Parents know intuitively that this announcement will unleash some, if not all, of the Five Furies. If your spouse-to-be is unable to tell his/her children because it might displease them, that's a red flag. It indicates a serious reluctance to face the consequences of personal choices, and marriage to you is unlikely to make that reluctance disappear.

If you begin a marriage under these circumstances, beware! You are giving your stamp of approval, albeit passively, to coming in second whenever your spouse has to make a choice between you and his or her children. You are signaling that you are the one who is willing to be disappointed. Be sure that you can live with that.

FROM THE VIEWPOINT OF THE ADULT CHILDREN: FEAR OF LOSING A STRONG CONNECTION TO A PARENT

Now, let's look at these same issues through the eyes of the adult children. Most adult children know they'll have to relinquish being the favorite when their parent remarries.

In the words of thirty-two-year-old Erin (a psychologist, as you might have guessed):

What I really want to know is do I still have the same strong connection with the parent I've relied on all my life, the parent I depend on? You don't want to lose that ability to count on your parent still cheering for you when you've had a success and being in your corner when you need emotional support. This can be mistaken for wanting to be on top, but that isn't the case. A very insecure new spouse can confuse continuing that bond with being number one.

Most mature adult stepchildren are more concerned about Fury #2, Fidelity to Family, than with Fury #3, Favoritism. That said, there are also cases in which a son or daughter has been a special favorite of the remarrying parent. Then, it may be very difficult for the child to surrender the *numero uno* position because it previously led to many wonderful privileges.

THE ADVANTAGES OF BEING A DAUGHTER OR SON WHO IS LOVED BEST OF ALL

If you come from a family in which your parents had an unhappy marriage or if your parent has been widowed, you may be the only bright spot in your parents' lives. If your parents have given up on having a loving marriage, one or both parents may have chosen a certain child on whom to focus all their unspent love.

If you are the chosen one, you may feel you are in a glorious and magical situation, in which you can do no wrong. This may give you a feeling of power, leading you to assume you'll be a star in the world beyond the family, too.

For a daughter, becoming your father's favorite and winning out over your mother can create a lifelong feeling of having special power over men. For a son, a mother's intense affection can make a man a confident lover of women for the rest of his life.

Let's be clear. We are not talking about a sexual relationship with your parent. Just being a parent's special favorite can bestow on you a sense of power and expectations of success.

Winning more love from one of your parents than they give each other can be intoxicating and empowering. The downside, however, is dangerous: It can set the favored child up for a disastrous pattern of unrealistic expectations in future relationships.

THE DISADVANTAGES OF BEING ON TOP WITH YOUR PARENT

Children who receive this kind of preferential love from a parent may face disappointment as adults. In the adult world, you usually have to make some effort in order to be adored. You aren't usually worshipped simply for existing. Moreover, the expectation that you never have to make a real effort to satisfy another person's needs almost guarantees you'll have trouble forming solid, loving relationships, including marriage.

Successful marriage is a partnership. Children who emerge as winners in the familial love affair may become lifelong losers when they try to create their own marital partnerships. They haven't had to learn that a spouse doesn't automatically love you as if you were a darling child from whom nothing is ever expected in return.

SURVIVING THE LOSS OF BEING THE FAVORITE

Mature adult children may be hurt by a much-loved parent's remarriage, but they get over it—just as Paul McCartney predicted his children by Linda Eastman would. Thirty-six-year-old Donna told us:

I thought I was the closest to my father. He was divorced and traveled a lot in his work in the entertainment industry. I arranged to have lunch

with him to tell him about my wedding, which I was planning for the fol-
lowing month. He showed up with some ding-bat with crisp hair.

At first, I thought she was just his assistant and there in a business
capacity. But then, she told me very casually that they couldn't come to
my wedding because they were going to be married in Las Vegas on the
same weekend. That's what really did it for me. Men really roll over for
these relative newcomers. I wanted to say, "You've had a relationship
with me for twenty-five years, and this idiot just walked into your life." It
almost discounted what I had to say. And that hurt. Of course, his mar-
riage lasted one year, and mine is still going on.

Twenty-five-year-old Eric says:

When my father told me he was getting married to Anna, the woman he'd
lived with for five years, I felt sick. He used to say that Anna was his live-
in companion for life and that he didn't need to marry anyone. When he
said that, it was always a relief to me. He told us, "You marry to have a
family. I already have my family." She loved my dad, but she always knew
that we came first and that she wasn't family. The one good thing about
my parents' divorce was that my father got closer to me. Now, I was los-
ing my father. She was taking him away from me.

I thought we would never get to do things alone again, just the two of
us and nobody else. Going to ball games, shooting baskets, playing com-
puter games, camping out in the canyon . . . then, I realized we hadn't
done those things together since I was a little boy.

But a parent's remarriage may devastate the child who hasn't developed other
relationships. Andria, fifty-five and unmarried, told us:

My father and I were always so close to each other. He was my protector.
Particularly from my mother, who always found something wrong with my
behavior. I could be absolutely sure he would support everything I wanted
to do. Whenever I was in trouble, he figured a way out. If I slept late in the
morning and missed the bus and was late for school, he would write a
note to excuse me for illness and drive me to school. If my mother criti-
cized me, he would defend me.

When he and I were alone, he used to confide in me about how
unhappy he was about his marriage to my mother. He told me he really

didn't know how incompatible and unhappy they would be until it was too late. We both agreed that mother was impossible to satisfy. Our secret conversations always ended with him assuring me that he would never leave the marriage because he wouldn't ever leave me. It was too awful for him to consider leaving me in the hands of my mother.

Years later, when my mother died and I had a job in another city, I never expected my seventy-year-old father to fall in love. I was very upset when he told me he had found a wonderful woman, who was intelligent and sensitive and adored him and that he was probably going to get married. When I met her and saw him so affectionate and admiring of her, I couldn't believe it was happening. He'd never been like that with my mother. He was treating this new woman the way he used to treat me! I said to him privately, "Dad, why don't you just live together, why do you have to get married? You're not going to have any children."

FINDING OUT THAT YOUR PARENT IS GETTING REMARRIED IS A UNIVERSAL TRAUMA

It doesn't matter how old you are. Finding out that your parent is getting remarried may cause a brief and uncomfortable psychological slide back to childhood. It might temporarily trigger fears that you haven't been aware of for many years.

The most prominent fears have to do with being replaced and forgotten as a consequence of your parent choosing a new life partner. This change can revive childhood feelings of dependency and arouse unanticipated anger. You can't count on that parent anymore, at least not in the same way. You will be on the lookout for changes in your parent's loyalty and behavior to you. How much will your wishes count now? Someone else, who has never been a part of your family, is now number one in your parent's life. This person, who usually hasn't come close to knowing your parent as long as you have, is now going to intrude on your family life, with a special seat at the family table. It's not easy, and you don't like it, but you still have to find a way cope with this new reality.

A biological parent's remarriage is as stressful as a parent's divorce. It's far more traumatic than having a parent decide to live with someone without being officially married. The legal power and social legitimacy of marriage hits the unprepared child like a bomb. Seeing your parent with his or her arms around a new spouse is worse than being your second grade teacher's favorite and then unexpectedly seeing her in the supermarket with her own children. Remember how terrible that felt?

USING THE SKILLS OF TACT AND TACKING

Several of the eight skills of Tact and Tacking that we discussed in Chapter 2 are useful tools for dealing with the painful loss of position and importance that an adult child feels when a parent remarries. You are too wise to complain and be sulky or vengeful. So how, then, do you deal with your immediate pain? Consider these possibilities. They'll be more useful than simply thinking of yourself as a victim, who has been ousted from the number one position in your parent's heart.

Tact and Tacking #1: Reframe the Issue

Your becoming less important helps loosen your ties with your parent. You can now pay more attention to your own life. After all, you've got to prepare for the eventual loss of your parent through death. Better to start now and gradually adjust to being on your own. Maybe, you've been putting it off too long.

Tact and Tacking #2: Let Time Pass

Right now, the love affair your parent is experiencing is very intense, just like yours when you first got married. There is not much room for anyone else. Probably, with the passage of time, he/she will come back down to earth and begin to see the imperfections in his/her new love. A spouse can't satisfy every need forever. Eventually, you will have more of a role. You've got to remember that this stage of total focus on their marriage will pass. This is the hardest time because you feel so unimportant, but this stage is temporary.

Tact and Tacking #3: Taking the Role of the Observer

Pretend to be a cultural anthropologist studying your own family. This allows you to create some emotional distance. Observe everyone's behavior, including your own. Keep a journal detailing how you and the rest of your family are dealing with this important change. Reading it later will help you see how far you've come.

Find a buddy who is in the same boat to discuss these typical stepfamily problems. Ventilate together privately. Feel free to talk about all the things your parent and new stepparent do that bug you. Schedule a regular time to share horror stories if you have any, validate feelings, anticipate hot spots, and give each other all the support you can muster. When you listen to your buddy's complaints, you may begin to see both sides of your own story. Ask yourself what you now expect of your parent, stepparent, and yourself. Ask yourself what you can do to adapt to this new family tribe.

Tact and Tacking #4: Tenacity

You may decide, "This is the time to put some things I haven't said to my parent into words. I'm going to let my parent know how important he/she is to me and that I want us to keep our love for each other strong, no matter what new ties each of us makes. I'll wish him/her happiness in marriage and recognize the prime importance of that union. After that, I need to take responsibility for showing how much I value maintaining the uniqueness of *our* bond, which is different, but also important."

Tact and Tacking #5: Trading and Negotiating

Some of your wishes may not get the priority from your parent that they did up until now. You'll miss that. Having your mom always available to baby-sit for your children made life so easy. On the other hand, now there is someone to take care of Mom as she grows older. She has someone to take her to her doctors' appointments or to go out with socially. You won't need to feel as guilty and responsible now that she has someone there for her.

Tact and Tacking #6: FEAT (Forgiveness, Empathy, Apology, and Tolerance)

Forgiveness means that you can maintain a positive relationship with your parent despite his/her acting selfishly. *Empathy* allows you to put yourself in your parent's shoes. Celebrate with the new couple. Invite them to your home. Try to remember how you felt when you met the love of your life. Or try to think ahead to when you will. If you were sulky or hostile to your parent when you heard about the marriage or during subsequent interactions, *apologize* promptly. Remember that a successful apology includes acknowledging your culpability. Don't hold back. The final FEAT component, *tolerance,* is the ability to see that your parents' views or needs have validity, just as yours do.

Tact and Tacking #7: Transformation Through Wisdom

Figure out what specifically upsets you about your parent's or stepparent's behavior and develop some useful insights into yourself. If you feel ignored, try to determine why you feel that way. Does it have to do with experiences in your past? Do those feelings still make sense today? If you think the new spouse is manipulating your parent, is that because you see ways in which you have manipulated your parent? Do both of you use the same techniques, and are you really upset because the spouse, and not you, is on top as a result? Do you feel powerless to influence a parent whom you previously felt was under your control? Was that a healthy relationship for you and your parent to have—for either of you?

Tact and Tacking #8: Turn Away from It

If you can't move to Australia, settle for making the time you must spend with the newlyweds as painless as possible. Use a friend to role-play ways you can avoid being hurt or hurting others. You probably know the whole script for any family occasion. Act it out with your buddy so it has a happy ending for everyone.

If your parent or stepparent makes you crazy, remember that you don't have to take the bait. You can change the subject. When things get tough, announce you'll be in the living room reading or take the dog for a walk. Chill out. Buy a copy of *Newsweek* and catch up on world events. These Tact and Tacking skills will help put family battles in better perspective.

You don't have to stay trapped in the older couple's plans on holidays. You and your siblings can rotate hosting holiday celebrations. Break the spell. Don't sit around being glum. Plan to go on a hike that the older folks can refuse easily. Schedule activities that you enjoy and can gracefully choose when you don't want to do what the family has planned. It's easier to operate on your own turf—don't be passive and don't feel victimized. Take charge and come up with a better plan for yourself.

TWO DIFFERENT CHALLENGES FOR TWO GENERATIONS

Adult children and their remarrying parents have different psychological tasks to accomplish in addressing the issue of who comes first in the new stepfamily line-up. Older couples may need to find ways to take into account the opinions of their spouses when making an important decision, even if they cannot agree. If the couple relies heavily on secrecy in making social and financial decisions, this may represent an attempt to avoid conflict at any cost. Such secrecy should probably be confronted before it causes more damage.

Unfortunately, handling conflict by secrecy usually endangers the marriage. Instead, the couple should learn to accept that being the first to know is a more realistic goal than always coming first. Facing up to and tolerating the differences between you can help your marriage grow and endure. Some older folks are afraid to talk these tough issues through for fear that the relationship will be destroyed. We have discussed some ways in which the more open spouse can start the process.

For their part, adult children are usually shaken by a reordering of their parent's priorities. This shuffling is not of their choosing. Initially, they have to concede, at least temporarily, some of their previously unchallenged importance to their parent. At a minimum, this requires greater maturity. Certain Tact and Tacking skills are very useful here. It is hard to be tactful when the outcome is so emotionally important. Nonetheless, learning tact is invaluable. Diplomacy is not just for public occasions. It is a way to make any family function more successfully.

Whom does your remarried parent love the most? Sam Goldwyn once said of a movie script he turned down, "It's so bad, don't even ignore it." Don't even waste time on the question. In happy families, including happy stepfamilies, there is plenty of love to go around.

Coming up next: What issues drive stepfamilies apart and what pulls them together. In short, can the words *mine* or *yours* ever become *ours*?

---

*This at last is bone of my bones and flesh of my flesh; Genesis 2.25, *New Oxford Annotated Bible,* 3rd Edition, p. 14.

CHAPTER 9

Your Children and Mine:
Can They Ever Become Ours?

My children are grown up. They're out in the world. They're on their own. This book should be about us, not them—our new life, our relationship. If they were small and lived with us, that would be different. What I need to know is how the two of us can find happiness together in these later years. So, why bother with a chapter about adult children? The children can take care of themselves.

Would it were so in the real world, but it's not! The "children" may be grown-ups, and they may live a thousand miles away, but they're also right in the middle of your new relationship.

Like it or not, they're his children or yours, and as you grow older, they don't become any less central to your lives or you to theirs. They're always there, for you or against you, and you're always there to them. Indeed, the issues among the complex role quartet of stepparent, spouse, his children, and her children are incredibly varied and often explosive.

To get a fix on the issues central to this chapter, let's begin with a few short illustrations of the wide variety of issues we saw and heard as we interviewed stepparents and adult stepchildren. Let's examine a sample of the enormous variety of problems that arise in the many facets of adult stepfamily relationships:

- He always criticizes *my* children, but he gets mad when I say anything at all about *his.* (Fury #3, Favoritism)

- Her daughter is getting married. But my wife's ex is alive and well. Why should *I* have to pay for the wedding? (Fury #4, Finances)

- She thinks my children don't like her, that they ignore her, and that they don't appreciate what she does for them. She's Italian. She expresses her feelings! My kids are typical English WASPs. They keep their feelings to themselves. She just can't accept the fact that that's just the way they are.

The way we see it is that two Furies are involved in this example. "She" (the wife) thinks that *his* kids are self-centered (Fury #5, Focus on Self) and, secondly, that he is defending his kids' behavior as culturally grounded, not selfish, on the basis of Fury #2, Fidelity to Family.

Here are some problems identified by stepparents about their spouses' children:

- I try and try, but his children will never really accept me. Whenever they call, they're disappointed when I answer the phone. They just want to talk to him. (This is a case of Fury #2, Fidelity to Family, which, by definition, promotes feelings of exclusion in the new family.)

- I never had children of my own, so I looked forward to this chance to be a mother. I guess I was naïve. It's taken almost ten years of patient work and, finally, at least one of them picks up the phone to call me instead of always waiting until I call. (Fury #5, Focus on Self)

- I know they have a real mother, and I certainly don't want to compete with her. Yet, they always make me feel that I'm some kind of vixen, who broke up their happy family. I just don't know how to deal with them! And my husband just doesn't seem to understand. (Fury #1, Fear of Abandonment and Isolation, and Fury #2, Fidelity to Family)

Here are some concerns mentioned by adult stepchildren about their stepparent. Concerns about a parent's new emotional ties weakening loyalty to the old family predominate. (Fury #2, Fidelity to Family)

- She's not our real mother. I wish she'd stop trying to act like she is. (Fury #2, Fidelity to Family)

- When I telephone to talk to Mom and *he* answers, he tries to be nice, but we have nothing to say to each other. I just want to talk to my mother. (Fury #2, Fidelity to Family)

- I'm glad he's found someone he cares about. But how could he care about someone like her? She's so different from Mother—and *not* in good ways! (Fury #2, Fidelity to Family)

Stepsiblings have their own concerns:

- I wish Dad and his wife would stop trying to make us all one big family. (Fury #2, Fidelity to Family)

- Her kids are okay, but I wouldn't pick them as my friends, and they wouldn't pick me. We're miles apart in every way! (Fury #2, Fidelity to Family)

- I think her son wants the family piano, but that belongs to us. (Fury #4, Finances)

The list is endless. It would grow even longer if we were to add in a lot more about some of the Furies we cover in separate chapters.

Unfortunately, most of the stories we heard—like those examples—were about trouble, not about joy. They expressed feelings of frustration, disappointment, and stress—all the way around the circuit: from stepparents about each other, from stepparents about stepchildren, from stepchildren about stepparents, and from stepparents about the behavior of their biological children, and from stepsiblings about one another.

Nonetheless, we must remember that most of the examples we listed above are snapshots, not movies: these snapshots capture what's bugging those interviewees right now. As we shall see, "right now" will be followed by tomorrow and—with sensitivity, hard work, and a little bit o' luck—right now's seemingly intractable relationships can move on to tomorrow's understanding and bonding.

THE MINUSES, THE PLUSES, AND THE "PLINUSES"

We've chosen a venerable psychological method for organizing the rest of this chapter. First, we consider some of the most prominent *minuses*—pressures that tend to drive stepfamilies apart, the minefields, the sources of suspicion and anger. Then, we'll look at the opposite end, at the *plus* forces, the things that tend to pull members of stepfamilies together, to unify them, to build love, trust, and respect. Then, come what we've called the *plinuses,* the mix of plus and minus forces that inevitably coexist in the real world—love intertwined with anger, hate conjoined with gratitude, resentment mixed with relief.

THE MINUSES: FORCES THAT TEND TO PULL ADULT STEPFAMILIES APART

At 4:00 A.M., the phone rings. You answer it sleepily. It's a social worker at the women's facility. Your twenty-three-year-old stepdaughter, Janice, is in jail, charged with drunk driving. This isn't the first time something like this has happened. She's had drug and alcohol problems before. Reluctantly, you wake up Judy so you can both drive over to see about bailing her out. On the way, Judy weeps. She apologizes for burdening you with her child's problems. You reassure her. You tell her it's okay, that life is like that. "Things happen. Let's stay calm. Together, we'll figure it out." Judy hugs you. She says she doesn't know how she could get through this without you.

That crisis passes. Together, you and Judy work out the best ways you can find to help straighten out Janice. Still, you know it will never really be over. Janice will generate stresses and strains for a long time to come.

The emotional shadows linger on. Down deep, you really feel that Judy and her deceased husband did all the wrong things while Janice was growing up. Yet, there's no use saying that now. It would only cause useless pain and anger. Even deeper down, there's another feeling, one you may not quite want to acknowledge: the who-needs-this feeling:

I'm sixty-six years old. I've already paid my parenting dues. I've sweated my way through problems with my own children. I thought I was just marrying Judy. Now, I find I've married her whole family and a bagful of new problems. I know Judy feels terrible about laying her kid's problems on my plate, but still . . .

Of course, some husbands (or wives) don't feel that way. A few may even welcome such complications. It gives them a chance to contribute, to help out, to get involved. That may be especially true of some women, who don't mind taking on the problems of their husband's children. For most men, however, whether they admit it or not, it's a drag—almost literally. It's a drag on their new relationship, an irritant, a nagging sore that's very slow to heal.

The Janice incident is, of course, just one small example of a much broader set of divisive issues, issues about children that tend to cause trouble between stepparents. Here are some others:

- You treat your children your way (the wrong way!), and I treat mine my way (the right way!).

He feels you should support the children with money and other help whenever they really need it. "After all," he says, "they're family, and family comes first. Besides, you can't take it with you. So, if we can help them with a down payment on a house or a car, let's do it."

She feels children "should learn to take care of themselves, to become independent and cope with their problems by themselves." Otherwise, they will always remain dependent little children, even when they're forty years old. That's how she was brought up, and it's how she brought up her own children.

So, when one of his kids asks Dad if he would help pay for furniture for their new baby's room, what does she feel? Perhaps, this way:

"If those kids are so broke that they can't buy the baby a crib, how come they took that expensive vacation in Hawaii last year?"

That may be the way she *feels,* but what she *says* is probably a little closer to this: "Do you really think it's a good idea for us to pay for *all* that stuff? Shouldn't they at least pay for some of it? It's not the money, but don't you think they should take some of the responsibility?"

He gives his usual reply—the one she's begun to expect, but also the one that's begun to irritate her more and more. He says: "You only live once. We can afford it. Let's buy them the damn crib and the bassinette and the other stuff. They're just getting started."

She says? . . . Perhaps she may not *say* anything at all, but she *feels* like saying a lot—and saying it quite loudly. Besides, that feeling hangs on, too.

- *Your children resent me. They don't like me.* No matter how much I try, they avoid me. I know they come for Thanksgiving, but I always feel they can't wait to get away. I feel like some alien invader. (Fury #1, Fear of Abandonment and Isolation)

- *No matter how your children treat me, you always defend them.* That's Fury #3, Favoritism, poking its head up again. Who comes first, I or your spoiled kids?

WHEN COUPLES KEEP SCORE

In remarriages (as in almost all marriages), keeping score is dangerous business. Negotiating about which family burdens I assume and which ones you take on is usually a bad idea. It emphasizes separateness, not togetherness. Most relationships do much better when both parties think *ours,* not *yours* or *mine.*

- *When you do something nice for my kids, you never let me forget it. You use it as a bargaining chip.* So, you helped my daughter find a job. Now, do I have to pay you back by helping your son find an apartment?

- *You give whatever birthday and Christmas gifts to your kids you want to, and I'll give mine whatever I want to.* This announcement promotes separation of stepparents from each other and stepchildren, too. If your goal is to build a solid family unit, such unequal treatment is almost sure to be seen by the children as unjust and divisive. Eventually, such seemingly clear, simple decisions are also likely to produce tensions between parents.

WHEN THE PARENTS TRY TOO HARD

From the children's perspective, stepparents may seem to be trying too hard to fill the parental role. Whether the stepchild's other biological parent is deceased or still living, coming on too strong as a new or extra parent is over-reaching. This process requires a delicate touch. Again and again, we heard the following comments from stepchildren:

- *He tries too hard to act like a textbook dad.* So, the children complain privately to Mother, "He wants to take us fishing and to ball games. That's Ozzie and Harriet stuff. Besides, we're adults. It doesn't fly. It's demeaning. Tell him to lay off, to quit playing *Father Knows Best.* Tell him to leave us alone. He's not our dad; he's just your husband."

- *She tries too hard to play Mother.* So, the children complain to Dad, "Ask her to stop trying so hard to mother us. We don't need another mother. Tell her to back off and leave us alone. She's not our mother; she's just a woman you live with."

Even when you walk on tiptoes, even when you're making offerings to them, his children (or hers) may see your behavior as overbearing and intrusive.

THE STEPPARENT AS A BODYGUARD

Another minus force that pulls stepfamilies apart comes into play when stepparents don't understand a stepchild's need for private time with the biological parent. This, too, requires a fine sense of balance on the stepparent's part. This classic case occurs when a stepchild telephones and the stepparent answers. Chatting long enough to demonstrate genuine interest before calling your spouse to the phone takes practice. Monopolizing the conversation and not offering to put your spouse on the phone can make your stepchild feel you are playing bodyguard.

- *She acts like she owns him!* "Every time I want a little time alone with Dad, she acts like I'm invading her territory. She always barges in between us. I suppose she thinks she's protecting him, taking extra-good care of him. Dad doesn't need protection—and certainly not from his own children. He must feel like he's in jail."

Of course, you feel you're not really overly possessive of your man. Check to be certain that you're just paying him the attention he deserves, even if that isn't the way the children may see it.

Those are a few—only a few—of the minus issues that arise between stepparents and their adult stepchildren. There are plenty of others, many of them covered in other chapters, but let's not get overwhelmed by the downsides. It's time now to accentuate a few pluses.

THE PLUSES: SOME FORCES THAT TEND TO PULL STEPFAMILIES TOGETHER: THE SAVING GRACES

Many of the pluses appear in the form of one or more Saving Grace. Here's a not-too-unusual story from Lisa, age forty-two:

I was just delighted when Dad married Ruth. And I'm still delighted. My mother died before either of my kids was born, and Rick's parents both passed on years ago. So, my children didn't have grandmothers on either side until Ruth came along. I think children need grandmothers, and Ruth is a great one. She loves my children as though they were her own, and they love her. They always want to go there, and when Rick and I can take a weekend away, Ruth and Dad are always ready to take care of them. Ruth is the best thing that could have happened to our whole family. (Saving Grace #3, Friendship)

Q: Did you feel this way from the first day you met Ruth?

A: Oh, no. Of course not. My husband and I and my children, too, were very suspicious of this woman who was moving in with our dad. Now, when I look back, I feel guilty. We didn't welcome Ruth at all. We talked about whether she was really after Dad's money, and we didn't like her taking our dad away from us. But Ruth is so kind and decent. She just let our not-very-nice behavior slide right off her back. There was no particular incident that made us change our minds. We just gradually came to like her and then to love her. She's just a great, unselfish person. Nobody could dislike her for long. (Saving Grace #2, Facilitating Maturity and #3, Friendship)

And here is another positive story from Tony, age thirty-eight:

The truth is my father is a tyrant. He's semialcoholic, and he's got a temper like you wouldn't believe. I don't know how my mother stayed with him as long as she did. My sister and I certainly got out of that house as soon as we could—probably too soon for Beth. She would have been better off at least to stay long enough to graduate from high school. But he was impossible. He'd blow up for no reason at all. Anyhow, Mom finally had the good sense to get a divorce, and we certainly supported her decision. She's never gotten a penny from him. Then, came some tough years, when she went back to work, barely making enough to survive. But she was sure happier than when they were together. We tried to help. We kept telling her she was still a very attractive woman and she ought to start dating. But she just sloughed that off and kept struggling by herself.

Then, unexpectedly, she met Frank, and they hit it off. It's the best thing that's ever happened. She's blossomed into the lively, good-humored person we knew as kids, and Frank has been great. He's convinced Beth to get her high school diploma, and he's helped me with a few problems I had. Thank God for Frank! (Saving Grace #1, Fulfilling Remarriage and #3, Friendship)

That feeling is expressed quite often by adult stepchildren—the feeling that the new stepparent is a blessing, a welcome addition to the family. If the new stepmother or father reciprocates, the net effect can be extremely positive. And grandchildren's needs are not the only ones that can be fulfilled by a stepparent.

Consider this example from Jack, a seventy-eight-year-old stepparent:

When my son Jim married Doris, my wife Donna was still alive and well. Doris had lost both her parents, and except for a sister who lived in England, she was pretty much alone. And Doris was sort of unsure of herself—on matters of taste in clothes and things like that. Anyhow, Donna and Doris really hit it off. Doris became Donna's new daughter. I mean that literally. I really think Doris felt that Donna was her mother. Then, Donna got sick and finally died. It was a terrible year. Doris was just as shaken by it as Jim and I.

So, some three years later, when I married Martha, I know Doris wasn't happy about it. I think she and Jim wouldn't let themselves like Martha, as though that might be a kind of betrayal of Donna's memory. It took another year before the two of them got to like and respect Martha. Doris really had to try hard. But, then, it was like Donna all over again. Martha has become Doris's guide and adviser. She likes taking her out shopping and going to the theater with her. It's a good match. And I think it's made Jim feel better, too. So far, so good!

These stories involve two of the Saving Graces discussed in Chapter 4: #1, Experiencing the Joy of a Fulfilling Remarriage can increase the capacity to be generous to new and old family members. Forming a Friendship with a Stepparent, #3, can be a partial replacement for a deceased parent.

Of course, there's another far more common positive force that often pulls stepchildren and a new stepparent together: gratitude. As we've noted earlier, the children are grateful that dear old Dad now has someone to be with him, to take care of him—or her. Here is an example of Saving Grace #5: Freeing from Filial Responsibility. It takes a load of responsibility off their backs—usually.

Hildegarde, a thirty-eight-year-old stepchild:

After Dad died, Mom was all alone. But Tom and I lived just a few blocks away, so I could get over there often to keep an eye on her. Then, Tom learned he was being transferred out of state. We thought about taking Mom with us, but she just wouldn't have it. She had her friends, and all her activities right there. I was really in a quandary. I didn't want to leave her all by herself. I just didn't know what to do.

That's when Peter appeared. It was a miracle! Mom was only in her late fifties, but she hadn't gone out with anybody since Dad's death. But Mom and Dad had both known Peter since childhood. It turned out he had lost his wife a year or so ago, and he had just come around to look up his old friends. Thank heavens!

I must admit that I was relieved. A lot of tension was building up between Tom and me, because I was so upset about leaving Mom. I probably wouldn't have cared who Peter was, as long as he solved the problem. Fortunately, though, he's a great guy, and they're very happy together.

Sometimes—thought not often—that plus-type scenario gets played out in reverse, as a minus. This next story really belongs in the minus section, but the world is complicated and what's positive in one setting can be negative in another, even when it looks very similar. Instead of a plus-type "thank heavens for our new stepmother," this one is a negative: "How dare she steal my father from me?" Fury #1, Fear of Abandonment and Isolation, and Fury #2, Fidelity to Family, outweigh Saving Grace #5, Freeing from Filial Responsibility.

This story was told to us by Marybeth, age forty-six:

I have—or rather I had—a very close relationship with my father. He came to live with us several years ago, and it worked out fine. He's no youngster, but he's perfectly healthy. My children adore him. He takes them to all sorts of things, rodeos, ball games, fishing trips, etc. I adore him, too—or I did, until she came into our lives.

Can you imagine? She picked him up at a supermarket! I couldn't believe it. He didn't mention her at first, but I noticed he was a little more careful about how he looked when he went out. Then, he started going out at night, saying he was going down to the Elks Lodge.

Well, it went on from there, until he asked if he could bring a friend home for dinner. "A friend," he said. He didn't say a girlfriend. So, in she flounced, and from then on it was all downhill. Now, he wants to leave us and move in with her! He's like a kid in a candy store! I know he's making a big mistake, but I don't know how to stop him.

Let's get back to pluses. Certainly, from the stepchildren's point of view, most new stepparents seem to ride in on a broomstick. The first reaction is often negative. Who is this invader? This usurper? Sometimes, however, the newcomers enter on a graceful white horse, tossing flower petals, easing preexisting tensions, and even helping to solve some chronic problems of the troubled biological families they have now joined.

Here's a case in point. Sam, age seventy-five, related this story to us:

Sam and his biological daughter, Elaine, have had a long history of ups and downs. Sam doesn't approve of Elaine's attitude toward money—especially other people's money. He thinks she is irresponsible, and he has told her so more than once. It's true that Sam's standards are very high. He has a strong general sense of integrity and honesty, a sense that extends to financial matters. He has a sterling business reputation, and the family has always lived well within their means. He always pays his credit card debt promptly and fully.

Sam has tried hard to inculcate the same values into Elaine and Elaine's older brother, Stan. And Stan has, in fact, internalized those values. Stan is just as meticulously honest and ethical in all his dealings as his father.

Elaine, however, looks at the world a little differently. She's married, and the couple makes a good total income. Elaine, however, and her husband, too, tend to overspend. They have one young child whom Sam thinks they are in danger of spoiling. They like to take cruises and generally enjoy life.

That would be fine if they could afford it; however, they simply cannot meet their obligations. Legal complications and courtroom visits ensue, and things get rather unpleasant. Elaine and Harry, her husband, are in danger of losing their cars and their home, and the burden of debt just keeps growing.

Elaine, finally and reluctantly, has to tell her father and brother about the whole situation and ask for financial help. But when that happens, Sam is more troubled about Elaine than about the couple's immediate financial crisis. He feels that Elaine is—once again—not telling the whole story, even to him. He worries that Elaine and her husband might not have "played it quite straight."

In any case, Sam does send Elaine some money to help her. More importantly, brother Stan spends a lot of time (and a lot of his own money) helping to straighten things out for Elaine and Harry. Between Stan's know-how and a large loan from him, Elaine and Harry finally resolve their financial problems.

From Sam's point of view, the key word in the above sentence is loan. Stan is reasonably well off, but far from wealthy, and he has stretched his own resources to lend all that money to Elaine.

Two years pass. Harry has a new job that pays well, and Elaine is working, too. They are meeting the mortgage payments on their house and maintaining their one car. But they have not paid anything back to Stan, who, incidentally, now happens to be having financial problems of his own.

Sam calls Stan. Stan's quite depressed. Things aren't going well for him. Sam offers to help, but Stan, characteristically, refuses. He says that he'll work things out. Whereupon Sam, worried about son Stan, calls Elaine. He suggests—gently at first—that Elaine ought to start paying Stan back, even if it's only a few dollars a month. Elaine agrees and says they'll start sending him monthly checks right away.

About six weeks later, Sam asks Stan if he has received any repayment from Elaine. "No, but don't worry about it," says Stan. "They're struggling, too. She'll pay me when she can." Sam is incensed.

That same evening Elaine calls. She announces enthusiastically that she and Harry have started a complete remodeling of their condo. "This place is a mess. It really needs to be updated. We've got great plans. We're taking out the wall between the living room and dining room, and we're putting in a whole new kitchen, and we're going to install one of those six-burner stove tops and—"

Sam reacts! "How can you spend all that money on your condo when you haven't paid back a single cent to Stan?" That question only infuriates Elaine. The conversation becomes an argument; the argument descends into anger on both sides, and it all goes downhill from there. Finally, Sam shouts, "I'm ashamed of you. How can you be so immoral?" At which point, Elaine slams down the phone, and so does Sam.

"Immoral." That was the word that causes both of them to shut down. After that episode, for month after month, Sam and Elaine do not speak to one another. There is no direct contact of any kind between them. Sam sends some money to Stan. He tells Stan to treat his check as a partial repayment of Elaine's debt. At first, Stan protests, then reluctantly he accepts.

Here, we pause for a moment, to make room for one more character to enter our story: Sam's relatively new wife, Louise. She has been in the background all this time, listening to Sam as he vents about Stan's financial troubles and his concern that Elaine "doesn't have any sense of responsibility about money. And it's so unfair to Stan!"

Louise is the kind of person who gets along with everybody, with her own children, and with Stan and Elaine, too. She doesn't like to see Sam and Elaine at loggerheads, but, sensibly, she hesitates to interfere.

Nevertheless, a few weeks later, as they drive to dinner at a friend's, Louise puts one toe into the very hot water:

"Have you heard from Elaine?"

A sharp, definitive response: "No!"

"It's been a long time. Why don't you call her?"

Louise has lit the wrong fuse. Sam almost shouts, "Why should I call her? Why doesn't she call me to apologize? I might call her after she sends a big check to Stan! And why are you butting in? They're my children. Please mind your own business!"

Louise has no trouble reading that danger signal. It's not like Sam to snap at her like that except when he's really upset. So, she backs off—for now. But she doesn't give up. She waits for the right moment, then tries again—carefully—about a week later.

"Sam, you know this is not good," she tells Sam. "What about little Martha? Martha's birthday is coming up, isn't it? She'll be seven, won't she? She sent us that sweet e-mail last week. She's really a great kid."

Sam replies—wearily this time, not angrily: "She'll be eight, not seven. I think she knows about Elaine and me."

Louise, sensing the mood change, becomes more daring. "Come on, Sam," she pleads. "Enough already. Elaine is wrong, but not talking to her won't solve anything."

From Sam: Silence.

One week later: Louise to Sam, at breakfast (because Louise knows Sam is one of those rare people who always feels up in the morning): "Any news from the eastern front?"

Sam: "No news, and, for God's sake, Louise, stop bugging me about Elaine. I'll handle it."

Five days later: Sam to Louise, over dinner: "I talked to Elaine today. I wanted to send an e-mail, but I didn't have her e-mail address."

Louise, still stepping carefully: "How did it go?"

"It was okay. We both apologized. I still don't like the way she acts about paying back what she owes Stan, and she knows I think it's terrible. But she and I can get back to that problem later."

"I'm very glad you talked to her," Louise says, "and don't you think this dessert is really delicious?"

The simple moral of that tale: Stepparents can sometimes help resolve problems in their spouse's biological families—if they do so with sensitivity and caring. They can help move the whole family toward greater unity and mutual understanding, illustrating Saving Grace #2. In this instance, the new spouse is able to Facilitate Objectivity, Maturity, and Wisdom.

Clearly, one can't easily predict whether a parent's new, late-in-life relationship will have a positive or a negative effect on the families involved until one gets close enough to see the details. So, don't jump to conclusions too soon.

THE "PLINUSES": THE EMOTIONAL PLUS/MINUS MIXTURES OF THE REAL WORLD

This brings us to a perhaps obvious reality: In every complex situation, there are positives and negatives, yins and yangs, goods and bads. In adult stepfamilies, both tend to be exaggerated.

For example, in our experience, adult stepchildren often feel relieved when a lone, aging parent finds a new relationship. That's a positive. They feel unburdened—though often they don't like to admit it—because someone else has assumed responsibility for poor, lonely old Mom or Dad. The kids may feel this way even when Mom and Dad feel neither lonely nor old and wish the kids would stop pestering them.

Yet, even as children may feel relieved by the arrival of a blessed nurse, they are also likely to resent such newcomers, viewing them as intruders who may displace them from their own number one position in their parent's affection. Such mixed feelings can last for a long time. Besides, they can work in either direction: children feeling both grateful and resentful of a stepparent and—albeit less often—parents feeling both grateful and resentful toward stepchildren.

CRISES CAN CLEAR THE EMOTIONAL AIR

Perhaps, more than any other single force, crises are the realities that tend to end such ambivalences. Crises often force family members to make up their hearts and minds either to come together or to break apart.

Mixed feelings, like relief and resentment, affection and anger, can go on for a very long time. They can seesaw back and forth, month after month, even year after year, leaving a continuing trail of tensions. Often, it takes some unexpected crisis to end that game, to show us what's really basic (and *who* is a real family trooper) to help us distinguish the important from the trivial.

Gayle, a seventy-three-year-old stepmother, described her crisis experience in the following way:

Rick's son and daughters were wary of me at the beginning. They didn't like the idea of their father getting remarried. They had tightened the fam-

ily circle after Rick's first wife died, and they didn't want to let anyone else in. They had managed to defend that family circle against two previous girlfriends that Rick had after Glenda died. They were doing pretty much the same with me, until the car accident. That changed everything.

It was really terrible. Rick and I were driving on the turnpike in New Jersey when an oil truck rear-ended us. Before you knew it, the car started to smoke. You could smell all the oil. Rick's door somehow had jammed in the crash, and he couldn't get out.

He kept telling me to get out and run. He has a very bad back, and there was no way he could climb out of his bucket seat and over the console to my door. He was afraid of an explosion. I did get out, but then I ran around to his side of the car. I kept trying to open his door. He was motioning me to get far away from the car and to watch out for all the cars that were whizzing by, but I wasn't going to let him stay there.

Somehow—don't ask me how—I managed to get his door open just enough and pulled him out. We got out just in the nick of time, because we had barely gotten to the edge of the road when the car blew up. The explosion was fantastic. We were both knocked to the ground, and we were burned, but not too badly. The truck driver was seriously burned. He had been knocked unconscious and was stuck in the truck. Then, the ambulance and police cars began to arrive. We were both in the hospital for a few days, but we feel lucky to be alive. That poor truck driver was in very bad shape.

Rick keeps saying I saved his life, and 1 guess maybe I did. I certainly wasn't going to leave him to get blown up. How could I have lived with that?

When Rick's kids heard about the accident, they were scared, but they were also grateful that Rick was alive. Rick kept telling them how I managed to open the door, even though he was telling me to run for it. He calls me superwoman because the door was really jammed.

After that, I think their attitude toward me changed. They understood that I loved Rick enough to risk my life for him and that he'd be dead if not for me. Every now and then, we all talk about the accident, and they thank me for saving Rick. When Janey, his oldest daughter, talks about it, her eyes fill up with tears. Mine do, too.

That incident changed how Rick's kids felt about me, and, I must admit, vice versa. I don't feel left out anymore. I appreciate that now they treat me like a real member of the family. That doesn't mean we don't have our moments. But, then, don't all families go through ups and downs?

All families encounter crises over the years—accidents or illnesses, sons or daughters going off to war, teenagers getting into trouble. Families, biological and step, struggle with such crises, and usually they cope, leaving the family's foundation shaken but intact.

The big crises—unexpected death or life-threatening illness—act as psychological earthquakes. They shatter old family relationships and force the construction of new ones. They cause family members to "unfreeze," to question, to reexamine their lives, and to search for some new level of stability. That crisis-driven, "unfrozen" period is a time of disruption, uncertainty, unclarity, emotionality, and tension—all those within each of the people involved and also within the relationships among them.

The Chinese symbol for *crisis* becomes relevant here. That symbol has two parts. One part, *wei,* means "danger." The other part, *chi,* means "opportunity." Crises are always accompanied by dangers—by fear, anger, and all the rest. Yet, they also open the door to new worlds.

Many stepfamilies, like many biological families, work their way through the effects of crises and come out with stronger, less ambiguous emotional bonds than ever before. Even frightening crises can produce such silver linings. Here is a case in point, as told by Mildred, age seventy-two:

I love Paul's daughter Betty, and I know now that she loves me. Oh, she was wary of me at first, but so was I of her. In fact, she really kept me at arm's length for a long time. She had very different tastes and attitudes, completely unlike mine. And I think she felt I had somehow stolen her father away from me. I thought we could never really build any kind of bond between us. We couldn't be more different.

But you know what really brought us together? Betty's baby developed meningitis, and she was admitted to the hospital. I was down in San Diego at the time, at a conference, and Paul was in Boston on business. Paul called me on my cell phone. He was very upset. He called from Logan Airport to tell me he had talked to Betty, and things were very bad. It was really touch and go for the baby. Paul was beside himself. He had managed to get a seat on a late plane to Seattle to go to Betty.

I immediately canceled everything and took the first flight to Seattle, too. I got there about ten at night, five or six hours before Paul got there. I took a cab right to the hospital. Then, Paul finally arrived, and we stayed there for four days until we were absolutely sure the baby was going to be okay.

But before Paul got there, I sat with Betty in the hospital room by the baby's crib. The baby was feverish and weak. Betty was scared for the baby. Frankly, so was I. Scared to death, in fact.

I think just those few hours when Betty and I were alone in that hospital room, and I was holding her hand and reassuring her—that somehow that short time did it. We just bonded. We knew we felt very, very deeply for each other. Nothing could split us after that! And after that, Paul and I knew we had really become a family.

Crises can be defining moments, crucibles that can mold great relationships. But they can also burn previously positive relationships to ashes. What determines which way a crisis will lead? You do.

Suppose, for example, that Mildred had not grabbed that first plane to Seattle. Suppose, when Paul called her that day, she had made another decision. Suppose she had said, "Okay, you go to Seattle. I'll come up tomorrow night, when the conference is over." What then? Even in times of crisis—perhaps *especially* in times of crisis—weak relationships can be welded together.

WRAPPING IT UP

This chapter could go on and on. The varieties of relationships between stepparents and adult stepchildren are endless and diverse. Perhaps, the most important thing about them is that they are always there, whether we want them or not. No matter whether you cherish those relationships or just wish they would go away, they will play an important role in the lives of both parents and children. So, here are a few closing suggestions:

1. Life in families with adult stepchildren seldom starts out as a bowl of cherries—but it can become one, though an occasional cherry is almost sure to be sour. Late-in-life loves *can* provide great rewards for both stepchildren and stepparents. But there *will* be stresses and strains along the way, especially at first. Expect them, but don't just accept them as inevitable. Whether you are a stepparent or stepchild, you can change them.

2. Don't think all the difficulties you encounter (either as a stepparent or a stepchild) are due to the fact that yours is a stepfamily. Look at the biological families around you. Don't they also have family problems? Don't children get mad at their *real* mothers, or vice versa? Do all the adult children in every family just love one another? How about sons- and daughters-in-law? No stresses and strains there? Don't they, too, have problems about who goes where on holidays? Do all your friends

think their daughters married exactly the right husbands and their sons exactly the right wives? Are sons- or daughters-in-law always welcomed wholeheartedly into their spouses' families? Or is it just that your friends can't blame their family problems on wicked stepmothers or conniving stepsons?

The step relationship gives all the parties involved an emotional escape hatch. It allows all family members to attribute perfectly normal and common stresses within families to the fact that theirs is a stepfamily. An adult child might have trouble with her biological mother, but she can't blame it on "that woman" whom Dad so foolishly married. And a biological father might have serious conflicts with his son, but that's his own son. So, he can't easily blame his son's nasty behavior on his new wife! Keep that escape hatch locked! Using it doesn't solve problems.

3. If you're a new stepparent, be sure to keep your priorities straight. Remember that your relationship with your new spouse (or domestic partner) comes first. The children are important, and you should certainly do everything you can to build positive relationships with all of them, but they should *not* be your number one priority. The person you sleep with is.

4. Remember that relationships can change. Bad ones can be repaired, and if they can't be repaired, they can at least be defanged. Try to think ahead about what you would like your family relationships to become and work—patiently—toward that goal.

5. Crises—unforeseen, unscheduled, and usually unwanted—are the testing points of any relationship. Crises will happen. How we handle them can strengthen or destroy the relationships between stepchildren and stepparents and between spouses, too. Expect that even small crises will be accompanied by tension, anger, finger-pointing, and irrationality. Still, realize that you have the patience, the will, and the power to make things better.

6. A strong recommendation to adult children in stepfamilies: Let your parents live! Give them the space they need to rebuild their lives!

7. An equally strong recommendation to stepparents: When your stepchildren are being their most difficult or immature, try looking at them as if they were your own biological offspring. Now, how do you

feel about them? Maybe, viewing them through the lens of biological acceptance, you can begin to see them not as *yours* or *mine,* but *ours.*

While adult stepchildren can present all kinds of problems and dangers, their children—your stepgrandchildren—can be a special source of love, pleasure, and reconciliation. How so? The next chapter charts the territory of stepgrandchildren.

CHAPTER 10

The Grandchildren:
Pawns or Bridges?

There are three main sets of characters who appear and reappear in this chapter: grandparents (step and biological) and their adult children (also step and biological), who are the parents of the third set, grandchildren. These last characters are *almost* always biologically related to their parents, usually young and often unaware of the strife that's going on among the adults. Moreover, there is no question about which of these three sets of characters must play the starring roles in this chapter. The stars are neither sweet old grandma and grandpa, nor the adorable little kiddies. The stars of this chapter are the men and women in the middle, the adult stepchildren.

WHAT'S IN A NAME?

When we began this book, we promised ourselves and our families we wouldn't write about them. Still, because we loved the following story so much, we asked and received special permission to use it. When Rosie, one of our granddaughters, was in the fourth grade, she was asked to write an essay about her family. She found herself puzzled about how to label her grandfather's relatively new wife, Jean, her nonbiological grandmother. Rosie knew that Jean wasn't her *real* grandmother. Her own mother's real mother (and Rosie's real grandmother), sadly enough, had died several years earlier.

How then, in her essay, should Rosie identify this new person? What was the appropriate label that would communicate Jean's place in the family? Rosie pondered for some time. She finally found a hint—one of her friends was always talking about her "stepbrother" and "stepsister." Rosie understood, albeit only vaguely, what "step" meant in this context. As a result, in her essay, she referred to Jean as her grandfather's "stepwife."

Stepwife was a brand-new term, at least to us. While it may not set kinship experts on fire, the term reflects a much larger nonsemantic problem common to many adult stepfamilies. That is, not just what grandchildren *call* their step-grandparents, but how do they *relate* to their grandfathers' new wives or grand-mothers' new husbands?

What forces determine whether these stepgrandparent/stepgrandchild relationships will flower and flourish or wither on the vine? How close can these two generations become, separated as they are by another in-between generation? How important a role should grandparents and grandchildren play in one another's lives, particularly in stepfamilies?

ADULT STEPCHILDREN GUARD THE GATE

As we said earlier, the adult stepchildren are the key players in this chapter, the sentinels who guard the bridge that connects grandparents to grandchildren. In stepfamilies with grandchildren, the parents of the little ones are the gate-keepers and sometimes the toll collectors. They have the power to open or close the road, pretty much at will, between new stepgrandparents and the grandchildren. The adult children have so much power that they can, if they choose to, destroy that bridge altogether. And sometimes they do just that.

GRANDCHILDREN AREN'T POWERLESS

The grandchildren, however, have countervailing power, although they may not even be aware of it. Many times, we have found, young grandchildren force open the gates their parents have locked, reaching out for the affection and support of their stepgrandparents.

By their very presence, such grandchildren can even heal deeply wounded relationships between their parents and their own remarrying parents. Yet, it's wise for the adults not to lay all the burdens of bridge building on the grandkids.

FIRST MEETINGS COUNT

Here is a story about three generations of one family from the grandchild's perspective:

Jessica was six years old. So was her dearest friend, Becky. Becky had something that Jessica didn't have. She had a grandmother. Jessica wasn't sure exactly what a grandmother was, but she knew Becky loved her grandmother. She talked about her grandmother all the time. She would spend weekends with her grandmother, and when she came back, she would always have a new doll or a new dress or some special cookies.

Jessica, listening to and watching Becky, began to think a grandmother was like a fairy godmother. She wished she had one, but she didn't. Jessica had a grandfather, but when she asked her mother about her grandmother, she learned that once, before Jessica was born, one of her two grandmothers—Daddy's mother—had died. And Mommy's mother—Jessica's other grandmother—had also passed away when Jessica was just about one year old. So, Jessica had no grandmother.

Then, one day when Jessica was seven, her grandfather came to visit. He came to visit a lot, but this time was different. He brought a woman with him. Her name was Virginia. Then, Grandpa asked Jessica if she would like to have Virginia as a grandmother. Jessica couldn't believe it! She shouted "Yes!" about five times and ran over to sit on Virginia's lap.

Virginia just shook Jessica's little hand, and said "Hello." That was all. Then, she went right on talking to the other adults. Jessica's eyes filled with tears.

When Grandpa eventually married Virginia, Jessica and her parents did not attend the wedding. She and Virginia did not become great friends. And Jessica's mommy and daddy were less than delighted that Virginia had come into the family, because, although they felt that Jessica had really missed the great experience of having a loving grandmother, they were quite sure that Virginia would not fill that bill.

As for Jessica, she still wished she had a grandmother like Becky's.

That's an unhappy, but common, story. Now, let's rewrite it and brighten it up. Go back to the sentence that reads, "Virginia just shook Jessica's little hand. . . ." Let's rewrite that paragraph, transforming Virginia from a Distancer into a Joiner. The story now continues:

Virginia smiled and picked Jessica up on her lap. Then, she reached into her big handbag and pulled out a beautifully wrapped little package. It was a gift for Jessica. Jessica opened it eagerly. Inside was a little necklace with a gold heart on it. Jessica loved it.

Later, when Grandpa married Virginia, Jessica was the flower girl at the wedding. She and Virginia became great friends. And Jessica's parents were delighted that Virginia had come into the family because they felt that Jessica could now have that vivifying experience of growing up with a loving grandmother.

Now, Jessica had a grandmother just like Becky's. And they all lived happily ever after!

Of course, in real life, people often don't change just because they remarry and enter an established family. The first Virginia, the Distancer, just didn't reach out to Jessica. She probably did not reach out to anyone in her new family. That might be true, even if she weren't a natural Distancer. Perhaps, like so many modern grandmothers, Virginia had a very busy life, with friends and a career to which she was deeply committed.

Whatever the reason, the first Virginia's behavior that day created lasting negative consequences for the whole family. It may even have hurt her impending marriage. She didn't have to behave as effusively as the second Virginia—a classic, even stereotypical grandmother. But couldn't she have been insightful enough to know this was the time to bend a little?

Wasn't this the time to be a bit more welcoming so she would be more welcomed? Wasn't it in everyone's interest, including her own, for her to do so? We all know how initial meetings are etched into people's memories. We have to work extra hard to repair any inadvertent damage that results from early mistakes.

Patty, a sixty-eight-year-old bride of two months, told us about a first meeting with Ruth, her twelve-year-old stepgranddaughter, who was having a birthday party. As Patty and her new husband stepped onto the patio where the celebration was taking place, she overheard Ruth in the swimming pool pointing her out, and saying, "That's my grandpa's new wife, but when my grandpa dies he's going to be buried next to my grandma." Hard to recover from that one.

This vignette reflects an important point that we commonly saw with very young stepgrandchildren: Their behavior reflects their parents' feelings toward the stepgrandparent. So, adult children, give your own kids a fair chance to establish a loving relationship with this new grandparent. We all need all the real love we can get.

GRANDPARENTS, THE TWENTY-FIRST-CENTURY MODEL

Many of today's grandmas, and grandpas, too, just "ain't what they used to be." They don't sit on rocking chairs on their front porches, Grandpa with newspaper and pipe and Grandma hunched in her shawl over her crochet hook. Some of today's grandparents wouldn't think of taking a young grandchild for the weekend. They're more likely to say, "Sorry, but we can't baby-sit Saturday night. We're going dancing!"

So, the middle generation has to get real! If you're lucky enough to have doting grandparents for your new child—that most beautiful, intelligent, and charming of newborns—enjoy it, but don't expect too much. If little Mary's new stepgrandma is eager to baby-sit, or if she showers thoughtful toys and adorable clothes on the baby, enjoy that, too. Just don't count on it. That kind of grandparent is becoming rarer every day.

Moreover, if your child does have such grandparents, be prepared to pay a modest bill for services rendered. If Grandma feels that closely connected to the baby, she may also feel she has the right, even the duty, to make sure that the child is raised "properly," at least as she defines it. As a result, she may make suggestions that you find intrusive, suggestions like, "You're spoiling her. She needs more discipline."

There, alas, is the rub! You wanted all that old-fashioned love and affection between grandmother and child, but perhaps you didn't want the "old fash-ioned" child-rearing notions that are sometimes part of the package. As a young parent, you've read the books and attended the parenting seminars. You're quite sure you don't need child-rearing advice, especially from a stepmother! So, you wish she would butt out, and maybe you tell her so. Then, what happens?

Suppose, instead, that Stepgrandma is *not* falling all over herself to help you with the new baby. Suppose she loves the baby, but she also loves running her business, or teaching her high school classes, or working at her office. Or per-haps she and Granddad prefer tours of Europe, African safaris, and cruises to Tahiti to baby-sitting. Then, as young parents, you might resent Stepgrandma for different reasons. You may think she *doesn't* spend enough time with the baby, or, heaven forfend, that she is insufficiently interested in the baby's new tooth.

Maybe—for a grandparent and especially for a stepgrandmother—there's no way to win the grandmothering game, unless the gatekeepers, the adult chil-dren, have the maturity to understand both the costs and benefits of the complex role they want Stepgrandma to play.

DISTANCE, TECHNOLOGY, AND THE GRANDCHILDREN

In today's world, grandchildren and grandparents are often separated by hundreds, even thousands, of miles. Grandpa doesn't live next door. He lives with his new wife in Florida, and the grandchildren live in Chicago, or Little Rock, or Phoenix, or, for that matter, London or Hong Kong.

Modern technology, especially communication technology, can partially compensate for such separation. E-mail, instant messaging, camcorders, and the telephone can reduce distance. The baby, when he or she gets to be eight or nine, will probably be more familiar with all that technology and more facile in its use than most grandparents.

So, something like this may happen:

Kathy is now eleven years old. Her parents, Estelle and Robert, are having difficulties with her. She's become quite rebellious and sullen. She claims her parents don't understand her. Estelle and Robert really got upset when they dis-covered she had been "chatting" on the Internet with a strange man. They insisted that she stop and grounded her for a week. This isn't the first time they've had to ground her. The tension between Kathy and her parents is now quite high.

Kathy has a good relationship with her stepgrandmother, Pam, even though Pam lives far away. In fact, Kathy's relationship with Pam is a lot better than her parents'. Robert was not at all happy when his dad decided to marry Pam. Robert and Estelle are rather quiet types, and they really disapprove of Pam. She is too outgoing, outspoken, and ebullient for their taste, a kind of Auntie Mame character. And she has a rather colorful past.

But Pam and Kathy get along fine. Pam sends Kathy lots of little gifts and funny cards. When Pam comes to visit, she takes Kathy to lunch at white table-cloth restaurants and buys her clothes and costume jewelry. Kathy feels Pam is really with it, that she's much more fashionable and up to date than her mother and dad. She thinks that even though they're a lot younger than Pam, her parents are sticks-in-the-mud. They seldom go to parties or the opera or do other interesting things like that.

So, one day, when Kathy has had a bad time with her parents, she sends an e-mail to Grammy Pam. She doesn't tell her parents she's sending it. The e-mail reads: "Dear Grammy Pam, I hate it here. My mother and father are always telling me what to do. Can I come live with you? You're much nicer than they are. Love, your grandchild, Kathy."

Pretend you are Grammy Pam. How do you respond to that message? Would you tell Kathy's parents about the e-mail? Would you invite Kathy to come live with you and Grandpa Mac for a while? Would you e-mail Kathy and tell her that her first duty is to talk to her own mother and dad? Would you not respond? What about those chats with a strange man over the Internet? Can you help prevent Kathy from going down that dangerous path? What's the *proper* role for a stepgrandmother in a situation like this—a situation that is becoming increasingly common as technology improves and older folks become younger in spirit, if not in years?

There's a temptation to enjoy being idealized by Kathy. That is, until you remember that you don't live 24/7 with her and that she views you as a fairy godmother. Just as you don't like being the evil stepparent, resist teaming up with Kathy to make her mother the evil mother. "Do unto others . . ."

TEENAGED GRANDCHILDREN AND DRUGS, ALCOHOL, AND SEX

Drugs, alcohol, and sex are a potent combination under any circumstances. In stepfamilies, they are not any easier.

This is a story told by a stepmother, Elaine, age sixty-nine:

My stepdaughter, Louise, called the other day. She was distraught, but covering it up. The call was a jumble. She was concerned about her sixteen-year-old son, Joe. Here's roughly what she said: "We found drugs in Joe's room. First, he denied it. Then, he admitted using them. His grades have been going to hell, and it's his senior year in high school. Now, he says he doesn't want to go to college. Don (Louise's husband) and I told him he couldn't drive the car. He got very mad about that and said he hated us all. He wants to work in a restaurant. Don't tell my father. He'll have a heart attack!"

I like Joe, and he likes me. So, after that phone call, I thought about calling him or inviting him to visit for a few days. But he's at school, and it's a five-hour plane trip. And I certainly wasn't going to keep this from my husband, Mel. It would upset him, but he had to know about it.

Mel did get quite upset, but he calmed down, and we talked it over that night. We knew Joe had been acting up for a year or so. He got ticketed for speeding within a month after he got his driver's license, and, one night, he apparently didn't come home at all. The fact that Joe's school grades had dropped, that he seemed a little too familiar with drugs, and that he didn't want to go to college made us think he probably needed to talk to someone other than his parents—a therapist, for example—about his feelings. We knew therapy was expensive, and we knew the kids couldn't pay for it, but we could. So, we decided that we'd underwrite it if Louise and Don thought it was a good idea.

I called Louise the next day and told her about what we'd been thinking. She said that they, all three, had made an appointment to talk to the guidance counselor at school. She didn't seem to want to talk about therapy. That night we got a call from Louise's husband, Don. He was quite angry. He said this was their family problem and they would handle it. His anger was really directed mostly at me, telling me to back off and stop interfering. I felt I had done just what I would have done for my own kids.

Perhaps, the kids were right. Joe is their child, in their immediate family. They know him better than anybody and are directly responsible for him. Don might have said it more gently, but he was right in telling his stepmother to mind her own business. Wasn't Grandma's proper role—especially stepgrandma's role—to listen sympathetically to everyone concerned and to offer help only if they wanted it? In short, shouldn't stepgrandparents stay out of the action unless explicitly invited to participate?

Grandchildren may try to drag grandparents into squabbles with their parents. Sometimes, parents may, unintentionally, drag *their* parents in more than either generation really wants or means to do. For the most part, however, we've found that it is usually best for grandparents to hold back and let parents try to cope with their children's problems—especially when one grandparent is a stepgrandparent.

ADULT CHILDREN: REVISITING THE SENTRIES AT THE GATE

The story about grandson Joe's episode with drugs illustrates what we meant when we said earlier that the parents—the middlemen and -women—are this chapter's stars. They are not always lovable or heroic stars, but they are the key characters, nevertheless. They stand—sometimes loom—between grandchildren and grandparents. That's true in biological families, as well, except perhaps in those families, rare in Western culture, in which all three generations live under the same roof.

Grandchildren's parents are, of course, much more than mere gatekeepers. Parents do—or can do—much more than that. They can actively reach out to invite stepgrandparents into their nuclear families, or they can padlock the family gate to make sure that stepgrandparents never get anywhere near the grandchildren.

Here's what Esther, age thirty-six, told us:

I just can't figure out how my good, sensible dad could have gotten himself involved with that woman—and while Mother was still alive! Amy's just a little redheaded hussy, and she's hardly older than we are! She's a predator. I'm sure she has her eye on his money. She's already had two husbands. And, now, he wants to marry her. Less than a year after Mother passed away! It's terrible! He's besotted! I really think it's just sex. He'll be tired of her pretty darn soon.

When Esther told us this story, we responded: You have two children. And you told us that they feel very close to your dad. How are you going to handle all this with your kids?

I wish I knew the answer to that. My husband, Hank, and I really don't know what to do. I do know that we will not go to any wedding they may have. And I'll do everything I can to keep the children away from her.

Question: Even if that also means keeping the children away from their grandfather?

Yes, I guess that's the price we'll have to pay. She seduced Dad, but I don't want that witch to seduce my children, too. I can only hope that Dad will see the light and get over this teenage infatuation.

Telling us this disturbing tale, Esther was adamant. She has decided to separate the biological grandfather and his grandchildren because he is about to marry someone she despises.

Is Esther right? What about the long-term consequences of her behavior? As we've already suggested, small children often internalize and adopt the attitudes of their parents. Isn't Esther's lockout of "that witch" also likely to turn the children away from their granddad? Does Esther's dislike of her father's new love justify depriving young children of a grandfather, whom they love, and of his wife, who might grow into a real grandmother?

The key question is *why* is Esther so adamant about "that witch," Amy. Consider several possibilities:

- Is Amy really a predatory she-devil, marrying Dad only for his money?

- Does Esther, herself, have an eye on that money?

- Is Dad really "besotted" by Amy's sexual wiles? Or does Esther just find it too painful to acknowledge her father's sexuality?

- Or is all the fuss because Dad has chosen a much younger, obviously sexual partner? We all know that parents often find it difficult to accept the fact that their "babies" have become sexually active. But, as we discuss in Chapter 13, many adult children also find it difficult to accept the fact that their aging parents are still sexually active.

- Is Esther is really angry at her father? Is she angry because she feels he betrayed her mother by having an extramarital relationship while she was alive? Does Esther feel her father has compounded that betrayal by deciding to marry Amy so soon after her mother's death?

Esther might do well to have a long private talk with Dad, leveling with him about her feelings in all this (without overpowering him with her anger) and trying to understand his point of view. If Esther doesn't initiate that talk, then Dad should. It may be hard for him to talk to Esther, especially about his feelings for Amy, but even a bumbling effort is better than nothing. Realistically, such a talk will be tough for Dad to take part in, but its potential healing power far out-weighs its difficulty.

We haven't often recommended counseling, but in this case, Esther, and her dad, too, could certainly profit from a few sessions—and *soon,* before the bridge between the generations is closed forever. For while the active players in all this are certainly Esther, her dad, and "that woman," the grandchildren are the ones who must live with the long-term consequences.

Just as the grandkids will suffer if the adults don't resolve the situation, the grandkids will profit if the adults can work out some better resolution than sep-arating the grandchildren from their grandfather. Let's also not forget that Esther will be cutting herself off from a father whose wisdom and affection she may need more than she knows. He, too, presumably loves Esther and may need her now more than ever.

There are, of course, happier stories out there in the step jungle, stories about grown sons and daughters welcoming new stepgrandparents. Some adult children welcome newcomers because they bring happiness to old Mom or Dad. Others welcome the newcomer for more personal reasons, perhaps because the adult children want someone who can, at least partially, fill the emotional void left by a lost mother or father. Some adult children welcome a new granddad or grandma so their small children can have that sense of belonging to a rich, extended family, a sense that greatly enhances the children's feelings of self-worth and self-esteem.

Most of the tales we were told and the ones we observed firsthand cannot be put simply into a box marked "happy" or "unhappy." The single best descriptor for them is "complex." Sometimes, for example, the grandchildren are, them-selves, young adults, occasionally with a fourth generation of children of their own. Most of the grandchildren are the biological descendents of their parents, but sometimes the children have been adopted. Sometimes, one of the middle generation, a parent of the grandchildren, has also been adopted. So, stepgrand-parent/grandchild relationships can be very varied indeed.

As with the rest of life, the good and the bad of these complicated relationships are inextricably intertwined. Yet, despite all the variations and complications, we found a few strategies almost always helped ease tensions, rather than exacerbat-ing them: Sensitivity, thoughtfulness, and patience—especially from the middle generation—coupled with a little luck, almost always led to more positive out-comes.

Consider, for example, the following rather complicated situation:

George has just married for the second time. His first wife, Marion, the mother of George's two adult children, is alive, well, and living rather far away. She has not remarried and shows no sign of doing so.

One of those two children, David, and his wife, Mary, have a baby girl, about six months old. They live very close to father George, but far away from mother Marion. Unfortunately, David and Mary have had marital problems and are now legally separated. They alternate custody of baby Johnny.

Stepson David loves baby Johnny dearly, but he is not exactly competent at such things as diapering and feeding small children. In fact, he's rather old-fashioned in all his attitudes about marriage and family. For example, he did not want Mary to work outside the home. Until now, he had left all domestic duties to her, while he acted as breadwinner—which may, of course, have contributed to his recent separation.

Now, let's get back to David's father, George, and his wife of two years, Marcy. The plain fact is that son David doesn't like Marcy and has shown it in many not-very-subtle ways. He seems to blame her for the breakup of his parents' marriage. So even though they lived close by, he and Mary seldom visited them and rarely invited them to visit. On holidays, David and Mary went to mother Marion's or to Mary's family. They never accepted the frequent invitations from father George and stepmother Marcy.

But all that was before David and Mary split up. David's attitudes have changed recently and rather fast. If he was going to take care of little Johnny for weekends at a time, he knew he had to learn a few things. And, to his credit, he did just that. He read and practiced and got on the Internet to learn more about child care. He called mother Marion often, asking for advice. But mother Marion was physically far away, so she couldn't really help David take care of the baby.

George and Marcy, however, were practically next door. Fortunately, Marcy—who feels no great affinity for David—does feel considerable affinity for little Johnny. So, she, for little Johnny's sake, steps forward to help. So, without invitation, George and Marcy begin to drop by when they know the baby is with David.

David, knowing he needs all the help he can get, reluctantly accepts Marcy's help with Johnny. It soon becomes obvious, even to David, that Marcy knows what she is doing and has a kind of competence that he lacks. Soon, Marcy and little Johnny are getting along just fine. Johnny has begun to recognize Marcy and is delighted to see her.

The next step: David begins to bring Johnny over to visit George and Marcy. Often, they stay for dinner. Marcy arranges a little place for Johnny to take his nap. She keeps some diapers and clothing on hand. David even leaves Johnny with them while he goes out to do some errands.

George, Marcy, and David begin to talk to one another, at first only about the baby, but gradually about other things, about marriage and divorce, about Marcy's life and David's relationship with George and with his biological mother. George couldn't be more pleased with this trend toward reconciliation.

This is not a fairy tale. Marcy and David do not become best friends and live happily ever after. Marcy still thinks David has a lot of growing up to do. And David still cherishes many of his macho qualities. But they have managed to accommodate each other, and they are accommodating still. And, of course, Marcy has developed a deep affection for little Johnny and vice versa.

In an earlier chapter, we suggested that crises were times of opportunity, as well as times of danger. This case is another example of that. The crisis of George's separation from Mary, with all its stress and pain, also opened the gate that was separating little Johnny from his grandfather and step-grandmother.

What would have happened if David and Mary had not separated? Would there still be an enormous gulf separating generations number one and number three from one another? If so, who would have been to blame? Was it up to Marcy to force that gate open? Or should George have taken a more active role? Or, even from far away, might George's first wife, Marion, have helped to get David to loosen up? Or should David have recognized the chasm and tried to bridge it himself?

In this case, the crisis of David's separation, the existence of little Johnny, and Marcy's quiet determination all pushed open the gate and let in the grand-parents. In many other cases, too, common sense, realistic expectations, patience, and a little serendipity can work wonders—not fairy tale wonders, but the authentic wonder of realistic, working relationships across the gene-rations.

STEPGRANDCHILDREN: BRIDGES OVER TROUBLED WATERS

As we have said before, grandchildren, at least those past early childhood, are not just powerless pawns. They don't have to acquiesce passively to what-ever their parents do vis-à-vis their grandparents, step or otherwise. In fact, we heard several stories of how stepgrandchildren built bridges between their par-ents and their stepgrandparent. Here's one, told to us by Lena, a seventy-year-old stepgrandmother, that may make you smile:

My stepdaughter, Felicia, and her husband, Ed, had always been quite cool to me. We simply weren't on the same wavelength. I think when Kerry and I got married, Felicia was still mourning the death of her mother, who had been gone about two years or so.

To make matters worse, her mother had died early in Felicia's preg-nancy. Felicia had always had a close relationship with her mother and was looking forward to sharing this wonderful event with her mother, as mothers and daughters often do. So, Felicia was devastated when her mother died quite unexpectedly in Felicia's third month. As I've heard the story from Kerry, when Alicia was born only six months after Peggy's death, Felicia was still very depressed. She felt cheated and thought that Alicia, too, had been cheated out of a loving, warm grandmother. It really was a shame.

When Kerry and I began seeing each other, I heard much about Felicia, Ed, and Alicia, but I didn't see much of them. I'm not sure why. They never seemed available when Kerry called. Maybe, Kerry was nervous about pushing our relationship too much with them. Truly, I don't know exactly why. We simply didn't see very much of them. When we did see them, they were always polite, but really quite distant.

After we married, they continued to be quite distant. Alicia, however, had a mind of her own. And she is an adorable, absolutely adorable, child. You can't help but love her. When they came to visit or we visited them, she always wanted to sit near me, and I welcomed her sweet little presence. She was the one who made those "required" visits bearable. In fact, I would get so involved with her that I barely noticed how aloof her parents were.

Little by little, the ice began to thaw. I think that Felicia and Ed could tell that I genuinely loved Alicia. Who wouldn't? And I think that Alicia loved me, too. She didn't resent me as someone who was taking her real grandmother's place. After all, what makes someone a grandmother—blood or love? I've seen some of my friends who don't particularly like, much less love, their own grandchildren. My daughter is a lesbian, so she'll probably never have kids. Alicia is Alicia. She feels like my own flesh and blood. Next to Kerry, Alicia is the light of my life.

As I said, Felicia and Ed have begun to thaw toward me. They seem much less distant than they used to be. That doesn't mean we'll ever be kindred spirits. But I think they respect my genuine feelings for their child and vice versa. Maybe, they even respect it more because it happened despite their lack of encouragement. You know the old saying, "Dogs and children really know people."

Stepgrandchildren, particularly if they were very young (or not yet born) when the older folks marry, don't usually carry as much emotional baggage from their parent's biological families. They respond to people as people, particularly if the air is not polluted with their parent's anger and resentment. Unfortunately, when the atmosphere has been tainted, the children, too, may succumb to their parent's negativity.

WHEN SENTRIES CAN GO OFF DUTY, TRAFFIC FLOWS BETTER

If the adult stepchildren (that is, the grandchildren's parents) are wise, they'll appreciate that a grandparent's affection is a precious commodity. They shouldn't squander it casually. They should think twice, even thrice, before dynamiting any bridges the youngest generation has built with a grandparent or stepgrandparent.

As for the stepgrandparent, remember that the grandchildren have a right to be responded to in terms of their *own* behavior and personalities. Avoid the temptation to see them as representatives, willing or otherwise, of their less-than-welcoming parents. It's not their fault if their parents need to grow up a bit more.

Older grandchildren, particularly preadolescents or adolescents, may be looking for a safe haven now and then, if only in cyberspace, with a sympathetic stepgrandparent. Let's be very clear: We are *not* suggesting that stepgrandparents gang up with stepgrandchildren against the in-between generation. But grandparents, step and biological, can offer an important loving buffer between their kids and their grandkids when things get rough.

The parents of adolescents, too, may welcome a respite from their parental duties now and then. This can mean a teen's weekend away or a calming telephone session with grandpa or grandma.

If you are the stepgrandparent, your spouse will appreciate your support, even when he or she doesn't ask for it. The older generation often worries that their adult children are not as wise in their parental roles as they were. True or not, the oldest generation needs some supportive handholding and nonjudgmental understanding as it watches, sometimes helplessly and with hair on end, as the two younger generations work out their problems. And, in truth, the child-rearing challenges that their adult children face today may be much greater— with drugs, alcohol, sex, AIDS, gangs, chat rooms, and much more—than those they confronted with their own children.

SUMMING UP

This chapter has been about the relationships among three sets of actors: grandparents (step and biological), their adult children (who are, themselves, parents), and grandchildren, some young, some not.

The key actors in this cross-generational drama are almost always the adult children. Like Janus, they face in two directions, back toward their aging parents and forward toward their own children. Calling them "key" players is appropriate, because they almost always hold the keys to the gate that can separate grandparents from grandchildren. Theirs is the power to block the connection between the first and third generations or to throw it open and smooth the way for a rewarding relationship between the oldest and youngest family members.

That middle generation's power exists in both biological and stepfamilies. In stepfamilies, however, some parental gatekeeping may be driven by such negative motives as active dislike of a stepparent or steadfast loyalty to a deceased or divorced parent.

The next most powerful members of this hierarchy are not the grandparents, but the grandchildren. They have the capacity to build bridges. They also have more leverage with the sentry than the stepgrandparent does. They also may have the innate wisdom to realize that children flourish with and need a grandparent's love, even a stepgrandparent's love.

Still, it's important to remember that the world has changed, that grandchildren and many present-day grandparents are quite different from those of generations past. They may not be retired and sedentary. They may be living their own busy, active lives, just as their children are doing. So, the middle generation, parents of the grandkids, can no longer expect the stereotypical grandparents of Norman Rockwell's old *Saturday Evening Post* covers. Nor should they expect that their own offspring, however extraordinary, will automatically become the centers of their grandparents' world.

The technological revolutions of recent years have also caused the relationships between the generations to change. Parents and their young children may live many miles away from grandparents, but the telephone, jet aircraft, instant messaging, and e-mail have eliminated much of the isolation once caused by physical distance. Grandparent/grandchild relationships can flourish even when the participants are thousands of miles apart. Indeed, these relationships—like other less desirable e-mail relationships—may even flourish when parents do not approve of them. We heard of several cases where the Internet served as a way of bypassing barriers that parents tried to erect.

A bond between grandparent and grandchild can add to the full development of any child, to his or her sense of belonging, and to the richness of the world in which the child lives. When grandparents (step or biological) and their adult children sever that bond, for whatever reason, they do so not only at their own peril, but at the peril of the third generation, as well. Once severed, the bonds that connect grandparents to their children and grandchildren are very difficult to repair.

Intergenerational issues in stepfamilies are complicated and often painful. As we'll see in the next chapter, so are the many thorny issues related to inheritance.

CHAPTER 11

Who Should Inherit My Property?

For four hundred years, the tragedy of *Romeo and Juliet* has been emblematic of a fundamental conflict between younger and older generations. Romeo and Juliet represent the ultimate star-crossed lovers. Emboldened by a great passion, they refused to be restrained by material interests or social concerns. They married secretly within a day after they met and fell in love, knowing full well that their parents would oppose their marriage. As love-struck teenagers, they struggled against the calculated social and financial interests of their powerful aging parents. Tragedy followed when they chose love over the common sense demanded by their families.

Their parents were not evil. They were just "practical" and "realistic." They had other plans for their children, plans better suited to their families' interests. Romeo and Juliet's break from their parents ultimately cost them their lives.

Romeo and Juliet failed, but they also triumphed. In the course of the play, they accept the consequences of their own choices, thereby becoming mature, independent adults. The price of their adulthood, however, is the loss of their secure, but dependent, childhood pattern of trading obedience for parental approval and support.

Today, the situation is often reversed. Romeo and Juliet, the eager, passionate lovers, are not the children, but the parents. The older bride and groom are thrilled by the prospect of their new marriage, while the children play the more practical and materialistic roles.

In fact, many older, star-crossed couples marry in direct or indirect opposition to their children's wishes. Unlike Shakespeare's teenagers, adult lovers are keenly aware of their mortality. They long to enjoy the intimacy of love again, or in some cases for the first time, before they shuffle off this mortal coil. They see this as their last chance for love. They view their marriage as a celebration of renewal.

In this role-reversed conflict of generations, the more sober younger generation may fiercely oppose the impatient older lovers. The older couple may find themselves having to fight off the restraining forces of their down-to-earth, economically savvy, hardheaded, and, in some cases, calculating adult children.

Many in today's younger generation have come to see inheritance of their parents' property and money as a birthright. They fear that birthright will be diluted or disappear altogether as a result of their parents' late-in-life marriage. We now see many instances of children trying to prevent their aging parents from entering what they sincerely believe to be overly impulsive marriages, marriages that may cost the parent—and cost them—financial, as well as emotional, pain. They urge their parents to stop and weigh carefully the potentially disastrous consequences.

At times, in the new generational reversal of the old Romeo and Juliet tragedy, the children may even threaten the parents with social exile. Some parents come to realize, as they grow older, that they have become dependent on their middle-aged children for approval, emotional support, and advice. Such parents may be forced to choose between their new love and continued reliance on their children.

It is those complex intertwinings of love and money in adult stepfamilies that will be the foci of the rest of this chapter and the next.

FOR THE PARENTS: A DIFFERENT COMING-OF-AGE DRAMA

We live in a culture that has, for many years, affirmed an inborn right of adult children to declare independence from their parents. By choosing their own careers, lifestyles, and lovers, young adults still risk disapproval and possibly even disinheritance, but we don't dispute their right to make their own choice. We even celebrate this painful, but courageous, process in movies and novels as a coming-of-age drama. In those fictional plays and tales, the prodigal daughters and sons are forgiven, either grudgingly or gracefully, by their crusty parents. A familiar scenario? Well, forget it. That was yesterday!

The heroic figure at the center of today's coming-of-age story is the vigorous aging parent. Such parents have typically acquired some financial independence. They are determined to remarry and make other bold changes in their lives, even at the painful price of incurring their adult children's disapproval. Typically they have worked hard for many years at career building and child rearing. They believe they have earned the chance for a second life, free of responsibility to bosses and children.

A BENEFIT OF AGING: EXPRESSING YOURSELF RATHER THAN PROVING YOURSELF

If the first two-thirds of a long life is a time in which to *prove* yourself, then the last third can be the time in which to *express* yourself. As a consequence of greater health consciousness, prophylactic medicine, and other advances, the average person has more life chapters to live than ever before.

The years from fifty to ninety are being redefined as a period for self-actualizing, at a time when you finally have a better sense of what life is all about. This life stage can be a Paradise Regained, when you can put into action the ideas and activities previously put aside or even sacrificed for others.

Retirement and widowhood, which used to be considered the closing period of an active life, can be the beginning of new possibilities for learning—intellectual, social, and emotional. The drive to regenerate and express yourself fully, however, also requires you to achieve your independence once again.

Some adult children applaud their parents' mature surge into independence. Thirty-five-year-old Kate told her seventy-year-old stepmother:

> *I'm so excited that you and my dad are taking courses, and becoming students again, and getting so stimulated by what you learn. And that you go to a gym and stay in shape. It makes me feel that there is always hope, no matter what age we are.*

On the other hand, becoming more independent when you are older may mean being disinherited emotionally by your adult children, a disinheritance that may be subtle or explicit.

Forty-two-year-old Kevin told us:

> *My dad can't baby-sit anymore because he is going to things like jazz classes or taking ballroom dancing lessons. Why can't he act his age?*

Forty-year-old Kelley told her mother (sounding much like a parent talking to an errant teenager):

> *I feel that you are just not interested in me and my children anymore. For years, you were over here all the time. And we got to depend on you. Now,*

I have to make an appointment to see you. Don't expect me to jump when you need me.

Within the next few years, the boomers will swell the numbers experiencing this phenomenon of elder liberation. A new coming-of-age drama is becoming increasingly common, one that literally comes *with* age.

IS THERE SOMETHING FOUL IN THE HEIR?

Many problems regarding inheritance in stepfamilies are quite similar to those in biological families. The problems, however, are often intensified by the addition of nonbiological family members. Today, owing to the enormous wealth created in the past twenty years, adult children are probably more aware of being potential inheritors than any prior generation. Those who have already begun to count on that money commonly resist losing some or all of it by virtue of a parent's remarriage.

Of course, a parent's remarriage is not the only threat to a child's inheritance. An economic downturn or a long illness could wipe out a stock portfolio or retirement fund or force the sale of family real estate. Nevertheless, adult children frequently believe that whatever wealth a parent has amassed has their name written on it.

Meanwhile, the parents who earned the money may develop new priorities. They may decide to put it to their own use or even to put the new spouse's name on it. The subsequent conflict of wills (that's literally what it often comes down to) may be intense.

Upon hearing that his widowed father was remarrying, Charles, an English barrister, jumped into his car and drove all the way from London to his father's home in Cornwall. There, Charles walked his father around the sea wall of the town insisting, "Live with her, but for God's sake don't marry her!" To a rather traditional and proper father, this response from his son was "simply frightful."

We found that the most difficult issues to discuss between the two generations come from Fury #4, Finances. The most raw and savage conflicts between parent and adult child often come down to that simple, materialistic question: Who "owns" the parent's money?

Forty-two-year-old Bob told us:

Don't let the new spouse "rape" the family assets. You've got to badger your parent into planning wills and living trusts.

The parent, the adult children, the grandchildren, and the new spouse will all insist that fairness and equity are on their side when they argue her/his/their case. Each, however, has a different, frequently self-serving, definition of what is fair. How then does one figure out what is truly equitable? Finances is a particularly difficult Fury to assuage because it simultaneously arouses and agitates all of the other four Furies, as well: Fear of Abandonment and Isolation, Fidelity to Family, Favoritism, and Focus on Self to the Exclusion of Others.

Many times, we heard children oppose a parent's marriage supposedly on the basis of Fury #2, Fidelity to Family, when the Fury that actually held sway was Finances. The real motivator behind an adult child's anger at parental "selfishness" and "lack of interest" in their children's welfare was often Finances.

HOMEWORK FOR PARENTS: HOW MUCH IS ENOUGH?

The truth of the matter is that none of us knows how long we are going to live and what our exact financial needs will be. Most of the time, we don't think about it unless we are forced to do so.

Remarriage in later life is one thing that makes us finally confront these thorny issues. That means we must look squarely at some of the nastiest aspects of human nature: selfishness and greed. Some parents are remarkably clear-eyed about those issues. Most are not. Remarriage makes parents spell out how they will divide their property, however large or small it may be. It also pushes them to take the legal steps necessary to execute their wishes.

Most people drew up their current wills many years ago, either when they got married or when the children were born. When their children were young, their parents' primary motivation was to protect and educate them. Many other people simply put off making a will. They find it too painful to think about their own deaths and how to divide property among their children. You may have been too busy for too long earning enough to keep up your lifestyle, pay your bills, and fund retirement. The prospect of remarriage may be the first occasion in many years when you have even thought about your net worth, let alone put it down on paper.

Remarriage means, among many other things, redefining your responsibilities and obligations in light of your new marital status. Inevitably, this leads you to think about your adult children's economic stability. Your "baby" girl may now be forty-five, married, with two children and a husband who doesn't really have any ambition, but, nevertheless, likes to live well. Now is the time to think clearly about whether you want to support their current lifestyle when you are gone. Whether you wish to think about it or not, what you decide to do now—or what you don't do—will have serious consequences later. Better to act and have the consequences be those you intended.

THE BIG CHILL: PRENUPTIAL AGREEMENTS

The warm and cozy planning of a wedding and a future together can be frosted over by the prior need to settle important financial issues. Prenuptial negotiations involving property can test the strength of even the most passionate relationship. They may threaten the development of trust in a relationship that has not had time to solidify.

Most people highly value their own honesty and trustworthiness. You may see your new love's request that you sign a binding legal agreement before you marry as an insensitive challenge to your integrity. Besides requiring both of you to reveal all your financial assets, a prenuptial agreement also spells out in advance the financial consequences of dissolving the marriage. Thinking about divorce when all you want to do is plan for a happy marriage is unnerving at best.

The "prenup" also requires you to consider the financial consequences of your death, something else most of us try hard to avoid contemplating. That simply adds another unpleasant complication to what should be a blissfully happy time.

Margaret, a forty-five-year-old bride-to-be, told us:

When Don suggested that we each consult a lawyer about a prenuptial agreement, I became incensed. I couldn't believe he would ask such a thing of me. How could you be planning to enter into holy matrimony where you promise to be together for richer, poorer, in sickness and health and have so much basic mistrust for your wife? I went home, and, the more I thought about it, the angrier I got. The next morning, I told him that if he needed me to sign a prenuptial, the marriage was off. He backed down.

Lawyers are often the first people we consult to help us make these critical financial decisions. The legal steps they suggest frequently bring the first chill into what may be the warmest and most mature love relationship of your life. If either would-be spouse perceives the other as behaving in a cold, calculating way, the relationship may be threatened, even permanently damaged. That means the lawyer you choose is as important as the surgeon you would select for a major operation. We recommend that you take your time on this one. Make sure you find an attorney who is both sensitive and creative, as well as an expert in estate planning, family law, and the division of marital assets.

Barbara, age fifty, told us:

Ken insisted on a prenuptial agreement and told me from the beginning that he wouldn't marry without it. Ken is extremely close to his son, Jim, and wanted to be sure Jim and his sister, Carol, inherited absolutely everything that Ken had acquired prior to our marriage. He and his son made sure that every piece of property, every dollar he owned, was accounted for in the document. Ken had always spoiled Jim. So, of course Jim felt that everything his father owned belonged to him by divine right! They were at their lawyer's office for so many hours that I began to think that the legal fees would be greater than the inheritance. They discussed and made provision for every contingency you could imagine. So, every penny was out on the table. Every penny Ken earned before our marriage was to go to Jim and Carol upon his death. I would get half of anything Ken acquired after we married. My lawyer advised me not to sign it.

Although there were days when I thought the relationship wasn't worth it, I also knew that, since the financial settlement with his children was hammered out so completely and aboveboard, I could trust Ken to live up to his word with me, too. We had all our arguments about money openly and up front before we married. I knew exactly where I stood. It seemed highly unlikely that Ken would sneak around and do anything secretly with his money after that.

We are a legalistic society, and we naturally turn to our attorneys to tell us what to do to protect our assets. Prenuptial agreements represent an attempt to reach some fair and equitable distribution of property, especially when children from an earlier relationship are involved. Just as you would if you were divorcing, we recommend that each party retain his or her own attorney in preparing a prenuptial agreement. It is important that both parties feel that they have an expert looking out for their interests when their future quality of life is at stake.

Various kinds of trusts can be created in conjunction with a will drawn up at the same time. These ensure that your assets are distributed as you wish and in the most tax-efficient way. An estate planner can show you how income from your assets may be used for the benefit of your spouse for a period of time, while the principal remains intact and ultimately passes to your children.

In this process of thinking about finances, you have had to decide things you may not have anticipated. Making sure that your surviving spouse can live rent free in the home you share is easy. But do you really want your son to be the executor of your living trust and have the authority to lean over your bereaved husband's shoulder to see what he spends on clothes and travel?

Is it wiser to change your IRA into a trust for your grandchildren, rather than your adult children, given the fact that more than 50 percent of marriages end in divorce? Do you want to discourage legal battles after your death by stipulating a large financial penalty to hinder any challenge to your will? On the other hand, how much time do you now want to spend in your lawyer's office with his/her meter running?

Within a decade, the economy may change radically, and your net worth may sink. Or on the contrary, your wealth may increase substantially. Add to this the change in estate-tax laws to be phased in over the next decade. It will remove the long-standing advantage of tax-free spousal inheritance over direct bequests to the adult children and grandchildren. It is also wise to remember that the tax laws themselves will probably change in the future. While people of great wealth can revisit lawyers with impunity, most people want to get these legal matters resolved as efficiently, economically, and humanely as possible. Then we want to close the door on those issues for as long as the economic climate allows.

Anna tells us:

The worst time I had was during the negotiations about the prenuptial agreement. Up to that point, there had been no conflict between us. Life was idyllic. I was sixty-two, and John was sixty-five. We were so grateful and overjoyed to have found each other so late in life and to be spending whatever remained of our lives together. During our courtship, it seemed as if John's children were not of any real worry to him. They were grown up and living independently. But when it came to the prenuptial, he was adamant about protecting his children's interests.

I had assumed that, when one of us died, we would want the survivor to have use of the other's property and money if needed, for as long as needed. For me, it was a part of casting our lot together and protecting each other when we got really old. I thought that when the survivor of the two of us died, our money could go to the next generation. I believed that my children could and should wait to get money from me. He believed that his children should inherit right away when he died, no matter what the circumstances. It was the first time I felt his heart was closed against me. Somehow, we got through the negotiations to a compromise. The lawyers told me the best time to negotiate is before the marriage. I suppose they are right. Later, it would have been much more difficult because the romantic idealization wears off.

NO PRENUPTIAL AGREEMENT? THEN AT LEAST HAVE THAT DIFFICULT TALK ABOUT MONEY

Many people don't want to incur the expense of a prenuptial agreement. They may feel that they don't have enough property to warrant the legal cost. It may not make financial sense.

Still, deciding you don't need an expensive legal document doesn't mean you shouldn't share vital facts about your financial status with your spouse-to-be. Otherwise, there can be disastrous surprises.

We have discussed the problems of prenuptial agreements in such detail because the topics covered in such an agreement are the very same ones that should be raised in your two-way conversation about money. It is very important for you and your mate to ask and answer some fundamental questions about how you will deal with financial matters once you are married. You are not being nosy by wanting to find out about your future partner's financial life. You both need to know what income and expenses to expect as a couple. When you get to the stage of deciding where to live when you are married, you should also be discussing how to live financially. Who pays for what?

Discussing money is one of the most difficult conversations couples have, but they can be conversations with an enormous payoff. You will probably talk about salary and/or social security and/or other retirement benefits or funds. In that way, you can plan how and where to live, whether and when to retire, and how much supplementary income you might have to earn. If you are currently receiving social security or a pension, it is important to call and find out the consequences, if any, that remarriage will have on future payments. It's worth getting answers in writing since information from help lines can be unreliable. Remember, you will be making decisions that will influence how comfortably you will live. (We'll return to this issue when we talk about living together in Chapter 14.)

On the obligation side, the essentials to tell your spouse-to-be are such items as outstanding debts, mortgages, condo fees, property taxes, and insurance costs. At this time, it is also important to inform each other about any agreements either of you has made to adult children to help with their mortgage payments or other financial needs. This includes such costs as school tuition for grandchildren. These can be touchy issues that can generate more intense feeling than discussing even sexual issues, but wise couples address them candidly and thoroughly.

CHECKPOINTS TO DISCUSS WITH YOUR SPOUSE

All these items are meant for both you and your spouse to contribute to your discussion. Once you agree to the process, be brave and volunteer to be the one to start. Don't expect to do it all in one session. Initially, simply raising the important questions will be enough. Those questions require each person to think it through and prepare.

- *What are your assets?* These include salary, home and other property, bank accounts, and retirement funds, other financial assets, etc.

- *What are your debts?* These include mortgages, loans, alimony, credit card debts, promises of funds to children and grandchildren.

- *How will you share living expenses?* This means food, rent or mortgage, cars, health and other insurance, clothes, entertainment, and travel.

- *What do you wish to happen when you die?* This requires a will that spells out what you want to do with your home, savings, pensions, and bequests.

Writing down a complete list of assets and liabilities, including financial promises made to adult children, will enable both of you to see the big picture. Both of you then can understand what you will be gaining and/or giving up financially when you cross the line into marriage.

If you are so strongly motivated to marry that you are willing, say, to delay your retirement in order to help support your spouse's adult children, so be it. Still, it's best to know exactly what the deal is before you commit to it. Lesley, age fifty-five, didn't know beforehand, because she hadn't asked:

Dick never told me that he planned to help his daughters out financially. Of course, I have to take responsibility, too. I never asked. He's completely honest and would have told me. He is a government worker, and our combined incomes appeared to leave enough money for us to live on, with a little more left over than before we got together.

If I had known the extent of his feelings of obligation to his grown children, I don't think I would have married him. I was so in love, and it was the most exciting time of my life. I didn't want to make things go sour by asking him questions about how much time and money he would spend on his daughters. Big mistake. The way things worked out, Dick spends all his discretionary income contributing to his daughters' mortgage payments.

Lesley either goes on vacation by herself or with her female friends. When Dick goes with her, she has to pay for both of them. In either case, she feels resentful, and the resulting stress has taken a toll on their marriage.

A QUESTION FOR PARENTS IN BOTH GENERATIONS: WHAT IS YOUR PHILOSOPHY ABOUT INHERITANCE?

Why has inheritance become such a difficult topic to talk about with your children? It's even more difficult than sex! It may be because people have very different ideas on the subject, and any one of us may have internally contradictory feelings about it. As a parent, perhaps you want to spare your children the financial pain you went through in order to go to college or buy a first home. At the same time, you know that these same sacrifices helped make you a stronger and more resourceful adult.

Parents like to be providers and protectors, but they may not like the spoiled child whom they've raised. You may fear that your children won't work hard if they feel sure that they will inherit your money. We found that families, including stepfamilies, were happiest when parents in both generations—those remarrying later in life, as well as the younger generation of adult stepchildren who are themselves parents—shared the same philosophy about inheritance.

Much of adult children's attitude toward inheritance stems from the way a parent managed expectations about money long ago. Have you raised your children with the idea that you would pay for their college educations, but, after that, they should be ready to support themselves? Or have you somehow encouraged great expectations on your children's part? Have you communicated to your children that they will inherit significant family money and property at your death? If so, have you also led them to believe that their inheritance will all be managed for them, without requiring them to develop any money management skills of their own? In some affluent families, children inherit the services of money managers, along with their parents' wealth.

We have found that parental attitudes about money and inheritance can be organized into five basic categories:

1. **We don't have enough money to worry about inheritance.** We supported our kids the best we could when they were young, and, since then, they have been on their own financially. They may have student

loans, perhaps they have mortgages, but they are responsible for their own financial lives. Because we were never able to put much away, our children may even have to help us out financially as we get older.

2. **We earn a good income (often two good incomes) and live pretty comfortably.** We have always told our kids that they could count on us for financial support, including their college tuition, but that after that they would be on their own. We let them know that we shall almost certainly be able to take care of our own financial needs as we age without turning to them for additional support. We have told them, if there is money left over, they will inherit it, but not to count on it. We have raised them to be self-sufficient adults and expect them to continue as such, with or without an inheritance from us.

3. **We are very fortunate and have real wealth.** We shall be able to buy our children their first homes. They have always known that they have trusts and will have a lifestyle that comes with a guaranteed income. Although they will never have to struggle to support themselves and their families, we have instilled in them a sense of noblesse oblige and expect them to give something back to society.

4. **We have no consistent philosophy about money.** We don't budget, save, or spend according to any plan. We live entirely in the present. We spend money as we need to and don't think much about meeting future financial needs. We may be in debt, or we may live within our means. We don't have any clear sense of where our money goes. Sometimes, we lavish gifts on our children; sometimes, they get nothing. Our economic behavior is unselfconscious and natural. We don't think money is important.

Please note this behavior should not be confused with being dedicated to a strong antimaterialistic philosophy. The latter is usually based on religious beliefs (e.g., Buddhism, certain Christian groups, etc.) or a personal or political philosophy that discourages the acquisition of money and personal property.

Some of our interviewees had no financial plan and kept money matters fuzzy to postpone confronting difficult economic realities and decisions. You might be unconsciously following your parents' similar lack of clarity about money. Of course, in previous generations, adult children frequently had to support parents who hadn't made their own financial provisions for old age. Maybe, you were in that situation and it upset you, and, now, you don't want to think about money and aging either.

If you have no plan about getting, spending, and saving money—or you realize that you have not been a good money model for your children—getting remarried (or reading this book) gives you an opportunity to make changes. This doesn't mean you have to reveal every detail of your financial life to your children. You do need, however, to become aware of what you own, what you owe, and how you want to use the financial resources you now have or might have in the future. If your new spouse is good with money, you might ask him or her for some consultation.

5. **Money is a big secret. It's definitely there, but it is none of the children's business.** We never discuss money. We think it is an improper topic for discussion. We buy what we need but avoid ostention.

If you tend to keep money matters a *big* secret, you may want to think about why you do that. It may be a way to hold on to children. By making a mystery of money, you may unconsciously be creating financial dependency in your children. Perhaps, you want to maintain control over them by keeping them in the dark about the family's financial situation. By doing this, you may actually be trying to bribe them into catering to your needs. You may be threatening implicitly that you will retaliate by cutting off their inheritance unless they curry your favor.

Beware this strategy. Whether conscious or not, it undermines children in two ways: First, it discourages them from becoming financially independent. Second, it denies them the freedom of choice that comes with knowing that they will probably inherit some money.

The failure of children to grow into financial independence is especially crippling. Parental secrecy about money leads adult children to expect too much or too little and makes it infinitely harder for them to make their own informed financial decisions. This is particularly so during the crucial years when children are choosing and pursuing careers. Besides, they can legitimately blame you for allowing them to proceed without fully understanding the family's true financial picture.

HOW TO TALK ABOUT INHERITANCE

Remarriage gives you another chance to clarify your philosophy about money. You might not have done so for any number of reasons, including not having much money to talk about in the past. Now, you must prepare yourself for this often difficult conversation with your children.

You would be wise to start by first discussing the topic of inheritance with your new spouse. Then, you might turn to old and trusted friends for ideas about how and what they have communicated to their children. Find out what worked for them and what they would have done differently.

One thing you know for sure is that, by remarrying, you are probably disrupting your adult children's unspoken assumptions about inheritance. If you have been as up front as the first two examples we described, you have handled expectations about inheritance realistically. Then, everyone knows not to expect too much, barring your winning the lottery.

If you have been a nonplanner where money is concerned and now considerable money is at stake, you have the opportunity to clear the decks before you remarry. You may decide to simplify matters by giving your biological children and any stepchildren from a former marriage their entire inheritance *before* you remarry. If you decide on that approach, you should tell your children that they are getting their inheritance now and should not expect anything more. For your part, you don't have to worry about having them look over your shoulder in the future to see what you are doing with *their* inheritance.

A warning is appropriate here. If you choose to give your children their inheritance now, you may find that they respond to you very differently when they have your money in hand and no longer expect any future financial largesse. By taking the money off the table, you may discover the true extent of their attachment and affection. Like King Lear, you may not like what you see. In our experience, however, few people exercise this option, if only because most people who remarry don't have enough financial wherewithal both to give these bequests and guarantee their own solvency.

Seventy-five-year-old Martin was in a position to give his biological children their inheritance early. He told us:

> *I've been fortunate in business and have accumulated a good deal of property and money. When I decided to marry Kathy and start a new family, I didn't want to leave her at the mercy of my children and their lawyers in the event of my death. I thought it was a cleaner solution to give my children their inheritance outright before I remarried and eliminate everyone's need to worry and wonder about it.*

Few people are in Martin's circumstances. The rest of us have to continue to keep control of our financial resources and, therefore, of any inheritance that our adult children might ultimately receive. We don't have enough money to be confident we won't need it for ourselves.

What is the right thing to say to your children about the financial consequences of your remarriage? Maybe, your children need to hear something simple and straightforward.

Here are some suggestions:

First, you might tell your children that, by getting remarried, you have taken on a new responsibility. You have also gained all the benefits of having a helpful and loving partner. You can point out that this new responsibility is the same as the one they have or will have to their own spouses or partners.

Second, if the two of you have agreed to help each other financially should one of you predecease the other, you might make that clear to your children. This is something that they would probably have assumed if their biological parents were still married, but it may be unclear under these circumstances. The less ambiguity about your commitment to your new spouse's future financial security, the better.

Here is an example in which these matters had not been discussed. Sixty-seven-year-old widower Leonard tearfully told us,

After the funeral service for Lois, her three married children came back to the house and proceeded to take the silverware out of the dining-room drawer and pack it into their suitcases. I said, "Say, could you leave it here. Lois and I ate with that silverware for fifteen years, and I'd like to keep using it."

It is wise to tell your children, if it is your intention, that you want your spouse to continue to live in the home you share, with the furnishings as they are, and as comfortably as he/she can, if you die first. You can stop right there, because there is no law that says you have to tell your children your net worth. Remember that your children don't generally let you see their annual income tax return. You are under no obligation to put all your financial cards on their table.

An additional step is required for widow(er)s, if they remarry after inheriting their deceased spouse's property. Adult children are usually keenly aware of things that belonged to a deceased parent. Of course, you are under no obligation to give them the property that you inherited. Still, you can avoid problems by letting them know that you are aware that they might have questions about anything you inherited from their deceased parent. Your remarriage could prompt you to tell your children explicitly that you will continue to control the income you inherited. You may or may not promise to earmark what remains to be inherited by them when you pass on—or when you and your new spouse have both died. Wise, compassionate parents are sensitive to the feelings of their children, but do remember that you have the right to use the money left to you by a deceased spouse in any way you see fit.

As the new wife of a widower with four adult children, sixty-year-old Martha told us:

> *Of course, financial issues are terribly important because children expect to inherit from their parents. But it all depends on the circumstances if this will happen or not. We were extremely lucky that I was financially independent through my own family. The first things Ben and I sorted out were our financial affairs. I felt it was important for his children to know that I wasn't grabbing everything.*
>
> *Their mother had died two years ago, and my husband was a cash-poor widower when we met. Since we decided to live in my husband's home, I bought half of the mortgage and gave his children the money directly. I've spent a lot of my money decorating the house. Every single piece of furniture we own has been chosen in advance by each child in case we are both killed in an accident. I'm not a grasping stepmother. I know money isn't everything, but you can't get by without it.*

Many parents and stepparents give generous monetary gifts each year, but say nothing about inheritance as such. That may be a sign of fear. Some parents use money to assuage their anxiety about how their biological children will feel about them after remarriage.

We all face the possibility of being alone and physically dependent as we age. We've all seen coasters and bumper stickers that read, "Be nice to your kids. They pick your nursing home." The truth is that you have no real control over how your children will respond to you if you become physically and/or financially dependent.

Final suggestion for discussion: answering the spoken or unspoken question "How much am I going to get?" Admitting that you can't predict the economy and, therefore, can't really guarantee that you will have assets to leave to them is fair and forthright. You're no Alan Greenspan. Sometimes the obvious needs to be said. You can explain that you know they are capable people who can support themselves. Still, you hope you will be able to leave them something after you and your new spouse die.

Given life's uncertainties, raising these difficult issues and confronting them as best you can makes you a role model of integrity, honesty, and responsibility for your children. They may not thank you at the time, but you have illustrated wise principles by which to live. That, in itself, is a great legacy.

COMMONSENSE FORMULAS

It is useful to have a general idea of some common formulas or rules of thumb that people of average means have used to distribute their property.

For most people, *property* means the home, objects of sentimental value, maybe a retirement account, a bank account, and, perhaps, a modest portfolio of stocks and bonds. Often, the home and furnishings are given to the surviving spouse to use during his/her lifetime. Upon the death of the surviving spouse, the home—if it had been owned jointly—may be sold and the proceeds divided equally between each of the couple's estates. If the home was owned by only one spouse, it usually goes to his/her children or other designated beneficiaries.

The spouse who dies first may leave his or her retirement fund to the surviving spouse to use for the other's lifetime. After the second spouse dies, what remains in the fund usually goes to the adult children or other designated beneficiaries. Of course, there are other ways to do all this. These are just some of the most common arrangements.

In recent decades, largely because of 40l(k)s, 403(b)s, IRAs, and other retirement accounts, most people have some money invested in the stock market. Depending on how the funds are managed, problems may arise when the surviving spouse wants to invest in high-income investments, while the children prefer stocks that yield little current income, but have a greater potential for growth. Appointing a trustee who will be fair to both sides may be one solution. Frequently, couples who trust each other appoint each other as trustees. They know that the financial future is impossible to predict and that the surviving spouse may need to change the investment strategy that worked when both were living.

No solution involving money and inheritance is completely conflict free, but try to find one that minimizes potential disagreements and legal fees. Endless litigation serves no one, except, perhaps, the attorneys. One suggestion that many knowledgeable lawyers make is to create a life insurance trust that pays the biological children directly upon the death of their parent. That way, they don't have to wait to inherit money until after the surviving spouse dies.

Distributing objects of sentimental value can lead to conflicts having little to do with money and much more to do with feelings and fears about that old Fury #3, Favoritism. Before they remarry, some parents ask their children to tell them which favorite objects they would like to inherit. Of course, everyone may want the same object, and even King Solomon might be hard-pressed to decide who gets Dad's World War II flight jacket or the treasured pearls Mom inherited from her mother. It may be easier for everyone if the older couple decides who gets which mementos, rather than leaving it to the adult children to negotiate among themselves.

SOMETIMES A GOOD LAUGH HELPS

Disparities in financial lifestyles between parents and adult children can inhibit the older couple from spending their discretionary income as they wish. Sometimes, parents try so hard to avoid intrafamilial comparisons and envy that they behave absurdly.

For example, sixty-seven-year-old Agnes told us:

Every time my husband's son came to visit with his wife, they wore ripped-up old clothes and always talked about how they couldn't afford this or that. When they were around, I began to feel guilty about wearing the nice clothes that I owned. I started to wear blue jeans when they visited us. They liked to stay over in our beachfront apartment in Florida when we were out of town, because, of course, they couldn't afford to get away otherwise. I thought they might just go through my closets and my pantry to see what I was spending. Before I left town, I would remove labels from my good clothes and peel the price stickers off the wine bottles. I couldn't believe what I was doing.

ANOTHER LESSON FROM SHAKESPEARE

The intergenerational problems that cluster around inheritance bring Shakespeare back to mind. As we noted earlier, the difficulties that stepfamilies face are not very different from the conflicts between the generations in biological families, as this Shakespearean example demonstrates.

At the beginning of *King Lear,* the royal family is gathered happily around their respected, powerful, and contented aging father. The patriarch is proudly distributing his wealth, and the daughters expect to receive handsome bequests. At the end of *King Lear,* the stage is littered with the corpses of family members. Why the tragic outcome? Because Lear didn't think things through, and the family was destroyed by the deadly, if unintended, consequences of his failure to do so.

King Lear is a tragedy about a biological family—there are no stepparents to complicate things. Lear gives his great lands and fortune to two of his three daughters. He impulsively disinherits the youngest because she refuses to join her sisters in flattering him. He assumes he and his two *good* daughters will live together happily ever after and that his favored daughters will meet all his future financial demands because he has been so generous to them.

Very soon, King Lear's two favored daughters begin to object to what they now see as his spendthrift ways. Gradually, the daughters cut Lear's allowance and make it clear that he is no longer in charge of his own financial affairs. Rather than live in the situation he has created, however unwittingly, Lear goes mad, rampaging out of control in a storm that reflects his own disordered psyche. Although King Lear had been a very competent monarch who had acquired vast lands and wealth, he didn't apply the same astute judgment to his family affairs. He didn't anticipate the disorder and grief that would result from his unwise distribution of his wealth among his potential heirs. He thought he knew best and consulted no one about his estate plan. Even Lear's Fool knew that was foolish!

We can benefit from King Lear's blindness. Lear gave his money to two of his children on the assumption that they would care for him in the style to which he was accustomed. To his horror, Lear discovered that he couldn't maintain his independence after he had ceded responsibility for his financial destiny to others, even though they were his beloved children.

MONEY TALK FOR A REMARRYING PARENT

We have described some strategies, scenarios, and ways of thinking about family assets. We believe they will help remarrying parents make sound financial decisions that will affect them, as well as their adult children, grandchildren, and stepchildren. Let's not forget, however, that remarrying parents may be shattering their children's expectations of inheritance that they have held confidently, though silently, for many years.

Once again, we recommend that remarrying parents talk quite candidly with their adult children about money. This does not mean telling them the numbers or handing out copies of your financial reports, bank accounts, or tax returns, etc. This talk should include being explicit about your financial obligation to your new spouse. That discussion may be painful, but it will force you and your children to be more realistic about what they can expect from you financially in the future. For those of you who have been remarried for some time, but have never spoken about such matters, there is no better time than now to have this important conversation. Family members have been thinking about inheritance and related issues even if they haven't been talking about them. Finally confronting them, honestly and openly, can really clear the air.

We believe that parents can prevent many problems surrounding inheritance by helping their children, whatever their ages, to learn to be financially independent. An inheritance loses some of its almost magical centrality when your children feel that they are perfectly capable of supporting themselves and are happy to do so. You have bestowed the gift of your confidence in them as mature, responsible adults.

In this chapter, we've focused on inheritance and financial matters from the remarrying parent's point of view. In the next chapter, we'll see how some of these same issues look from the adult child's perspective. You may be in for some surprises.

CHAPTER 12

My Inheritance:
Great Expectations
Gone with the Wind

In the last chapter, we saw how some older couples think about money. In this one, we'll look at money matters through the eyes of their adult children. Money is one of the thorniest subjects for most families even to discuss. In these two chapters, we allow the two generations to eavesdrop a little on one other in hopes of avoiding the anguish and turmoil money and self-interest too often cause in stepfamilies.

During much of the twentieth century, most of us considered adolescence the most problematic period for the family. That was the time when family life turned into a battlefield of teenage rebellion. Today, a new contender is vying for the title of most dangerous period: the years when older divorced or widowed parents enter new love relationships. Older parents are coming of age a second time, a phenomenon that is confusing their adult children and upsetting some of their long-held financial assumptions.

IF IT AIN'T BROKE DON'T FIX IT

"Why do you have to get *married?* You're not going to have any children." "I think it's great that you found someone to love and you won't be alone. But why can't you just live together?" Such questions are seldom asked in anger. Those thoughts occur to many reasonable adults when their aging parent announces plans for remarriage. "Why is a legally binding commitment necessary at your age?" Whether spoken aloud or kept as private thoughts, such words often express the adult child's wish that the parent's need for companionship can be satisfied without disrupting the emotional and financial structure of the pre-existing family. Nonetheless, in some states, after living together for a specified length of time, couples are considered to be common-law spouses.

If you are an adult child, the divorce of your parents or the death of one parent has caused a permanent, painful scar in your life. You and your siblings have probably stood by, sharing all the emotional consequences of the loss and comforting one another. You have always assumed that you and your biological siblings represent the continuity of your family and are its rightful heirs.

As an adult, your view probably goes something like this: Okay, Mom or Dad has found a significant other. Fine. In anticipation of Mom or Dad's death, some reasonable bequest can be arranged to care for that surviving companion, but why do they have to get *married?* That's one way adult children can dampen two of the Five Furies—Fury #2, Fidelity to Family, and Fury #4, Finances. Cohabitation outside of marriage is an increasingly accepted social arrangement, one that will preempt future problems. Nasty legal battles can be avoided from the start by not setting new allegiances in stone.

Thirty-five-year-old Russ, twice divorced himself, says this:

My aunt did it the right way. She had a wonderful companion. She never got married. They lived together for twenty years. This way, no one had to give up anything. They kept both houses. They did it so that all of their children could still have a family home to go back to. They were in love, and there was no need to legalize it. They did the Katharine Hepburn-Spencer Tracy thing. It was just perfect.

The situation may have been perfect from Russ's viewpoint, but many older couples want to make a home together. They want a traditional marriage, with its implication of a lifetime commitment. Living next door to each other doesn't feel all that great at 3:00 A.M. when you're lying awake worrying about something.

THEY'RE SQUANDERING MY INHERITANCE

Often, when a parent falls in love again, he/she is emerging from a period of feeling lonely and depressed. That parent probably wants to get out and enjoy life again. That heightened energy and renewed exhilaration may lead to dining out, buying new clothes or a new car, and traveling with a new companion. Of course, all of that costs money. To the children, that behavior may seem almost manic.

In a literary example, Prince Hamlet was horrified by his mother's rapid transition from widow's weeds to wedding gown. Hamlet felt that his mother's impulsive remarriage to his uncle weakened the political legacy from his father and threatened his own place in her heart.

Forty-year-old Harvey told us:

My father was a very successful businessman, and when he died, he left it all to my mother. He was dead for less than two years when my mother sold our home on Long Island, where I grew up, and bought an apartment in Manhattan for herself and the guy she finally married. He's ten years younger than she is. She couldn't move fast enough because he had to have a place in the city to entertain and be near the theaters and galleries and shops. I don't know where he lived before he met her. Every time my wife and I see him, he is wearing another designer jacket. My mother calls him her peacock! She never made a fuss over my dad. There goes my inheritance.

Thirty-five-year-old Bob reports:

My dad came over to my place looking really upset. He said now that he was remarried, the dream of his life was to buy a houseboat and would it be all right with me because it would have to come out of my inheritance. What could I say? It was embarrassing to me to have him ask my permission.

Some parents are deeply apologetic about spending their own hard-earned money on luxuries for themselves. They fear their children's disapproval. As an adult child, this role reversal may make you very uncomfortable.

Thirty-six-year-old Nancy told us:

My father didn't care what he looked like after my mother divorced him. He gained weight and didn't keep himself up and suddenly looked really old. I'd have to take him by the hand to go out to dinner with me. Other-

wise, he'd eat frozen food in front of the TV. But once that woman, Mary, found out he was available and went after him, he started to buy new clothes, joined a gym, bought a new car, and now he gets his hair styled. Of course, the dinners with me stopped. It's been spend, spend, spend, ever since they got together, and, since they married, she's moved him from the suburbs to an expensive condo in town. Every time I go there for brunch, they've bought a new piece of expensive furniture or are planning another vacation. Last month, he forgot my birthday, and, of course, he doesn't talk about buying me a new car anymore, the way he did right after the funeral.

BUT . . . WHAT IF I WERE IN MY PARENT'S PLACE?

Forty-year-old Linda says:

I've put a lot of my dreams on hold for my kids. It may sound strange, but I look forward very much to menopause and my postmenopause years. I will insist that things be different then. I'll finally have time and money for myself. My feeling that way is perfectly understandable to me. But my father and his wife are already at that stage, and I'm far less understanding of them. I don't know why that is. When they are busy spending time and money on their own needs, it annoys me greatly. I still think they should get most of their satisfaction from their rich, interesting relationships with me.

Linda has a different standard for herself and for her father and stepmother. She sees her children becoming adults as something that will liberate her, but she doesn't want to allow her parents the same freedom. She admits her bias, but she still wants it both ways.

WILL YOUR IRRESPONSIBLE PARENTS LEAVE A MESS?

Many adult children fear that their elderly parent is no longer able to think things through clearly. They worry that the new spouse will influence the parent in deciding how to distribute his or her property. Children also commonly fear that the death of the parent will change the relationship with the stepparent from cordial to combative.

Thirty-five-year-old Sarah tells us:

My mother always says, "Don't worry. My house will go to you children when I die." But we think there will be trouble about that with her husband if she dies first. It's a comfortable house, and he'll want to continue to live there. I tell her that he won't treat us right. She says, "No. You won't get cheated. I trust him." My mom hates confrontation and usually winds up saying, "Well, I won't be around, so it's one thing I don't have to handle."

Sarah's mom is engaging in some wishful thinking. By refusing to act now, she is leaving a big problem for her daughter. Sarah's mother needs to face up to the issue and make a real decision. One way the problem could be resolved is to suggest that Sarah's mother arrange to have the house sold on her death and the proceeds divided between her husband and her children. Of course, Sarah's stepdad needs to be in on the decision, and few mothers will look forward to such a discussion.

Another possibility is the creation of a trust into which the family home (and/or other real estate) could be put, with her mother's husband as the initial beneficiary and Sarah and her siblings as the final beneficiaries. Assuming Sarah's stepfather survives her mom, he would have the right to live in the home until his death. At that time, title would pass to Sarah and her siblings, and the trust would end.

With such an arrangement, if the stepdad wants to sell the house in order to buy something smaller or to move elsewhere, he must have the approval of the trustee. The trustee would be bound by the terms of the trust. If permission to sell is granted, the stepfather can't take the money and run. The proceeds of the sale and title to the new home remain in the irrevocable trust for the ultimate benefit of Sarah and her siblings.

The terms of the trust would prevent the stepfather from irresponsibly using the proceeds from the sale. The trust simply defers the benefit to Sarah and her siblings until her stepfather has passed away. Prior to his death, the arrangement allows Sarah's stepfather to remain in the house, subject to the terms of the trust.

WILL MY STEPPARENT EXPLOIT MY PARENT?

Many of the adult children we interviewed worried about passive parents, typically fathers, who, they felt, had been completely duped by their new spouses. From the adult children's point of view, their parents were being systematically exploited. They believed their parent eventually would be abandoned, in what amounted to a slow-motion bank robbery.

Barry, a fifty-year-old Vietnam vet, told us:

When I got back from the service, my parents were already divorced, and the house was gone, along with lots of my personal things. My mom had married a nice man. My dad had also married. . . . His new wife wasn't a nice person. She took Dad for all he had. She was just a money grabber. They were married for two years. She drained him, and that was it. She took off with her kids and all the stuff.

Such stories of predatory women stripping a father's wealth are told with a cynical laugh, as if the adult child were saying, "What do you expect of aging fathers?"

Forty-two year-old Frank told a similar story about his father being "cleaned out" financially by an attractive, younger woman. He added:

I keep remembering what Zsa Zsa Gabor always said: "I'm a good housekeeper. I marry a man. I keep his house."

Karen, thirty-two, recalled:

My dad's second wife was just a blip on the radar screen. . . . She lasted less than a year, and she ravaged him.

Some new spouses may, indeed, be predatory. If you are genuinely worried, speak to your parent about writing a prenuptial agreement. Keep in mind that your counsel is more likely to be heard if your motivation is clearly to protect your parent's assets for his/her own enjoyment, not for your benefit.

HOW DO YOU TALK ABOUT MONEY WITH YOUR PARENT?

Adult children often find it embarrassing and painful to show concern about such seemingly childish issues as loss of parental love, loss of importance to one's parent, and, especially, loss of family money. Most adults don't admit to such feelings—even to themselves.

We don't need Sigmund Freud, however, to remind us that money symbolizes many other important issues, including love, esteem, and preference for the recipient. If you are fortunate enough to have parents who have always been clear about inheritance, you can be fairly certain they will inform you of any changes. If your parent has *never* been clear about who will inherit what or is simply very private about money matters, then you are likely to be left up in the air after he or she remarries.

If your parent has a history of being impulsive about money, it is unlikely that you will be able to change that pattern. On the other hand, if you can tolerate some awkwardness and the probability of failure, why not open the discussion?

Practically speaking, how do you broach concerns about finances and inheritance with your parent? Often, it quickly becomes obvious that the parent is in no mood to answer questions about financial matters. Sensitive children may feel that it is inappropriate to bring up such mundane, even unpleasant, business when the parent is obviously experiencing great joy. It's all too easy to decide that the subject is taboo. Given all these constraints, how can you move forward?

Your first task is to decide the risk-to-reward ratio of initiating the discussion with your parent. How much can you actually accomplish and at what psychic cost? Before you say a word to your parent, gather information from people whose judgment you trust, such as your spouse and your siblings. Question friends who have been in similar circumstances.

Consider all the possible outcomes. In addition, think hard about the best means of communicating about this topic. The means can determine the result. You may write to your parent, as well as have a face-to-face meeting or a telephone conversation.

Sometimes, writing is better because it tends to be less confrontational than a conversation. Putting your concerns in writing has the advantage of giving your parent space and time to think and reflect. A conversation is more likely to evoke a quick, defensive reaction. A letter is less likely to make your parent feel that he or she is being put on the spot and is expected to answer immediately.

If a letter seems too formal, you may want to try an e-mail. But e-mails are rarely the best medium for setting a carefully calibrated emotional tone. If you do use e-mail, you probably want to arrange for a follow-up meeting or, at least, to schedule a telephone call if you are far away.

For the adult child, taking action—by asking questions that you believe to be polite, reasonable, and appropriate—allows you to avoid regret that you stood by passively. Unless you seize the moment, it can be lost forever. If your parent replies coolly or angrily to your questions, the tension may well be temporary. You need to make a judgment about his or her likely response in advance. Is your parent someone who holds a grudge? Is your parent someone who vents and quickly regains his or her composure, with no lingering consequences?

One bonus of expressing your concerns honestly to your parent may be a better relationship with your parent and stepparent. Your questions and your parent's answers may put the subject to rest, so that everyone concerned can get on with life. In the long run, respectful candor is probably your best strategy.

If you are angry with your parent about finances and don't deal with your anger directly, you will probably dump it on your stepparent. Directing your anger at your stepparent won't make anyone happy. What about the image you are presenting to your stepparent? Sure, displacing your anger may give you a certain infantile satisfaction that you can make your parent and stepparent as unhappy as you are. Still, if your parent's new marriage is here to stay, you will pay the price for your behavior in the long run. If the marriage ends, and your parent sees you as the cause of his or her marital breakup, there could be a permanent rift between you and your parent.

Ultimately, before you speak, you must decide whether you will get enough financial information to make any resulting alienation from your parent worthwhile. What specific information do you want? Role-play with a trusted person as a dress rehearsal to the actual discussion. This is an especially useful exercise if there are questions you are unsure about and you don't like surprises.

If you decide the discussion is worth the trouble it may cause, next ask yourself if there is a better time than the present to broach the subject. There probably isn't. We strongly recommend, however, that your *first* communication with your parent about his or her decision to remarry be congratulatory or at least respectful. If you don't think you can pull that off in person, do it in writing or over the phone.

WHEN DO YOU HAVE THE CONVERSATION?

The best time to raise financial questions with parents is *before* the wedding, when they are thinking about their changing responsibilities to their existing family and their new spouse. You may be able to raise issues that are important to you that your parent hasn't considered. If nothing else, your parent will know how you perceive things and may take your concerns into account in planning for the future. At least, you will feel that you had a fair hearing and weren't simply presented with a *fait accompli*.

If your parent suddenly announces that he/she has already gotten married, it's best to raise your questions sooner rather than later. Nonetheless, you can open a discussion about plans for inheritance at any time. We talked to people who had successfully raised the issue years after the parent's remarriage. In fact, if your parent and stepparent made their financial arrangements years ago, it may be easier to share them with you now because they have had time to adjust to their own differences on financial matters.

THE SINGLE BEST QUESTION TO ASK:
DO YOU HAVE A PRENUPTIAL AGREEMENT?

If you have siblings, consult them and jointly decide to appoint the most diplomatic, articulate, or business-minded sibling to initiate the talk about finances with your parent. What one sibling would make a mercenary interrogation, another may be able to turn into a low-key, if not routine, business meeting.

The safest question to ask is whether your parent has consulted with a lawyer about protecting his/her property before getting remarried. If the wedding hasn't yet taken place, you might say: "Mom/Dad, I know you're busy getting ready for this big change in your life, and I hope you won't be offended at my asking whether you have a prenuptial agreement." Asking your parent about plans for a prenuptial agreement (called an antenuptial agreement in some states) will elicit one of three probable answers: "Yes," "No," or "None of your business." You can expect one of the same three responses if you ask the question after the marriage has taken place.

What do you risk by asking the question? It depends. Once again, consider whether your parent has been frank in the past about inheritance and other financial matters. If so, the risk isn't great, because he/she doesn't regard the subject as "off-limits." On the other hand, if you already know that money is an area that your parent regards as absolutely private, he or she is not going to want to talk about a prenuptial agreement or any other financial arrangement. Some people would no more talk about their financial affairs than fling open their bedroom door. In any case, especially if you are tactless, your parent may be insulted and feel that you are inappropriately trying to play the parent role. That parent may feel you are being condescending by suggesting that he/she has helplessly fallen into the clutches of an acquisitive new spouse. In fact, *you* may be considered acquisitive for asking.

Still, even a terse "yes" can ease your mind. At least you know that a lawyer will explain the standard legal issues of living trusts and assignment of property involved in prenuptial agreements to your parent. A little anxiety at the outset may result in enormous peace of mind when you discover that your parent has already protected him- or herself.

In the best-case scenario, your dad or mom may welcome your opening the subject. It could lead to an in-depth discussion of plans for distributing property and investments that wouldn't otherwise take place. In the words of Wayne Gretsky, "You miss one hundred percent of the shots you don't take." Still, here's a word of caution. Responding to your parent's "Yes, I have signed a prenuptial" by asking to read the document could produce real discomfort. Don't do it without an invitation.

How your parent's remarriage will affect your inheritance is rarely clear at the outset. On the negative side, it may dilute or decrease the amount you receive because more of your parent's assets will go to the new spouse. On the other hand, it might actually result in your getting a larger inheritance than if your parent had not remarried. If your parent becomes healthier and more pro- ductive as a result of the love and support of a new spouse, there may be gains for you that you never anticipated. The data show that married men tend to live longer and healthier lives (the data about women are more ambiguous) during which their wealth may grow. Remember, happiness never hurt anyone. Besides, stepparents sometimes leave special bequests from their own assets to stepchildren to whom they feel especially close.

There are many possibilities, and the outcome is seldom predictable. Adult children may find themselves relieved of the obligation to support a parent with very limited resources because a new spouse takes up the slack. One likely downside: However much you finally inherit, your inheritance is likely to be delayed because of the new marriage. Your inheritance will probably follow that of the surviving spouse.

GIFTS AND BEQUESTS: WILL MY NEW STEPSIBLINGS GET TOO MUCH?

The fear that stepsiblings will get more than their fair share of the couple's property is one of the most pernicious problems of adult stepfamilies. It is prac- tically impossible to devise a formula that is truly fair when deciding the exact amount that should be disbursed to each adult child, stepchild, grandchild, and stepgrandchild. This holds true for Christmas, Hanukkah, birthday, and wedding gifts, too. What is truly fair and equitable is often hard to determine. Let's also remember that in those instances when a stepchild has been legally adopted, he or she usually gets gifts comparable to those given to the biological children.

In our experience, past behavior is the best predictor of future behavior. Par- ents usually continue the same pattern of gift giving after they remarry as before. If your parent came into the marriage with a good deal of money and has always been generous, he or she will probably continue that pattern. The parent who had less before the marriage will probably continue to give more modest gifts to his/her adult children and grandchildren. Sometimes, the more generous partner may influence his or her new spouse to follow suit. Of course, when your parents retire, they may need to scale back their gift giving.

Because the remarried couple may be sensitive about differences in financial status, they may make monetary gifts "under the table" to their biological children. These gifts are usually given according to a tradition set by the original family, in which a wedding, say, or the birth of new baby was always marked with a generous gift. As an adult child, you may not know exactly how much a brother and stepsister got for their birthdays and whether it was more than you received. In some stepfamilies, parents give simple token gifts on holidays, say, when the whole family is present, even as checks of different sizes are being sent through the mails.

The longer the marriage lasts, the more likely the couple will merge their resources. This may mean a move toward greater equalization of gifts to biological and stepchildren. In terms of inheritance, many remarried couples decide to divide the property acquired during the present marriage equally among all the children, biological and step. Usually, when there is a prenuptial agreement, it has been written to preserve property owned prior to the current marriage for the benefit of the biological children. Depending on the age of the remarrying couple, the bulk of each person's assets may have been accumulated before the current marriage and, thus, eventually would flow to his or her biological children.

WHAT ABOUT RECIPROCITY?

One of the basic difficulties with initiating a conversation about inheritance with your parent is the one-sided nature of the discussion. It's embarrassing to ask if and how your aging parent plans to provide for you after he/she dies. The embarrassment is natural because the conversation ignores your parent's needs and focuses exclusively on yours. By the time you are an adult, you are aware of the importance of reciprocity in all your relationships. Yet, this conversation about inheritance seems to lack mutuality.

You should tell your parent how uncomfortable the discussion's lack of reciprocity makes you feel. And you should do more than that. In fact, now is a good time to think long and hard about whether you have given something back to your parent and how you might do so in the future.

Perhaps, you are newly aware of how little time you have spent with your parent and how much your attention would mean to him or her now. Or, depending on your circumstances, you can let an aging parent know that you intend to help out should he/she run out of resources. Be warned that talking about inheritance with a parent with whom you have a difficult relationship generally causes old hurts and angers to resurface. These feelings will have to be managed by both of you if you want a constructive outcome.

ESSENTIAL ITEMS TO DISCUSS WITH YOUR PARENT

If you do open a discussion about inheritance with Mom or Dad, what are the other essential elements you want to clarify after the question about the "prenup"? Here are some additional items that should be on the agenda:

- Has your parent made a new will since he/she has remarried? Be appreciative if the response is yes and tactful if it is no.

- If the answer is no, it's a good time to let your parent know that you *would* appreciate his/her making a will. In that way, all the survivors can carry out your parent's specific wishes for distributing his or her possessions.

- Is there anything that your parent wants to tell you about helping his/her surviving spouse, if your parent should die first?

- This is a good occasion for a discussion of reciprocity. What financial aid or physical assistance does your parent anticipate needing from you? What do you feel you can offer?

APPROACHING YOUR PARENT

In this chapter, we have looked at how adult children feel about their parents' and stepparents' financial arrangements. Often, they feel shocked, even angry. We have recommended that direct discussion between parent and child is very much in order, albeit very difficult. We have tried to suggest the best approaches for discussing these very touchy topics with your parent.

Some adult children will be shocked to learn that they don't own their parent's money. The parent's remarriage may have shattered their great expectations of an inheritance. If this is the case, acknowledge, if only to yourself, that this possible change will take some getting used to, as well as some serious thought. Then, talk to your parent. Think about what you hope will emerge from such a conversation. Decide what you really need to know about your potential inheritance and how to ask the right questions with the least chance of hurting or angering your parent. Run your questions past your spouse or siblings.

If you haven't already done so, read the preceding chapter about finances from the parent's point of view. It offers useful glimpses into the mind of remarrying parents and their spouses. That chapter also may provide insights into the process that your own parent is going through as he/she considers the financial consequences of late-in-life love and remarriage. After you've done all those things, take courage and have that talk with Dad or Mom.

In the next chapter, we'll tackle another emotionally charged subject: how the couples and their adult children feel when a parent is involved in a new romantic and sexual relationship.

CHAPTER 13

Love Is Great the Second (or Third) Time Around, But Should the Old Folks Be Doing It?

In this chapter, romance, intimacy, and sexuality raise their lovely heads. The remarrieds are looking forward to a new life full of love and happiness. As we have already seen, they believe that the kids, since they are grown, will not make much of an issue of this new relationship; they are too busy with their own adult lives.

The older couple may joke about how happy the kids will be to get the newly marrieds off their hands. The remarrieds think the kids, of all people, should understand their joy at finding each other. They should be thrilled that Mom or Dad has found this fulfilling, new relationship.

HONEYMOON MODE

When the new couple is still in honeymoon mode, the adult children often have difficulty, as we noted earlier, dealing with the romantic and sexual aspects of their parent's new life. It's a mirror image of the family's situation a few decades ago. Then, the children were entering young adulthood, and the parents were the ones having a hard time dealing with the idea that the youngster was old enough for intimacy and entitled to a sex life.

The parents had something short of two decades to anticipate and prepare themselves for the eventual sexual blossoming of their children. They knew all along that they were awaiting the inevitable. Nonetheless, dealing with offspring who followed their hearts (or their libidos) and became sexually active was often hard on the parents.

The children, for their part, chose not to think about their parents as sexually active with each other. Nor did they ever anticipate they'd have to deal with their parents' sexual relationship with a stranger. Even when divorce or death opened new possibilities, the adult children certainly didn't expect to see their parent fall passionately in love. As growing children, they felt they had a divine right to take any romantic and/or sexual partner they chose. That, however, did nothing to prepare them for their parent's later-in-life love affair.

Since one's parents' sex life seems almost universally unthinkable, many children do just that. They bury that whole idea deep in their unconscious. Yes, maybe Mom and Dad used to do it, but that was years ago, and then mostly so they could have children. In fact, children of all ages cling to the myth that their biological parents probably haven't had sex since they were conceived. The biological parents may have so protected their sexual privacy that they inadvertently helped keep the myth alive.

The idea of older folks getting married is fine, even "adorable," when they are someone else's parents. Yet, when *your* older parent turns up with a new love, the thought can be downright appalling. Who can think of older people having sex? The young often can't imagine such a thing and don't care to, besides.

Still, older people do indeed have sex and more often than their children might have guessed. In 1999, AARP (formerly the American Association of Retired Persons) studied 1,400 people forty-five years of age and older. They found that 60 percent of those aged forty-five to fifty-nine reported having sex once a week or more. Among those seventy-five and older, 25 percent also said they had sex that often.*

Other studies concur. In 1998, 1,292 men and women in their sixties through eighties were surveyed nationwide. Half the participants over sixty reported having sex at least once a month. And this was not joyless sex. More than 70 percent reported that their sexual encounters were as "emotionally satisfying as when they were in their forties."** Despite the stereotype of older men dependent on Viagra, that same study revealed that "most seniors are satisfied with their sex lives without artificial aids."

Still more evidence: A 1990 report in the *Archives of Internal Medicine* stated that "nearly 74 percent of married men over sixty remain sexually active, as do 56 percent of married women."† Studies show that seniors in good health tend to have sex more often than those in poor health. So, it is highly likely that vigorous seniors who remarry—and active, healthy seniors are the ones who usually do—enjoy a reasonably active sex life. Ready access to the little blue pill (i.e., Viagra) no doubt increases the number of older people having sex.

FROM THE REMARRIEDS' POINT OF VIEW

For the newlyweds, romance is just as sweet—sometimes even sweeter—when it arrives late in life. The surprise of new love at a time in life when romantic possibilities have often been discounted only enhances the delight of older lovers.

Cecily, age sixty-nine, told us:

I never expected to fall in love again. I wasn't looking for it, because I didn't see it happening to me. When I met Jack, and when we fell in love, I felt almost light-headed. I couldn't wait for him to call me each day. It was like being nineteen all over again. He is a very attractive man. He keeps himself in good shape, and he is very sensual, besides. Our sex life is better than when I was younger. We don't have to worry about getting pregnant. We're monogamous, so we don't think much about AIDS, either. So sex is fun and unencumbered. We don't have to worry about getting up in the middle of the night with little kids, so we can sleep later if we want.

I think it was a little difficult for our kids to see us feeling so attracted to one another. But we're both very private people, so we are quite reserved that way in front of family and friends. We do hold hands sometimes, but I think everyone can deal with that. Or at least, they can learn to deal with that. After all, we feel happy when we see our kids being affectionate with one another. There's so much divorce these days that seeing them holding hands always reassures us.

Louis, age seventy-six, described his situation:

Ann and I have been married for three years. I've never been happier. My first marriage wasn't great. We stayed together for many reasons, but I was very unhappy for a long time. We hadn't had sex for years, and that was a trouble spot between us. I considered divorce off and on, but somehow that seemed like an immense ordeal to put everyone, including my kids, through.

When my wife died, I was sad, but, I confess, also relieved to have the possibility of a new life. I wasn't thinking about remarrying, just having a stress-free life, doing whatever I wanted. When Ann and I met, it was unbelievable. We had many of the same interests and values. She's damn attractive. And there was an amazing chemistry between us.

At first, I didn't think I wanted to get married again, given my past experience. But, eventually, we were spending so much time together, it didn't make sense not to. We are best friends and best companions. We love doing things and going places together, just being together. Our sex life is unbelievable, better than I ever thought possible, not only at my age, but at any age. Sometimes, I have to pinch myself to be sure this is all real.

I think my kids don't know quite what to make of their old man, in love in his old age. But, to tell you the truth, I don't really care how they feel about it. I've never been happier, and I think I am damn lucky to have this so late in life. I guess "better late than never" is how I think about it. I hope they understand and are happy for me, but if they're not, then being happy about this myself is enough for me. I sacrificed my own happiness for them during my first marriage to their mother. Now, I feel this is my time, and I plan to enjoy it, regardless of how my kids feel about it.

In both these cases, as with most of the people we interviewed, romance and sexual intimacy were just as satisfying, or more so, the second—or third or fourth—time around. Most of the participants in our research were delighted and a bit surprised at falling in love again and at feeling such strong sexual attraction and fulfillment.

IT'S MY TURN NOW

Louis struck us as somewhat defensive about his newfound happiness with Ann. He seemed to sense that his children were not as ecstatic as he was about his late-in-life love and active sex life. Yet, he was adamant about putting his own emotional and sexual needs first, after years of giving his parental responsibilities top priority. His somewhat defiant tone—he is saying, in effect, "I deserve to be happy after years of sacrificing for my children and that's what I intend to be"—reminded us somewhat of a teenager declaring his independence over parental objections. Still, like any other emotionally healthy adult, Louis is taking responsibility for his own happiness—and without causing his children any harm that we could see.

Many of the remarried parents we interviewed seemed oblivious to their children's attitudes toward their new love life. The most recently married couples, in particular, rarely mentioned their children's reaction to them as sexual beings. They were so caught up in their own happiness and sexual satisfaction that they simply weren't attending to any cues their adult children or stepchildren were sending. Some did notice the raised eyebrows of the younger generation but simply chose to ignore them.

The couples who were beyond the "honeymoon glow" seemed to take their sex lives as their due but made little fuss about it. They saw sex as a private matter that didn't concern their children, any more than their adult children's sex lives concerned them. They tended to treat their feelings for each other as a given, though not routine, aspect of their lives. This seemed to discourage any undue comment on it by their children or anyone else.

FROM THE CHILDREN'S POINT OF VIEW

Many of the adult children we spoke to had some quite negative feelings about their remarried parent's romantic and sexual life. Of course, most couldn't help noticing the signs of mutual attraction and affection between their parent and his or her new love. When that occurred, they had varied reactions.

Edith, whose seventy-two-year-old father had remarried, told us:

My dad remarried about four years after my mom died. By that time, we had gotten over the "please don't remarry" stage and were hoping he'd find someone to be with. Of course, we weren't quite prepared for what that all meant. So, when we first saw them in the "honeymoon phase," we were a little embarrassed. It also hurt me a little—I know that's silly—to see him in love with another woman who wasn't my mother. But I kept telling myself I couldn't have it both ways. I think he is better off than being alone.

On the other hand, forty-year-old Bob was thrilled with his remarried seventy-two-year-old father's interest in sex:

When my mother and dad lived together, their twin beds were two feet apart. The first thing I noticed when my dad remarried was that the beds were pushed together. I thought, Go, Dad. *It gives me hope.*

Not all adult stepchildren are as willing or able as Bob and Edith to deal with the realities of their parent's new romance, including their own understandable ambivalence toward it. As long as one's own parents are together, most children, including adult children, don't pay much attention to sexual cues between them. We've watched our parents hold hands for so many years, we hardly notice it anymore. Even when they are physically affectionate in front of us, we tend to deny the reality of their sexual relationship.

MOM, PLEASE CLOSE THE BEDROOM DOOR

When a parent introduces a *new* romantic partner into the family, however, the child's view of the parent as nonsexual is challenged. The parent's new relationship forces the adult children to acknowledge that their parent has sexual needs and appetites. That recognition may be difficult for adult children, especially if their other biological parent is still living or if the other parent has been dead only a short time. Most of the children who spoke about their parent's new love showed some degree of ambivalence.

Nelly, whose mother remarried at age seventy-three, was one of the few who thought the lack of obvious passion between her mother and new stepfather, was a danger sign. Nelly said:

> *My mum married Bob when she was seventy-three. He's a few years older. They seem pleasant to one another, but I've never seen them kiss or touch each other, except at the wedding. I'm a little worried about that. My mother is a wealthy woman, and I hope Bob has not just married her for her money.*

How demonstrative should one dare to be in front of one's children? That is a decision every couple must make for themselves. There is no universally agreed-upon formula for what is appropriate. It depends on many things: the couple's own comfort level, their sense of privacy, their family norms, their culture, whether they are shy or extroverted, the occasion, and much, much more. For the adult children, the choices are few: Get used to it and/or butt out. Besides, grandparents who love each other are positive role models for their grandchildren.

WHEN DAD MARRIES A YOUNGER WOMAN

We saw the greatest ambivalence—and the most outright hostility—expressed by children whose father had married the proverbial "younger woman." We had only two cases of a mother marrying a much younger man, and in those situations, too, the children had strong feelings.

When the "younger woman" had originally appeared as the "other woman" in an extramarital affair, tensions ran particularly high. Then, the marrying couple had to show unusual patience and forbearance to overcome the predictable resistance of the adult children, who tended to side with the mother they felt had been ill-used.

The surging emotions triggered by affairs-transformed-into-marriages probably warrant a volume of their own. Here, let us simply acknowledge that a marriage based on an affair, especially one that led to the parent's divorce, sets off fireworks in virtually every stepfamily thus created. Time and maturity, including emotional generosity, and letting it go are needed here in spades. Tact and Tacking skills once again!

WHEN YOUR STEPMOTHER IS YOUR OWN AGE

In our research, the greater the age difference between the parent and his or her new spouse, the more complex the situation tended to become. When older men married women of childbearing age, the issue of sex became even more emotionally charged, because the adult children had to face the prospect of new half-siblings. This, in turn, raised the possibility of jealousy about the amount of time and affection the father directed toward the new offspring. Adult biological children frequently complained that their father had not lavished that much attention on them when they were young. Some sarcastically criticized their father for "having his own grandchild" and expressed fears that their own children would not receive their fair share of Grandpa's attention.

Money often became an issue, as well. This concern frequently took the form of questioning the impact the new wife and child would have on the adult children's (and grandchildren's) inheritance. A father's post-affair remarriage, with the prospect of his having more children by the other woman, tended to set off all Five Furies. Fear of Abandonment and Isolation, Fidelity to Family, Favoritism, Finances, and Focus on the Self jostled one another for first place in line.

WHEN YOUR GRANDPA HAS A NEW BABY

In an earlier chapter, one grown son talked about his reaction to his father and young wife's new baby. This adult child from the earlier marriage was so distressed he couldn't even call the newborn by his given name. Instead, he kept referring to his new half-brother as "It." After several years, the adult son grudgingly allowed that his young half-brother (who was the same age as his own child) wasn't the one who should be held responsible. In this instance, it was the adult son's wife who encouraged her husband to accept his new sibling, both as a younger brother and as an important new age-mate for their own children.

Nancy, age forty-three, described her situation this way:

My father married Zena, someone he'd been having an affair with for several years before we heard anything about it. My mother didn't want a divorce, but he insisted. He said he wasn't in love with my mother anymore and that he loved Zena. My parents went into counseling and all that stuff, but nothing made any difference. He eventually moved out, and Zena moved in with him. You can imagine how we all felt—my mother, my two brothers, and me. We just hated her. She's much younger than he is. In fact, she's closer to my age than to his. It's clear that she plays the sexual card with him. It's sort of disgusting. Well, I mean embarrassing.

When my father married Zena, we thought that was the end of the world. What we didn't know was that that was just the beginning. It really felt like the true end of the world when he announced that Zena was pregnant. It seemed like he just killed off our family, and now he was starting a new family. And, if you can imagine it, he actually expected us to be happy about it. Obviously, we weren't.

It's hard for me to think of Irenee as my little sister, even my half-sister. She's actually younger than my own kids. Besides, she's a terrible spoiled brat. Of course, it's not her fault. My father dotes on her, so what can you expect? Whatever she wants, she gets. When we were kids, he didn't treat us that way. If I wanted a new dress for a party, my mother had to wheedle the money out of him or take it out of her household money. Of course, my parents didn't have too much money when we were growing up. A few years ago, my father inherited some money from my grandfather, so he's feeling easier about money, I guess. I don't think there'll be anything left when he dies. That sounds awful. I don't mean it the way that sounded. But, after all, we're his kids, too.

We see all Five Furies at work in Nancy's account. Since her father has established a new life, complete with a new baby, it is unlikely that Nancy will ever be able to go back to the "old days," real or imagined, before her parents divorced. For Nancy, the best strategy is to *reframe* the situation. Instead of viewing the birth of Irenee as the "end of the world," Nancy would do better to try to think of it as the beginning of a new, larger world, or at least a new and larger family, with more possibilities for family bonds of love and support.

Nancy may never become close friends with Zena, but Zena is not only her father's wife. She is, perhaps even more importantly, the mother of Nancy's half-sister. Regardless of whether her father remains married to Zena, Nancy and Irenee will be half-sisters forever. Nancy can continue to view Irenee through the lens of the Furies, or she can try to open her own and her children's hearts to Irenee. If she succeeds, everybody wins.

A NEW VARIETY OF SIBLING RIVALRY

If Irenee is close to Nancy's children in age, then thinking of her as one of their generation may ease Nancy's strong feelings of competition with Irenee. Psychologically moving Irenee into the next generation, and out of Nancy's cohort, may help eliminate the sibling rivalry that seems to torment Nancy. Developing a warmer relationship with Irenee, who is not responsible for her father's actions, will help Nancy increase her self-regard as a generous, wise adult, someone who can practice transformation through wisdom. In this way, the Saving Graces can help the members of the adult stepfamily become a closer, more integrated family unit with authentic bonds, not just genealogical relationships.

As we have said before, the adult stepfamily is a system. Nancy's acceptance of Irenee is bound to have an effect—probably a positive one—on Zena. In addition, Nancy's dad may be starry-eyed at the moment, but he is probably not blind. He surely senses Nancy's angry, envious feelings toward his newest child. As parents, we all feel uncomfortable with people—even our own relatives—who don't like our children or don't treat them very well. Rejection of our children is even harder to bear when other family members are the ones rejecting them.

Any residual guilt Nancy's dad has about the divorce may make it hard for him to demand that Nancy act congenially toward Zena, or even to expect it. But that's not the case with Irenee. So, Nancy can expect her relationship with her father to improve a notch or two when she lets go of some of her jealousy, anger, and preoccupation with self. Nancy might also bear in mind Saving Grace #1—a parent's fulfilling remarriage often leads to that parent's increased capacity to nurture all of his or her children and grandchildren. Nancy and her children could reap all sorts of emotional and other benefits from a happier remarried father—as long as Nancy's behavior doesn't create a new barrier between her dad and herself.

EMBARRASSMENT: WHAT WILL THE GRANDCHILDREN THINK?

When the adult children have preadolescent or adolescent children of their own, the grandparents' sex life can cause considerable confusion and embarrassment. Some adult children complained to us that their parent's sexual "acting out" came at the worst possible time—just as they were trying to teach their own children about responsible sex and/or sex limited to the context of marriage.

Although the next chapter addresses many other aspects of unmarried cohabitation, let's look at the sexual implications of that choice now. We found that when Grandpa or Grandma was living with a new love without benefit of marriage, that was the most difficult situation for adult children to explain to their own children. Major family fireworks are likely if Dad's younger girlfriend becomes pregnant before they are married, or if they simply decide to raise the child outside of marriage. Predictably, adult children who were most concerned about this were those with a strong commitment to traditional religion.

Rosa, a forty-year-old daughter, explained her concerns about her cohabiting father this way:

I have a fifteen-year-old daughter and a seventeen-year-old son. We have brought our kids up within a religious household. We go to church every Sunday. Most of our friends come from our parish. When my father left my mother, we were all humiliated. Now, he's moved in with his lady friend.

My husband and I have worked very hard to teach our kids that sex is part of marriage. In my book, living with someone without being married is wrong. It isn't easy to bring up kids today and guide them through all the dangers of adolescence. My father's behavior isn't making it any easier for us. My kids ask me how come Grandpa is living with Jill, and they're not married. I don't really know what to say. They ask if Grandpa's behavior is sinful. I feel caught. How can I say that to my children about my father? But how can I teach them not to do the same thing when he is setting such a bad example? Since we grew up in this town, my priest knows my whole family. My father doesn't go to church anymore, but I'm embarrassed when our priest asks how my family is doing. I guess I'm really angry that my father is putting us all in this embarrassing situation.

For Rosa and other adult children from conservative and religious backgrounds, a parent's sexual activity outside of marriage can pose real problems. Still, that does not mean that parents must engage in hypocritical behavior or feel forced to lie about their commitment to a new love. *Commitment* is probably the operative word in that sentence. Divorced or widowed parents who have casual sexual relationships may want to be more circumspect, in light of the distress they may cause their children.

Within healthy families, we believe, honesty and integrity always trump embarrassment and differences in values. In fact, an open family discussion

about the importance of respecting other peoples' values and trying to understand them would probably help everyone live more easily in our increasingly
diverse, but highly interdependent, world.

That doesn't mean the adult children have to condone their parent's decision
to live with their partner without being married. Learning to disagree with other
family members, but to love them nonetheless, is an important lesson we all
need to learn. Acceptance and tolerance of other people's behavior, beliefs, values, and customs can go a long way toward creating a better, more peaceful
world. Moreover, these lessons are best learned (and taught) within the safe
confines of the family circle.

When a grandparent is living in a committed relationship with someone he
or she loves, grandchildren can come to grips with the fact that their parents'
values differ from those of their grandparent. The grandchildren are most likely
to do this if their parents demonstrate that they can do the same.

A grandparent who parades a series of casual romantic relationships in
front of the grandchildren is a different story. That grandparent needs to consider seriously how that model of casual sex will affect the grandchildren,
possibly undermining what the parents of these grandchildren are trying to
accomplish.

David, a forty-eight-year-old, explained his concerns about his mother:

*My mother is a wonderful woman. She and my dad had a good life
together. They raised me and my four brothers and kept a happy home. We
were all wiped out when my dad got pancreatic cancer and died rather
quickly. He was still young, only sixty. My mother was left all alone, since
my brothers and I are all married, and we are scattered all over the place
geographically.*

*About two years ago, she met Earl, and they started to go together. I
didn't really expect my mother to take up with anyone after my father
died, but I guess she was lonely, all by herself. At any rate, Earl asked her
to marry him. My mother said she didn't want to get married. Earl is close
to eighty, and my mother told us she couldn't go through the agony of
nursing another husband and watching him die.*

*Instead, she moved in with Earl. Well, that was a shock! We couldn't
imagine our mother living with someone she wasn't married to. I'm having a hell of a time explaining that one to my sixteen-year-old daughter,
who keeps saying she thinks it's "cool." I certainly don't want my daughter to move in with some guy and just live with him. But I don't feel I can
tell my mother that she's a bad example for my daughter. Of course, she
has more judgment than a sixteen-year-old, so it's not exactly the same*

thing. I guess the fact that my mother lives far away helps, in a funny way. We don't have to deal with it on a daily basis.

The principal Fury that besets David is Focus on Self. He seems to have little concern for his mother's happiness or welfare, only how her behavior is having a negative impact on him and his ability to deal with a teenage daughter.

There are several ways that David might cope with this situation. He can candidly acknowledge to his daughter that he doesn't condone his mother's behavior, even though many other older couples are making the same choice. In fact, there has been a marked increase in older, unmarried couples living together, as we shall see in Chapter 14. While David doesn't have to agree with his mother's decision, he should know that it is no longer unusual. People's views of acceptable behavior change, but romance, love, and sex go on—whether people are young or old, married or single.

SEX ISN'T THE ONLY REASON SENIORS LIVE TOGETHER

David should also point out the difference between young, inexperienced people deciding to live together and mature people making the same decision. Seniors may choose to live together for a variety of reasons besides sex: love, companionship, safety, financial security, lower taxes, and concerns about health and health insurance, for starters. Religion, of course, makes a difference, too—the more religious a couple is, the less likely they are to live together without marrying, whatever their ages.

Although the decision to cohabit may seem much the same whether the couple is young or older, the factors that propel this choice are often as different as spring and autumn. David may choose to point out some of those differences, including the financial needs of a senior, if he thinks that will help discourage his daughter from following her grandmother's example. David may have to use his wits to make a compelling argument to his daughter, but he has plenty of ammunition. Besides, using your wits to keep your children safe is what much of parenting is all about. Whatever he says to his daughter, he should do it without being disrespectful toward his mother and her choice. As we said before, sexual norms and mores may change, but honesty and compassion—those absolute ground rules—don't.

In sum, late loves often sweep into seniors' lives with the force of a tsunami. Widowed or divorced parents may have given up any expectation of romance and sexual pleasure at this point in life, only to be delightfully surprised by falling in love again.

Almost all children have trouble acknowledging their parents as sexual beings. When a new love enters a divorced or widowed parent's life, the children may be forced to confront an issue they have kept safely buried in their unconscious since childhood. The adult child's confusion and mixed emotions can provoke many, if not all, of the Five Furies, but compassion and candor can turn them into Saving Graces.

As we have already seen, some seniors decide love is enough, and it need not include marriage. In the next chapter, we shall look more closely at cohabitation and how it affects adult stepfamilies.

---

*http://www.my.webmd.com/content/article/1687.50188?page=1.

**http://www.hollandsentinel.com/stories/092998/new_oldfolks.html. "The Truth: Old Folks Still Have Sex."

†http://www.my.webmd.com/content/article1687.50701. Blum, Jeffrey. "Can Good Sex Keep You Young?"

CHAPTER 14

When Couples Don't Marry

Some of us are old enough to remember when sex between people who weren't married was illegal and unmarried couples had to be as furtive as spies. In those days, there were a great many Mr. and Mrs. Smiths checking into the hotels and motels of America. Because of movie and television censorship, even married couples were never shown occupying the same bed, and the words *virgin* and *pregnant* were banned in mainstream media until the late 1950s. Happily, most adults today don't swoon at the thought of grownups falling in love and pairing off, with or without marriage.

It has become increasingly commonplace for older, unmarried couples to travel together, to socialize together with friends, and to live together (or almost together). The U.S. Census Bureau reports that the number of unmarried people sixty-five and older who were cohabiting rose 73 percent from 1990 to 1999.[1] Nor are seniors the only ones deciding to live together outside of marriage. In fact, today 5.5 million unmarried couples of all ages are living together in the United States, more than eleven times as many as in 1960.[2]

Of course, there are still communities that frown on cohabitation, just as they frown on divorce. Condemned as immoral, unmarried couples who belong to these societies must either leave them or find ways to keep their relationships more or less hidden. In most of the United States and most of Europe, however, the social tide continues to flow in the other direction, toward increasing acceptance of couples who choose not to formalize their relationship.

WHY DON'T THEY GET MARRIED?

Sometimes, when an older unmarried couple is asked why they haven't tied the knot, they say something like, "Why should we go through that hassle? We're doing fine just as we are." Here, for example is what Hilda, age seventy-eight, said:

People are always asking us if we're married and why we don't get married. What nonsense! They should look at it the other way around. Let them go and ask married couples why they bothered to get married. Are they better off than we are? We think not. A marriage license would only complicate our lives. Things are much more flexible this way. We both have children and grandchildren. We have our own homes and our own bank accounts. We can deal with our children and their inheritances in our own ways. Should one of us die, it will be clear who will get what. This way, we can stay together as long as we choose to, and we can travel together when we want. But, sometimes, we both like to stay separate for a while. Of course, there are a few old fogies who say we are "living in sin." What's sinful about a loving, lasting, faithful relationship like ours? If we're living in sin, they're living in the nineteenth century!

Intimate, ongoing relationships between divorced or widowed men and women often resemble marriages in everything except legal status. The families of such couples are, in effect, stepfamilies. Evidence of how commonplace such arrangements have become is the acceptance of the long-term relationship between former first lady Jackie Kennedy Onassis and her late-in-life love, Maurice Templesman, who was still legally married to someone else.

WHEN MEDICAL REASONS MAKE MARRIAGE IMPOSSIBLE

The increased prevalence of debilitating, irreversible, long-term diseases, such as Alzheimer's, Parkinson's disease, and others, raises many moral, as well as medical, questions. If one spouse, for example, has to be institutionalized for a long-term, irreversible disease like Alzheimer's, what is "appropriate" or "inappropriate" for the other healthy, vigorous spouse? Here's a story that illustrates the anguish that can accompany this increasingly common problem:

Esther and Henry had been married for forty-two years when Esther was stricken with Alzheimer's. She deteriorated very rapidly, often wandering out of the house and getting lost. Though Henry devoted himself almost exclusively to her, he reached a point at which he felt he could no longer cope. He became quite distraught. Finally, the couple's son, Martin, convinced Henry—with great difficulty—that Esther needed full-time institutional care. So, Martin arranged for Esther's admission to a nursing home. It was near where Martin and his family lived—more than a thousand miles from Henry and Esther's longtime home. Henry decided to move, too, so he could be near his son and grandchildren and visit Esther as much as possible. He sold the family home, then rented a small apartment near Martin's home and Esther's nursing home.

Henry did his best to adapt to the unfamiliar new surroundings. Though depressed by Esther's relentless decline, Henry was basically healthy and vigorous. Now, he found himself with almost nothing to do. Back home, he had been involved in local politics and church and community activities. In his unfamiliar new surrounding, he was restless and bored. His depression worsened. Finally, Martin and his wife, Elaine, were convinced that Henry would be better off back home, among his friends and political cronies. They promised to look after Esther and urged Henry to return to his old, familiar territory.

Though reluctant, Henry didn't really need much convincing. He returned to his old home and was soon running for the school board and helping out in local elections. Later, when Martin visited his father while on a business trip, the son knew that the family had made the right decision. Back in his own pond, Henry was once again a lively, energetic person.

About a year later, Henry flew out to visit Martin and Elaine and his two young grandchildren. Of course, he went to see Esther, too. But this time Esther didn't even recognize him. That visit devastated Henry. Martin, Elaine, and the children tried their best to cheer Henry up, but even when he flew back home, it was clear that he was beset with guilt, sadness, and an enormous sense of loss.

Another year passed. Again, Martin, on a business trip, visited his dad. This time Henry seemed energetic and upbeat, but also a little nervous and evasive. Finally, he blushed and told Martin, a bit hesitantly, that he had "found a friend." "A woman friend?" Martin asked. Clearly embarrassed, Henry nodded and smiled. He explained that when he and Esther were quite young, the Jamisons had been among their dearest friends. Martin remembered them, but not very well.

Henry said that a few weeks earlier he had bumped into Sarah Jamison at a political rally. Sarah told Henry that her husband, Joe Jamison, had passed away about five years earlier. Henry and Sarah had much in common, including fond memories of socializing as married couples. Henry said that he and Sarah had begun to meet each other for occasional dinners.

Martin could see that Henry was hesitant and conflicted as he recounted all this. Henry clearly valued his reconnection with Sarah. Yet, he also felt guilty and even ashamed at seeing another woman while his wife languished far away in a nursing home.

To his credit, Martin eagerly endorsed his dad's new relationship. "That's great!" Martin declared. "Elaine and I were hoping you would find someone. I want to call Elaine right now to tell her the news. She'll be delighted!" Henry was visibly relieved by Martin's enthusiastic support. It was apparent that he had worried about his son's reaction. Would the family be angry because Henry was enjoying himself even though his wife was still alive? Now, Henry relaxed and even smiled.

That night, the three of them—Henry, Martin, and Sarah—went out to dinner together. Throughout the evening, Martin made clear that he and the rest of the family approved of the fledging relationship between Henry and Sarah. The scene was reminiscent of what had happened years ago, when young Martin had brought Elaine home for the first time. Then, it was his parents who had made it clear that they supported him in his choice.

Later that night, Martin called Elaine from his hotel room. "Dad's like a little kid," Martin reported. "He's all shy and embarrassed and excited. It's quite wonderful! And Sarah's very nice. I think she was scared about meeting me. She seems gentle and kind. I liked her a lot."

A few months later, Henry and Sarah took a long vacation together. When they stopped to visit Martin and Elaine, Elaine showed them the guest room with a single double bed that she had prepared for the two of them. Without making the older couple uncomfortable, Elaine had let them know that she approved of her father-in-law's life-affirming decision and welcomed Sarah into the family, even if the couple could not get married.

Was Henry and Sarah's relationship improper? Should Martin and Elaine have disapproved instead of approved? These are difficult questions whose complicated answers depend upon various factors. Does the debilitated spouse recognize you? Can you and your spouse carry on a normal conversation? Or is that spouse totally disoriented, unaware of time and place? Your religion and moral orientation, as well as community standards, come into play here. So does your own heart. There are no easy answers. Perhaps, you will recognize the "right" answer for you when you feel you can live comfortably with that decision. If you feel you have to hide your new relationship from the world, then that probably is not a good choice for you.

Unmarried couples like Henry and Sarah, one or both of whom have a living, but entirely mentally disabled, spouse, are becoming increasingly common. As the population ages, and the lives of the robust old and the frail and infirm old diverge dramatically, we can expect to see more and more couples who try to rebuild their lives in this way.

A PLETHORA OF REASONS

Many other couples choose not to marry even when there are no medical or other visible barriers. Why? The reasons vary from couple to couple. Sometimes, there are legal difficulties, such as unfinalized divorces that make couples forego remarriage. Sometimes, there are financial problems. Perhaps, the state in which you live has restrictions against divorce under certain medical conditions. More often, the compelling reasons are psychological. Once widowed or divorced, some people hesitate to commit once again to all the responsibilities and risks of marriage.

Older couples are sometimes reluctant to agree to remain together "in sickness and in health." One member of the pair may have just gone through a protracted period of caring for a sick wife or husband. That individual may feel—usually incorrectly—that as long as their new relationship is not formalized, they can escape a recurrence of such terrible times. There is, however, little moral refuge from such responsibilities, married or not.

Stella, age seventy-four, told us:

Dave was sick and getting steadily worse for over three years. Those were, to put it mildly, awful years. After he died, I swore to myself that I would never remarry. I can't go through that again. I like Larry, perhaps I love him, but I don't want to tie the knot. I keep my own place, and he keeps his. We travel together, and sometimes I stay with him for a week or two. But I always go back to my own apartment. Staying a little bit separate makes me feel that, if anything bad happens, I can escape.

Dream on! Whether the couple has married or not, committed partners rarely avoid the emotional turmoil brought on by illness and the other exigencies of a long life. When two people have been together for many years, the issue of whether or not they are legally wed tends to evaporate. In a sense, they are just as married as if they had taken legal vows. The emotional bonds between the two drive them to behave as if they were one individual. Those around them, including their children and stepchildren, come to expect them to act as a couple. An example:

Connie and Ray, each widowed long ago, had been going together for almost fifteen years. They kept separate households less than five minutes from one another, but otherwise behaved like any older married couple. Ray ate all his meals at Connie's, except when they went out together. They spent just about every evening and most nights together. When they traveled, they stayed in the same hotel room.

Ray, however, was eleven years older than Connie. In his earlier years, he had lived, shall we say, a rather carefree life. Although he no longer drank, he continued to smoke and to eat poorly, despite Connie's best efforts. Those bad habits seemed to catch up with him all at once. He developed serious respiratory problems, requiring constant use of oxygen, and he was having more and more trouble walking.

Connie took care of Ray by herself as long as she could, but finally she realized he needed more help than she could give. She found a trained nurse's aide, a young man who moved into Ray's apartment. That worked for a while, but Ray hated having a "stranger" around all the time, and eventually the young man had to leave.

At her wit's end, Connie finally phoned Ray's son, Mac, in Wisconsin. Mac immediately insisted that his father come back to Wisconsin, where Ray had raised his first family. Mac said he would come get his father and bring him home. There, Mac said, Ray's extended and rather prominent family could arrange for his care. Distraught, Connie reluctantly agreed, and, despite Ray's protests, he was flown back to Milwaukee.

Some months later, we again spoke to Connie. She spoke poignantly about missing Ray. She said she felt as if "my right side has been chopped off." She also told us that Ray was complaining bitterly about being a "prisoner" in Milwaukee. In fact, he had confided to Connie that he was planning to escape and return to her. By now, Connie was in a state of depression. She lamented that she just couldn't take care of Ray by herself. Compounding the problem, she said, was the fact that each of them had condos with just enough room for one person. At that time, Connie was not considering taking a larger place where she, Ray, and a medical caretaker could live comfortably.

There's little use going further with this familiar tale. The point is that Ray and Connie, though not legally married to each other, faced the same complex problems of aging and infirmity that any older married couple might encounter. They struggled with the same uncertainties, suffered the same emotional pain, and were as devoted to each other as any loving, aging couple anywhere. Even inheritance questions—Ray had long since provided for Connie in his will—were essentially the same as for a married couple.

Still, why hadn't they ever married? Connie's concise answer: "What for?"

WHEN FINANCES COUNT

Some partners choose to live together because they had been seriously burned, emotionally or financially, in a difficult divorce. That was especially true of the handful of people we interviewed who had been divorced more than once. Other unmarried partners cited the financial complications and costs of marrying again.

Eleanor, a sixty-one-year-old widow, lives with Sam, age sixty-six. She told us:

Sam and I have been living together for two years, and we plan to continue this way. Marriage would just cost us too much. According to social security, if I had remarried before age sixty, I would have lost my widow's benefits. And, even though they are reduced benefits because I'm not yet sixty-five, they really make a huge difference for us. Besides, Sam's social security is less than what I get as a widow. So, it doesn't make economic sense to marry, at least for now. Our kids understand, and they're all in favor of our living together and not marrying. Without both social security checks, we might need help from our kids. Sam and I both like it this way, where we are financially independent from our kids.

The social security regulations are, indeed, complex and confusing regarding the benefits received by widows and widowers, including those who were previously divorced after at least ten years of marriage. At this writing, in general, a widow or widower who remarries after age sixty may keep her or his survivor's benefits. People who have been divorced after at least ten years of marriage can keep the benefits derived from their former spouse—if they remarry after age sixty-two. And, in a curious twist, if the former spouse then dies, the surviving former spouse may actually receive an increase in benefits. If that's not clear, and it certainly isn't, call and clarify your situation with your local social security office!

Social security benefits vary enormously, depending on many factors, including whether or not the recipient has worked for the Federal Government. In short, social security law is too complicated to try to untangle here. Instead, we recommend, once again, that you consult with the Social Security Administration on the Web, by phone, or in person about what benefits, if any, you are entitled to claim. The agency can offer you definitive help for your particular circumstances.[3]

Given the rules that limit benefits to remarrying former spouses, it is prudent to check *before* you divorce or remarry, especially if social security benefits will be a major source of your income when you are older. It is also prudent to do some independent research on benefits so you are not dependent solely on the information you get from a single agency employee, particularly over the telephone. We know this from our own experience in double-checking our facts for this chapter. We repeatedly received contradictory information over the phone. It took several iterations—by phone and by Web—to nail down the latest regulations.

WHEN RELIGION HOLDS SWAY

As we noted earlier, cohabitation was once relatively rare and widely frowned upon. Today, most social barriers to cohabitation in the United States have fallen—most, but not all. Indeed, in some locales—smaller towns and traditionally conservative regions, for example—prohibitions against unmarried living together are still quite powerful. To boot, most organized religions continue to frown on the practice.

People for whom religion and religious participation are less important have higher rates of cohabitation than their more religious counterparts.[4] Among nonreligious Americans, 44.8 percent cohabit without marriage, while cohabitation rates for those who consider themselves religious are much lower: 8.2 percent for Mormons, 20–24 percent for Protestants, 23.1 percent for Catholics, and 32.5 percent for Jews.[5]

As we saw in the last chapter, a cohabiting parent may create problems for adult children and stepchildren who are more religious than their parent. This is particularly the case when adult children believe that a parent is setting a bad example for the grandchildren. You'll recall Rosa, who had two teenage children and worried about explaining her father's cohabitating with his girlfriend to the children and the parish priest. Alternatively, religion may inadvertently push seniors toward cohabitation, especially when one partner's religion prohibits divorce.

Kelly, thirty-one, had no problems with her father's long-standing, live-in arrangement with his girlfriend. Her parents had been separated for more than two decades, and her father had been living with Amanda for twelve years by the time we interviewed Kelly. This was how she described the situation:

My mom and dad have been separated for a very long time. They would have divorced, but our religion doesn't sanction divorce. When they were living together, my dad was an alcoholic. He was a terrible husband, and I don't blame my mother for splitting from him. I think Amanda is a very good influence on him. Since he's been with her, he's gone to Alcoholics Anonymous and has been sober for more than ten years. He has a responsible job, and when he had a heart attack, Amanda took care of him. She was great! I think Amanda's a terrific person. She's great for my dad.

My mom has a good life. She doesn't have any man in her life, but she has a big family of sisters and brothers, and she stays busy. Amanda is very thoughtful of the family. She knows when to appear and when to stay in the background. When Joe and I got married, we invited her both to the shower and to the wedding. I really wanted her to come, but I think she was smarter than I was. Both times, she said that that was a family occasion, and it would be easier all the way around if she didn't come. My mom and dad came to both events. Things went very smoothly.

OTHER MEDICAL AND LEGAL FACTORS

Seniors who cohabit face a number of difficult medical and/or legal issues. Although they may consider themselves a couple, because they are not legally married, one partner may not be allowed to make emergency health-related decisions for the other. Consider Ray and Connie again:

Before Ray returned to Wisconsin, he had twice been rushed by ambulance to the emergency room at the local hospital. That was where Connie discovered that, because she was not Ray's legal spouse, she could not make decisions about Ray's medical treatment. They could only be made by his next of kin. As soon as Ray was released from the hospital, however, he and Connie made sure that wouldn't happen again. Each signed an appropriate formal medical proxy for the other.

Unfortunately, signing a few legal papers won't always solve such problems. Too often, other, more complex issues exist, as in this case:

Dick and Roberta had been together for about three years. Dick was widowed, while Roberta finally got a divorce, after years of wrangling with her ex-husband. Dick and Roberta both have adult children, all of whom seem to feel comfortable about the unmarried, but loving, relationship their parents have established.

The couple often took trips together. On one occasion, they were in New England to enjoy the autumn colors. At four o'clock one morning, Dick shook Roberta awake. "I hate to wake you, but I've got a terrible chest pain that won't seem to go away," he told her. Roberta's own heart began to pound, as she reached for the phone and dialed 911.

The paramedics arrived and whisked Dick off to the local hospital. There, the admissions officer, assuming Roberta was Dick's wife, asked her to sign the standard waivers and permissions. Roberta then had to explain why she could not. As soon as the staff discovered the couple was not married, they began to treat her differently, Roberta told us. She felt the medical staff ignored her suggestions and brushed off her questions. She said she felt angry and embarrassed. What upset her the most, she said, was that she wasn't as effective an advocate for Dick as she would have liked to be, because she had no legal role in ensuring that Dick got the best possible care.

Dick's chest pain turned out to be a minor digestive upset. He was released later the same afternoon. That evening, Dick tried to persuade Roberta to let him sign a medical proxy naming her his health care agent. Roberta refused. When we asked Roberta why, given that she is a trained social worker and understands the importance of medical proxies, she explained, to our surprise:

It isn't that easy. Remember, Dick has grown children. They feel very close to him and very concerned about his well-being. I wouldn't dare make decisions about Dick's health without their okay. They feel they're the ones who should do that, not me. In this family, I'm just Dad's girlfriend. I'm not their mother or his wife. I'm not a real member of the family. If something went wrong because of a health decision I made, I'd never be forgiven!

Other unmarried seniors we interviewed recalled their embarrassment, anger, and a sense of helplessness when they were unable to make medical decisions for a partner. Given that Roberta had expressed just those emotions, we were surprised when we learned she had refused to exchange medical proxies with Dick. Later, we discovered that many seniors, including those who were legally married, felt much as Roberta did. They feared that, if anything went wrong, they might be demonized by the children.

Take the case of Melanie, who became her husband, Hugh's, medical care-taker as he slowly succumbed to amyotrophic lateral sclerosis (ALS), or Lou Gehrig's disease. Melanie and Hugh had married in their fifties, so they had been together for more than twenty years when Hugh was diagnosed. She described the situation to us this way:

I took care of Hugh as long as I could. Those were five very difficult years. When I couldn't do it anymore, I looked for a good nursing home close by so I could visit him every day. His two sons were outraged. They felt I was throwing Hugh away like garbage. I wasn't! I just didn't have the physical, not to mention the emotional, strength to handle it any longer. They didn't pay any attention to how hard I had worked for the last five years. There was a big family blowup at that time, but Hugh went to the nursing home anyhow. I couldn't take care of him any longer at home, and, for all their complaints, neither of his sons wanted to take him into their homes, either!

Whatever choices an older couple makes, they can expect to be second-guessed, or worse, by their stepchildren and others who may have strong attachments to the original family. It doesn't always happen, but the couple should be prepared, particularly if they are not married.

The decision not to marry can have other unexpected consequences:

Julius and Lucille had been together for more than twenty years. When Julius was quite old and infirm, he had a talk with his daughter, Fran, about his financial situation and his will. In the course of the discussion, Fran asked her dad what he had arranged for Lucille. He answered: "I don't plan to leave her anything but this condo."

Fran was shocked. "But Dad, Lucille has taken care of you for twenty years. She's done everything for you. How can you do this? After all that she's done for you and meant to you, how can you leave her with so little?"

Julius replied: "Yes, she's taken care of me, and I've taken care of her. When one of us dies, all that will be over. I don't owe her anything else."

Despite Fran's protestations, Julius didn't budge. Whether Lucille was aware of it or not, Julius had an old-fashioned idea of what his obligations were to her. As far as he was concerned, the deal was no marriage, no community property. In some states, Lucille would have had a legal claim on the property that the pair had accumulated while living together, with or without marriage. Still, in many states, unmarried partners have no rights to the other's property, no matter how long they have lived together.

AND NOW, THE CHILDREN

Adult children's attitudes toward their parent's new partners are diverse. They range from being strongly against to strongly supportive of their parent's finding a new mate. Yet, we have found that, when it comes to remarriage, most adult children become negative. Even adult children who generally disapprove of cohabitation on religious grounds often don't want their own parent to remarry. They can accept the reality that their parent wants to date. At the same time, they are opposed to that parent living with someone new, and some oppose remarriage at all costs.

MONEY AND SEX

Frequently, the underlying reason for an adult child's opposition to his or her parent's remarriage is the one the child is most reluctant to own up to—money.

Children may think, even if they never say it out loud: *If Dad doesn't remarry, his fortune is more likely to remain intact—for us.*

There are other reasons, as well, for children's opposition. Sex is one we discussed earlier. Children, even sensible, sensitive adult children, are often reluctant to deal with the reality that their aging parent is a sexual being. The illusion is easier to maintain if the parent doesn't remarry. If Dad is only "seeing" Suzy, that's ambiguous enough to be palatable. An adult child can think of the couple as "just friends."

THE *UN*EXTENDED FAMILY: STEPSIBLINGS, THE OTHER PARENT, THE GRANDCHILDREN

There are other reasons for children's tendency to prefer something other than parental remarriage. Some don't want to have to deal with a flock of new stepsiblings. Some children continue to feel, for many years, if not forever, that giving their blessing to a parent's remarriage would be an unpardonable act of betrayal to their deceased or divorced biological parent.

That sense of betrayal may have been what was troubling one of our male interviewees, whom we introduced earlier. He repeatedly referred—often disparagingly—to his father's "new wife." You may recall that when we asked him how long his father and his new wife had been married, he answered, with no apparent sense of irony, "Thirty years."

WHAT'S GOOD FOR THE GOOSE MIGHT *NOT* BE GOOD FOR THE GANDER

Adult children may, thus, find themselves in the paradoxical situation of trying to influence their parent to live with a partner—without benefit of wedlock—even as they are simultaneously trying to persuade their adolescent children that doing so is wrong. Unfortunately, the adult children sometimes have more influence on their parent than on their own children. A case in point:

Phil, widowed four years earlier, has two sons and a daughter. Daughter Barbara is now twenty-two. She is still the apple of Phil's eye. Moreover, Daddy is still the apple of Barbara's eye. Although engaged to be married, Barbara spends almost as much time alone with her father as with her fiancé. In fact, she clearly resents anyone else who tries to become close to her father.

Two years ago, Phil started dating. For several months, he dated Bess, a woman who had been close to his late wife. It was clear that daughter Barbara had a hard time with the growing relationship between Phil and Bess. While Phil's two married sons didn't particularly care for Bess either, they had not interfered. They were rather relieved, however, when Phil and Bess stopped seeing each other.

Barbara, however, wasn't simply relieved. She was ecstatic. No one knows for sure why Bess and Phil broke up, but her brothers are certain that Barbara somehow had a hand in it.

About six months later, Phil met and fell deeply in love with Doris, a divorcée a few years younger than Phil. The two boys and their wives all liked Doris very much. They felt she was just what Phil needed to bring him out of the mild depression he had fallen into during their mother's long illness, a depression that worsened after her death. So, the boys did their best to welcome Doris into the family.

At the time, Barbara was completely absorbed in her own new love. When she realized that Phil and Doris were getting serious, she did not behave as her brothers had. She did not welcome Doris. In fact, when Phil brought Doris to a family gathering, Barbara was so cold and unfriendly that Barbara's brothers later scolded her. "Why were you so rude to Doris?" they asked. "She's been very nice to you and to all of us. It's obvious that Dad likes her very much. She's a sensible, intelligent, caring person. She's ideal for Dad, and God knows he needs somebody. He doesn't need this grief from you, and Doris doesn't deserve it. Just lay off, Barbara."

Barbara reacted with a mix of tears and fury. Phil and Doris continued to see one another. Thanks in large part to Doris, Phil gradually regained his old vitality and sense of humor. His sons were happy to see the twinkle return to his eye.

Four months later, Phil called a family meeting. He sat down to dinner with his two sons, their wives, daughter Barbara, and her fiancé, Steve. Doris was absent. Phil treated the occasion quite formally. He rose from his chair after dinner. "I have something to tell you all," he announced. "Doris and I are planning to get married. But before we take that step, I want to be sure that I have your blessings. Of course, we don't have to have your approval, but we would both be happier if we knew that all of you approved."

Both boys and their wives reacted immediately: "That's great, Dad. Doris is wonderful. She's just right for you. We couldn't be more pleased."

Barbara just sat there. Finally, she got up, went over to Phil, hugged him, and said, "Dad, this is a rather precipitous decision, isn't it? Don't you think you need to think it over more carefully? Doris is nice enough, but she may not be the right one for you. Besides, we don't really know that much about her. Promise me that you won't even think about marriage until you and the rest of us get to know Doris better."

Phil frowned. Then, he smiled weakly and kissed Barbara. "Okay, sweetheart," he said, "you know I wouldn't do anything to upset you. I'll hold off for a while, and we'll see how things go."

Phil's older son stepped in. "Dad, you certainly do *know Doris well enough, and so do we. I don't know why Barbara is so negative, but the rest of us think that you and Doris will be a great team."*

"Well," Phil replied, obviously conflicted, "Let's just see how it goes."

Two years later, Phil and Doris are still together, but not yet married. Daughter Barbara, on the other hand, had a huge wedding and is now pregnant with her first child.

As we have said before, adult children often have strong, unexpected responses to a parent's announcement that he or she has fallen in love again. Just because the children are grown-ups who like to make their own decisions doesn't mean that they will grant their parent the same privilege. Frequently, adult children try to influence parental decisions about their new relationships and, often, perhaps too often, the children succeed.

The parent who has fallen in love again should listen to his or her children but also should draw the line when children try to usurp the parent's autonomy. Remember how your children responded when they fell in love the first time, and you tried to make them think it over? They were quite adamant: "I love you, but it's my life, and I have to do what's right for me." Well, once you've given the relationship both time and thought, use your own judgment.

SUMMING UP

Today, when older folks fall in love, they don't necessarily remarry. Many choose to live together in relationships that parallel marriage in almost all respects but one: There is no marriage license. Such couples create and live in stepfamilies even when they remain legally *un*married.

These older unmarried couples confront many of the same issues as married folks in dealing with each other, their children, and grandchildren, as well as the communities in which they live. Gay couples face some of these issues, too. Unmarried couples also encounter a few problems married couples avoid, such as being excluded from medical decisions about their partners.

For many couples, not marrying is a difficult option. Extended families may frown on family members who choose to live together, whatever their age.

Friends may, too. Most organized religions disapprove. Even if they are not religious, some people, nonetheless, may feel guilty or embarrassed about living together outside of marriage. In other cases, marriage may be impossible because of an incapacitated spouse or some other legal or moral obstacle.

What are the common *benefits* of an older couple's decision to live together without marriage?

- Children often like it better if their parent doesn't remarry, even if they don't say so.

- Both the child and the parent may feel that nonmarriage is less of a betrayal of the other biological parent, whether that parent is alive or deceased.

- The seniors, particularly those who have survived a messy divorce, may want to avoid legal entanglements, if only because they dread going through another divorce if the new partnership fails.

- The unmarried option may seem simpler and more convenient. It may give the new couple a sense—often unrealistic—that this new relationship involves less responsibility and more autonomy than marriage.

- Financial and legal matters are cleaner and simpler without commingled resources and assets, except perhaps shared living expenses.

- Unmarried partners may feel more secure after pooling their resources and cutting expenses by owning just one home.

- Pensions, social security benefits, alimony, and other forms of support that one of the new partners needs or wants may be complicated or threatened by remarriage.

- Other issues, such as legal residence, that could complicate tax and estate matters may be affected by remarriage.

- One partner's religion may prevent divorce and thus may make it impossible for the new couple to remarry. Guilt grounded in religion may drive a couple toward cohabitation or away from it.

- One partner may still be married to an institutionalized spouse.

There are *costs* to consider, as well.

- Adult children may be embarrassed by a parent's living with a partner without being married, often on religious grounds. They may feel that the grandparent is a bad role model for teenage grandchildren.

- An unmarried partner, for psychological or social (including religious) reasons, may feel uncomfortable living together outside of marriage.

- An unmarried partner, especially a woman, can be made to feel like an outsider and maybe even disreputable if not legally married. Of course, new spouses may not be welcomed warmly either.

- An unmarried partner, unless legally authorized, cannot make emergency health decisions for the other or may be denied access to bank accounts and other shared assets.

- Unmarried partners may find they are left without resources if a partner should die without legally transferring assets to the survivor.

- Unmarried partners who have had recent health problems may feel more secure in marriage and less dependent on their children.

We think it's worth remembering that there's an asymmetry between the two choices. Marriage is a major commitment, both legally and emotionally, even if, as you already know, it doesn't last forever. If you live together now, you maintain the option of marrying later. If you marry, there's no uncomplicated way to *unmarry* and go back to living together.

Our advice on whether to marry or simply live together:

For the parents: Listen to your children and other people you care about and respect. Hear them out. Seek their counsel. *Then, make your own decisions.* It's your life!

For the adult children: Try to think about what's best for your parent. Worry less about your inheritance and more about your parent's happiness and well-being. Remember, they worried for years about yours and probably still do. Focus on your own adult life and how to live it constructively and independently. Be generous and kind.

Maintain your moral and religious values, but remember that tolerance is a virtue. You don't have to apologize for your parent's behavior or defend it.

Think long and hard before you condemn your parent, however you feel about his or her behavior. Even if you are religious, you can hate the sin but love the sinner. Try to empathize with other people's values and needs, including your parents'. Teach your children to respect other people's rights and responsible choices, even if they are different from your own.

FOR PARENTS AND CHILDREN:

Once again, remember to do unto others as you would have them do unto you—the Golden Rule endorsed by virtually every religion and moral system. Learn how to disagree without rancor—and teach your children that lesson, as well. The ability to live and let live is an essential skill on a small, diverse planet.

In the next chapter, we discuss strategies for dealing with some of the most difficult moments in the lives of stepfamilies—holidays and special occasions, such as weddings and other command performances.

---

[1]U.S. Bureau of the Census. (1998). *Marital Status and Living Arrangements,* March 1997. (Superintendent of Documents: Washington, D.C.).

[2]http://members.aol.com/cohabitating/facts.html. "A Few Facts on Cohabitation."

[3]Social Security's Internet Website: *"http://www.ssa.gov"*. Toll-free number: 1-800-772-1213; See also, Social Security Administration (2002), *Understanding the Benefits.* Publication Number 05-10024, ICN 454930, February.

[4]Markey, Barbara. (2000). "Cohabitation: Response Over Reaction." *The Priest.* (Huntington, IN: Our Sunday Visitor), November, pp. 19–24; Bumpass, Larry, and James A. Sweet. (1999). *Cohabitation, Marriage and Union Stability: Preliminary Findings from NSFH2,* Working Paper 65 (Madison, WI: Center for Demography, University of Wisconsin); Krishnan, Bijaya. (1998). "Premarital Cohabitation and Marital Disruption." *Journal of Divorce and Remarriage,* vol. 28, pp. 157–170; Lye, Diane N., and Ingrid Waldron. (1997). "Attitudes Toward Cohabitation, Family, and Gender Roles: Relationships to Values and Political Ideology." *Sociological Perspectives,* vol. 40, pp. 199–225.

[5]http://members.aol.com/cohabitating/facts.html. "A Few Facts on Cohabitation."

CHAPTER 15

Family Holidays, Celebrations, and Commemorations: The Banana Peel Beneath Your Heel

Thanksgiving and Christmas, weddings, bar mitzvahs, confirmations, graduations, and other special occasions test almost every family, biological or otherwise. Stepfamilies seem especially vulnerable to the tensions generated by these familial command performances. We have found, however, that they are much easier to bear if you prepare thoughtfully for them and learn something useful from them when they go wrong.

Predictably, the Five Furies often reveal themselves on these occasions. For all the celebratory air, pretty clothes, and good food, someone always feels abandoned, snubbed, or overlooked at the christening of a new grandchild or the party after a graduation ceremony. The new family members may feel isolated at a stepchild's or stepsibling's wedding, as they watch the old biological clan gather with affection and tell stories that exclude them. Or the biological family may feel the ache of parental disloyalty as they watch their father warmly embrace a stepchild, who has just given a lovely toast at his seventieth birthday celebration. The emotional intensity of these landmark events makes each suffering family member's pain or anger that much worse. Many of the deepest rifts in stepfamilies begin at celebrations that are meant to bring families together.

Why are holidays and other special occasions such danger zones for stepfamilies? The principal reason is surprisingly simple: They force you to come face-to-face with stepfamily members you don't like. Most of the time, you can forget about certain troublesome members of your stepfamily, particularly if they live out of town. Because family rites are typically planned long in advance, it is awkward to say that you will be busy and unable to attend six months before one of these major events.

Moreover, choosing not to attend won't guarantee your escaping any negative consequences of that event. In fact, saying no may assure that someone in the family will be furious at you.

There are other downsides to such occasions, as well. You may have to select gifts for (and spend your good money on) family members you dislike. You may have to share your parent or spouse with them. You may be inconvenienced by having to travel long distances and share accommodations with steprelatives you can't stand. In addition, you may have to deal with a stepchild or stepsibling who never helps with the household chores or behaves badly in other ways.

It is easy to feel like a human sacrifice in such circumstances. To avoid feeling victimized, remember the Saving Graces we discussed earlier (see Chapter 4). These are the potential positives that difficult family get-togethers can provide. The Saving Graces include opportunities to make new emotional connections with stepfamily members and to learn valuable strategies for including outsiders, instead of simply keeping them at bay.

Family celebrations can be occasions for becoming savvier about how best to conduct our lives. They can be festive practice sessions for honing the social skills we need to bring people together as allies—allies who bring additional resources to the table—instead of occasions that reinforce negative stereotypes about stepfamilies. Such occasions can make us more adaptive, more socially and emotionally flexible. If we allow ourselves to build on positive feelings that family celebrations can engender, all kinds of good things can happen. We may even begin to grow a friendship with the stepsibling we always dread seeing. At a minimum, we can become more adept at neutralizing hostility.

Finding the Saving Graces in special occasions requires conscious, creative effort on your part. Some people know intuitively how to do this. Most of us have to learn how to look for the positive possibilities in stressful situations and how to transform them into realities. The Furies come naturally on such occasions. The Saving Graces are quieter presences that require goodwill and a willingness to reach out on our part. As you get to know your way around in the land of stepfamilies, the wisdom and tolerance you acquire helps you to accept disappointment and adjust your expectations.

A VALUABLE CLUE

If, after years go by, a stepfamily's Furies remain much stronger than its Saving Graces, that is usually the telltale sign that some fundamental conflict within our own biological family is calling for resolution. That comes as a surprise to most people. We prefer to believe that all our current problems are caused by the stepfamily. Often, however, the troubled family dynamic began long before the stepfamily came on the scene. Giving you the impetus to put this earlier problem or problems to rest may be the single greatest benefit that a stepfamily can offer.

Think of this opportunity for your own healing and emotional growth as an unanticipated gift from your stepfamily. Often the stepfamily and your conflicts with it provide clues to the fundamental trouble spots in your biological family. By examining the things that distress you and make you critical of your stepfamily, you may suddenly recognize the strong points, as well as the trouble spots, in your biological family. These clues typically emerge after several days of just the kind of intimate contact with your stepfamily that happens on holidays and other special occasions. That's why this discussion is in this particular chapter.

EMOTIONAL DISPLACEMENT

Put another way, you may not be able get over certain problems you have with stepfamily members until you figure out why you need to project onto them the frustration and anger you feel about your own biological family. This psychological process is often called "emotional displacement." Here's an example:

When his mother remarried, Ned, age thirty-four, saw trouble ahead:

I found it very difficult to visit my mother and her new husband, Jack, at Christmastime. It seemed like my mother could never do enough for Jack's children. She gave them first choice of rooms. She agreed to everything they wanted to do, welcomed any friend they wanted to invite over, cooked whatever they wanted, and let them set the schedule for meals and come and go, however inconvenient it was for the rest of us. She let her four-year-old stepgrandson dominate the entire dinner table conversation because his parents thought he was so cute.

I found out that my brother was having a hard time, too. We consoled each other and agreed that Jack's children and grandchildren were spoiled and had no manners. We began to collect stories about how uncool and selfish they were and had fun imitating them when we were alone.

But then, the next Christmas, it was the same thing. We knew we could keep on being miserable or speak to Mom and make her aware of what she was allowing to happen. We would have to risk her being angry with us. Needless to say, Mom had never spoiled us that way. We had to toe the line when we were growing up because she had been a divorced working mother and needed her kids to cooperate. That's why her indulging Jack's children so much really bothered us.

UNMASKING HIDDEN TRUTHS

Understanding the real source of the problem gives you the opportunity to accommodate to the facts of life as they are today. That includes accepting the inevitable changes and disappointments in any parent-child relationship. In the example above, once Ned and his brother talk about family history with their mom and face the real reasons for their frustration, they can forgive her. There will be less emotional pressure to stay angry with their stepfamily, even if they don't have good manners. The older generation can go through the same exercise.

It isn't easy, but, at any age, we can develop self-control and master our tendency, often unconscious, to let the Furies dominate and destroy our chance for affection and trust in our stepfamily. An understanding and nonjudgmental spouse or friend can ask us a few questions that may bring out a hidden truth, as happened in the following story. Five years into an otherwise happy remarriage, fifty-eight-year-old Gloria told us how some unconscious feelings fueled her hostility toward her new husband and stepfamily:

I have always paid my own way in life, and I became very angry when my husband offered to pay all the vacation expenses for his thirty-five-year-old daughter and her family to have a winter vacation with us in Florida. I thought it was unfair of her to take advantage of her father and accept his offer when she knew that he didn't have that kind of money. It meant that the two of us wouldn't be able to take any other trips. And then, when they got there and we went out to eat, they ordered the most expensive items on the menu and the most expensive wines. They never once reached for the check.

Maybe, it was foolish, but after we returned home I told my husband

how angry I was about how he had been exploited by them. He had a
hard time believing that it mattered so much to me. He said it gave him a
great feeling to be in a position to treat them to a good time, just as he
enjoyed doing it for me. He wondered why I was so angry and asked me
to think about it. I realized that I had been indulged that way by my father
when I was young, and I missed all that. I was really envious of my step-
daughter. My husband was amazingly sympathetic and respected my
honesty.

Through our stepfamily, we can begin to deal directly with the remaining unsolved problems in our original family and prevent ceaseless repetition of the old patterns. Sure, your stepchild may, in fact, be greedy and deceitful. Still, once you know that to be true, why does his/her behavior continue to distress you so, unless it relates to something deep inside you, probably some unresolved issue involving your biological family?

DISCOVERING THE ORIGINS OF A FURY

You might have grown up in a family where you had to sacrifice your own self-interest for the sake of other family members. As a result, you may have a lasting resentment of people who do whatever pleases them, without considering anyone else.

Holidays and special occasions can bring these old, unresolved issues to the surface in painful ways. Perhaps, watching the warm way your stepfamily opens Christmas presents makes you feel very much like an outsider. After each gift is unwrapped, you observe that the recipient kisses and hugs the giver, instead of simply saying, "Thank you." Even if you like the idea, you may wonder why your own biological family never made this happy show of feeling. You may be torn between a Fury and two Saving Graces. You may see the difference in holiday style as evidence of the new stepfamily's Fidelity to Family traditions. At the same time, you have an opening to Facilitate Emotional Learning about Your Own Family, as well as to develop Fraternity with Stepsiblings.

Emily, age thirty-six, told us:

My stepfamily always expresses tons of affection at holiday times. They
sing and make toasts and hug each other and say whatever is on their

minds. There is much laughter. My family was so much more inhibited and restrained. Christmas was not a particularly happy time. My mother was always sick. We would open our gifts and that was that.

We have learned over the years from our stepfamily how much better it is to loosen up and join in the fun.

The same opportunity may occur during a first visit to a stepparent's summer home over the Fourth of July. The stepfamily's traditional water activities and spirited touch football games may be new to you and a little alien. You may sense that this is a tight-knit family in which you have no part.

You may actually *be* left out. You may not understand the rules of the games that everybody else knows how to play. At times, you may feel that you are undergoing some sort of sorority or fraternity hazing or that you are watching the rituals of some strange and primitive tribe. It is easy to blame your loneliness on your stepfamily.

What you may really be feeling, however, is regret that your biological family lacked the warm, cohesive spirit of your stepfamily. Your own family life may have been a joyless struggle to survive, with little fun and few games. Now, like it or not, you are forced to see that other families live differently. You may seethe with resentment, but wouldn't it be better all around if you decided to learn from your stepfamily and inject more warmth and brio into your own life?

DISCOVERING THE STRENGTHS IN YOUR OLD FAMILY

A stepfamily is inevitably an education. It always presents new possibilities for—or at least new understandings of—you and your biological parents and siblings. By taking time to talk alone with your biological siblings about the "other" family, you may recognize great qualities of your original family for the first time. You may truly come to appreciate the support and unity that you and your siblings have always shown each other when you see your stepfamily arguing and competing amongst themselves.

Maybe, you now understand that the irreverence for authority that your parents encouraged has contributed to your family's being more creative, experimental, and assertive than your goody-goody stepsiblings, who were raised more conventionally. Once you recognize that you can benefit from seeing your biological family in the mirror of your stepfamily, you can view stepfamily gatherings in a new, more positive light.

From now on, instead of simply getting angry, ask yourself why certain behaviors in the "other" family disturb you so much (or ask yourself what makes your stepfamily so charming, if that is what leaps out at you). Either way, your stepfamily presents you with an opportunity to make your own life more satisfying by understanding better—perhaps healing—long-held grudges in your family of origin.

Todd, age thirty-eight, told us:

I always blamed my parents for their uptight behavior and the strict rules they insisted on when I was growing up. Rules like "Kids should behave and do the chores." Like "Kids should clean up the kitchen, put junk away, and not interrupt adult conversations." But when we spent our vacation with Dad's new family, where anything goes and no one cleans up the kitchen and the kids order their parents around, I started to think my parents had done something right, after all.

Even years after stepfamilies have achieved a state of equilibrium, holidays can still unleash painful emotions. You need not think of yourself as a failure if these distressing feelings reemerge at the Thanksgiving table or your stepbrother's wedding. Issues of inclusion versus exclusion, fairness versus favoritism, arise in every family, not just those formed when a parent remarries.

Anguish over Favoritism, Abandonment, and Isolation has strained families since the beginning of time. The works of Homer and the great Greek tragedies are filled with examples. Electra never felt secure at home after her father, Agamemnon, went to war. She never felt truly loved by her mother. Once her mother's new husband, Aegisthus, came on the scene, she had a new target for the rage she felt toward her biological parents.

LEARNING THROUGH DISPLACEMENT: AN UNANTICIPATED BENEFIT OF ADULT STEPFAMILIES

Feelings of being insufficiently loved exist in virtually all biological families but are rarely expressed directly. Confronting a parent or sibling may seem far too dangerous, a threat to our very survival. Because we may have tolerated inequities in family love all our lives, we may believe we are stuck with our wounded feelings forever.

If we were to talk directly to our parent or sibling about feeling unloved, we might provoke his or her rage and feel even more rejected and abandoned. Dad may have always loved your baby sister more. Yet, it may not be until you see your father favoring a stepdaughter at this anniversary party that you realize the depth of your rage and jealousy.

Because you displaced your anger onto a stepsibling instead of your father and baby sister, your fury can be much less restrained. You may not be aware that the real target of your resentment is your biological sister. It is far safer to be furious with a disposable outsider—your stepsister—than with a permanent family member.

Displacement is a psychological defense in which we fail to recognize our true inner conflict. We then express the feelings that rightfully belong to one situation in another context. Displacement in stepfamilies is powerful. It allows us to enlist our siblings as our allies—even those siblings we most resented earlier in life. In the new stepfamily, it is *we* against *them*. We have no problem being furious with the *other* family, unleashing our strongest emotions on them in ways we would never behave toward our own.

Displacement is also convenient. It allows us to blame our stepfamily for causing us to be unloved. What if we recognized this psychological strategy for what it is: a way to reduce the pain of something that happened in our biological family, long before *they* came on the scene? Once we understand the true source of feelings, we can begin to deal with them. Now, as adults, we can share this therapeutic discovery with a sympathetic sibling, spouse, or friend. With help (perhaps, from a therapist), we may now be able to figure out why we continue to be burdened with a childish longing for a parent's love, long after our childhood is over. In short, we may be able to move on.

Inevitably, there is an unequal distribution of attention, money, and love among the members of any biological family. We believe those feelings of resentment from long ago often fuel the Five Furies that trouble practically all adult stepfamilies. Yet, our stepfamilies can help us achieve the self-knowledge we need to overcome those early wounds.

Twenty-seven-year-old Angela told us:

My mother is a schoolteacher, and she has always been so disappointed in me for not finishing college. My older brother graduated from law school, and she thinks he walks on water.

When she married Fred, she got real chummy with his kids, and I really feel she likes them better than me because they are more educated. One of them is a teacher, and the other is a social worker. So, you can see why I feel like shooting them down whenever I have a chance.

Thirty-four-year-old Judy reported:

I disliked my father's wife before I even met her, just from the excitement and thrill in my father's voice when he told me about her. Then, when I saw them together and she was so beautiful and friendly and he was so ga-ga over her, I mentally tattooed the letter P for "phony" on her. I couldn't like her no matter how many good meals she cooked for me. She was no fool and got the idea and even asked me out to lunch to find out what she was doing wrong.

It wasn't until several years later that I realized that it was easier to dump on her than my sister, who had always been my father's favorite over me. I'd always resented my sister, but, when my father got remarried, it was easier to team up with her against my father's wife. Finally my sister and I were on the same side.

SPECIAL OCCASIONS OFFER OPPORTUNITIES: THE BIRTH OF A GRANDCHILD

The birth of a grandchild can be a real Saving Grace for a stepparent who is feeling excluded. This happy moment can provide an opportunity for building permanent bonds within the stepfamily, even when all else seems to have failed.

Barbara, age fifty-nine, told us:

As soon as my husband told me that his daughter Leslie's first child had been born, we rushed to the hospital, some sixty miles away. It was a marvelous sight to see the tiny newborn and the pride on his mother's and father's face. After congratulating the parents and gazing at the baby, "Grandpa" was given the child to hold, and out came a camera, and many pictures were taken. When the baby was returned to its basket, I leaned down for my turn, lifted the little one and held him in my arms. The camera didn't come out again. I felt left out. On the drive home, I told my husband that I felt excluded, and he was sympathetic.

When my stepdaughter visited our home weeks later, the baby was passed to my husband, and the same camera routine happened. Everybody was included in the pictures but me. I was hurt but tried to hide it. This time I said, "I care about your baby, too, and I'd like to be included." Leslie said, "Oh sure" and handed him to me. It was clear to me then that if I wanted to be part of the baby's life, I was going to have to ask for it. Alone. I was disappointed in my husband for being silent but decided to let it go.

This is a case in which the Guardian Angel, who could have knit this stepfamily together, failed to appear. Even so, the birth provided an opportunity for personal growth and assertion on Barbara's part that she decided to grab. Lacking support from her husband and other family members, she decided, nonetheless, to become a Joiner, for her own and her new stepgrandchild's sakes.

STEPFAMILIES ON VACATION

Going on vacation as a family may be the first opportunity an adult stepfamily has to spend unstructured time together. Such open-ended occasions can be trying, to say the least. Still, they also afford opportunities to form new bonds.

A transparency inevitably develops as we shed our work clothes and manners for the more open, casual environment of a family vacation. Some family members will feel that they are *owed* a vacation and won't lift a finger to help. Others will plan meals and initiate group activities. Some will always be there to help when a beach umbrella has fallen, a jellyfish has bitten, or someone needs a ride. Others will never be available.

On vacations, an important question arises: Who should create the structure for the occasion? If the hosts announce at the first meal that family members are on their own for breakfast and lunch, but that volunteers are needed to shop, cook, and clean up for the group dinner each evening, then everyone has some guidelines. Uncertainty is reduced. Of course, questions, such as "Who gets the best room?" and "Whose preferences shape the daily schedule?" will still arise, just as they did when you were children. Drawing lots on such matters can go a long way toward reducing resentments.

LOCATION, LOCATION, LOCATION—IT DOES MATTER

During our interviews, we were struck by how effectively a new, neutral place for the stepfamily get-together reduced tensions. When everyone is new to the setting, there is a greater chance that responsibility will be shared by all, instead of being shouldered only by Mom and Stepdad. Everyone seems more comfortable when no one has a special claim on the meeting place.

The low-key atmosphere of a vacation may be better for developing new bonds than higher-anxiety occasions, such as weddings. When you are living with and observing stepfamily members *offstage,* so to speak, you may find ways to improve a relationship that has been stuck. In a freewheeling situation like a vacation, you may finally discover you have something in common with someone you had never really gotten to know. You and the stepbrother you never much liked may find common ground fishing together or as the winning doubles team at tennis.

On the other hand, too much unstructured time together may make some family members feel more vulnerable, not less so. A certain amount of emotional Teflon is invaluable when spending a week with your stepfamily in a mountain cabin in the rain.

As people let down their defenses and become more of who they are underneath, they may also become less civil. Biological family members may become more clannish and exclusionary. This is particularly true if the vacation takes place in one of their childhood haunts.

Even when you are not stung by feelings of exclusion, you will probably feel relieved when the vacation ends. For a maiden voyage, we believe stepfamilies should try no more than a long weekend together. A three- or four-day weekend should give you a good sense of everybody's quirks and habits, without making anyone feel that this is a jail sentence, not a vacation. If the first attempt goes well, you can always schedule a reunion.

Happy memories of a shared vacation can help build a sense of community within the stepfamily that occasional dinners together never can. Conversely, a nightmarish vacation can escalate family tensions, even cause permanent estrangements.

Vacations can also exacerbate socioeconomic differences within the family. Worries about paying for transportation and sharing lodging expenses can make people uneasy. Some family members may want to eat in to save money. They may be embarrassed that they cannot comfortably pay for expensive restaurant meals.

It takes real courage to speak up if you are on a tight budget. In the long run, however, family members who do so end up feeling good about themselves. They also can look back on the vacation with pleasure, instead of being stuck with overdrawn credit cards and bad feelings.

Ron, age forty, told us:

After the first day at the beach house, my wife and I could see that we couldn't keep up with the way the others were spending money. We decided it would be better to speak up and say that we weren't prepared to spend money on eating out and that we had always cooked our own food on family vacations. It turned out that my stepmother's son felt the same way, and that led to all of us making our own plans for eating. Everyone did what they preferred, and it worked just fine.

WEDDINGS AND SUCH

A special event, such as the wedding of a stepchild, throws families together in ways that inevitably create a new shared history. In today's world, there may be many families involved, not just the bride and groom's biological families, but any number of stepfamilies, as well. Even if a genuine attempt is made to include everyone, there are liable to be moments of distress. The more formal, traditional parts of the ceremony offer the greatest opportunities for stress. Who walks down the aisle with the bride and groom? Who sits at the head table with them? Who is in the wedding pictures? Any and all of these decisions may trigger feelings of neglect, exclusion, or both.

Even when everyone has been consulted, weddings are often painful, as fifty-four-year-old Ruth reported:

I fully expected my stepson's wedding to have some difficult moments, but I hoped there wouldn't be any bad surprises. My stepson was very considerate of me during the planning. He asked if I was comfortable with not being in the wedding procession. I told him that I felt it was absolutely the right way to do it and that I didn't feel I belonged in the wedding procession. The entrance procession was for him and his bride and their parents who were giving them away, so to speak, in marriage. I was happy to be told I would have a seat in the front row of the church.

I didn't have any problem until the wedding pictures were being taken after the ceremony. I stayed to the side while the various immediate family members were photographed with my husband together with his ex-wife and my stepson. When it came time for the picture with my husband and me and his children and their spouses, including the bride and groom, my husband pulled me into the picture. As I moved to join the group, my stepdaughter objected, "I thought this was just for our family." My husband didn't hear her, but I sure did, and it hurt.

It is always helpful if each family member knows beforehand how the event will be organized and who will be included in each aspect of the proceedings. Everyone doesn't have to have a vote. Ultimately responsibility for the event lies with the marrying couple. It is up to them to set the ground rules, with a sensitivity to the feelings of the people closest to them. The bride and groom may also have to explain to various family members why they have chosen to do things the way they have.

Weddings involving stepfamilies require the full repertoire of diplomatic skills. Explaining the plan to stepfamily members before the wedding is far more important than the couple's china pattern or choice of caterer. A stepparent who feels mistreated is likely to remember that long after everyone has forgotten what the orchestra played. If the couple does their work well and makes it clear to all the major players that their presence is valued at the wedding, everyone will be more comfortable. Let's remember, not everyone can be seated at the head table.

Surprises cause the most distress. If you are a member of the stepfamily, don't hesitate to ask the marrying couple what plans they have made. If the plan makes you too uncomfortable, discuss it with them. They may decide to make changes. If not, you may decide not to attend. Unavoidably, your absence will have consequences. Nonetheless, staying away may be your best option, if you know that the wedding is going to devastate you emotionally. People rarely ruin the weddings they don't attend.

ETIQUETTE FOR HOLIDAYS WITH STEPFAMILIES

Family holidays are almost always stressful. So why should we expect more from holidays when stepfamilies get together? On all family holidays and special occasions, your Tact and Tacking strategies can be lifesavers:

- Put the topic of gift giving on the family agenda before the holidays so there are no embarrassing surprises. Get some e-mail dialogue going. There are probably too many people to expect meaningful gifts at a joint Christmas celebration. Some alternative, such as token gifts, gifts for grandchildren only, or picking one name from a hat can work. Bring a small gift to a stepchild or stepparent hosting a holiday dinner or providing a vacation house. You know what to do about birthdays and weddings.

- Find out what is planned and what is expected of you by your host. Find out who will be there and who will have which responsibilities. If the event itself is painful, try to put some emotional distance on it by taking mental notes on what is happening. Pretend you are an anthropologist observing some strange holiday ritual and discuss the event later with a trusted buddy who has been in a similar situation. (Tact and Tacking #3, Take the Role of Observer and find out about the culture.)

- If you have participated in the same family event before, and it has become a boring or stressful chore, Reframe the Issue (T&T #1). Instead of thinking of it as another dreadful Thanksgiving with your stepfather, think of it as a chance to sightsee in Philadelphia. It is your responsibility to make the occasion interesting and personally rewarding for yourself. You may want to ask other stepfamily members to join you in a visit to a local museum or some other pleasant activity before or after the main event. Or you may make it clear that you will be going off on your own or with nonfamily friends at a specified time during your visit.

- Find out your host's minimum expectation regarding your attendance and limit your visit to that. If it's a meal, you can probably excuse yourself after a few hours. If you're planning an extended stay, your absence may be less objectionable if you are doing something that can't be interpreted as unfriendly, such as working out at a health club. Or let your host know you can only attend every other year because of other obligations or limited vacation time or budget (T&T #5, Trading and Negotiating).

- Take an active role in planning to do something different the next time. Perhaps, you would have a better time on your own turf. Poll the others about changing the venue. Float the idea of each family spending some time alone together. Encourage the others to make changes they want, just as you want to make some changes (T&T #4, Tenacity, Sticking Up for What You Believe, and T&T #5, Trading and Negotiating).

- If you can absolutely predict an unpleasant time, ask if you can bring along a friend who has no place to go on the holiday. If it is in your home, invite some of your friends in addition to the family. This will dilute the family tensions and put people on good behavior. Seat yourself between people you like. If it is all family, serve buffet style so you can all spread out to sit down and eat. Structuring it this way avoids one awkward formal table conversation. (T&T #7, Wisdom)

- Remember, when things go wrong, be generous, apologize immediately and sincerely if you are in the wrong, and forgive quickly, too. (T&T #6, Tolerance)

- Give yourself time to adapt. Give it another year. Time tends to dilute intensity, and now you know the drill (T&T #2, Time). If not, then:

- Turn away from it, literally (T&T #8). Don't attend if the occasion costs you too much emotionally and you can't dilute the toxic effects. Arrange to see your parent or siblings in some other way.

THE OPPOSITE OF CELEBRATIONS: VIGILS AND FUNERALS

Those moments when stepfamilies come together at funerals, memorial services, or to await a life-or-death outcome for a family member are often times of great pain and anxiety. Usually, there are no clear guidelines or precedents for how to behave in such circumstances.

Sometimes, stepfamily members don't come to such events or take part in such vigils because they don't know what their role should be. Often, the bereaved family is too upset to issue invitations or to articulate its expectations. The most notice you might get as a stepfamily member is a hurried telephone call.

This is no time to stand on ceremony. In almost every case, your presence at the funeral or memorial service will be welcome. If you cannot attend, a letter of condolence is always appropriate. If the service is for a member of the stepfamily with whom you had a cordial relationship, clearly you will want to attend. Doing so is also a powerful way of showing other stepfamily members that you care about them and value your relationship with them.

If a parent has died, the most problematic relationship at the funeral or memorial service is usually the one between the surviving stepparent and the deceased's biological children. If there has been conflict in the past, each may fear that the other will be cold or hostile. Even if all parties try hard to be kind and understanding, the funeral may reactivate very intense feelings of Abandonment and Isolation, as well as other Furies.

Matt, age forty-five, told us:

My brother and I had plenty of time to think about our dad's funeral because he had been very sick for months with heart failure and kidney failure and going in and out of a coma. Even though we disliked Dorothy, his wife, because she was so possessive, she had, after all, been taking care of him for the past fifteen years. We decided that we could have some kind words to say about her at his funeral. After Dad died, we talked with Dorothy about wanting to say a few words at the funeral, about five minutes each, and she said it was a very good idea. I thought the three of us could cooperate for the first time in a peaceful way.

When the day of the funeral came, we had rehearsed our speeches and thought we had our feelings about Dorothy under control. We also thought we could take the burden off her by printing up a little program of the order of the memorial service to hand out as people arrived at the funeral home. We were totally taken off guard when she marched over to us at the funeral home with both barrels blazing and the program in her hand. "How dare you two be the first to speak and put my son at the end of the service?" She made us feel so bad, getting into a fight like that in the funeral home, which my dad would have been so sad to see. I suppose when the relationship is fundamentally not good, it just stays that way to the bitter end. I had a hard time saying the part in my speech about what a caring and supportive wife she had been, but somehow I managed it for my father's sake.

Matt was sensitive, but he may not have understood his own lingering desire to be first in his father's life—or death. Understanding his part in the final competition with his stepmother might have increased his self-awareness and led him to consult her before printing the program that led to their argument at the funeral.

THE GREAT AWAKENING

Family celebrations and commemorations can lead to a great awakening. The two (or more) families find themselves in a situation in which they can't escape one another. As we've suggested, interacting with your stepfamily may give you insights into lingering wounds from your earlier life that continue to make you unhappy. Being able to see yourself and your biological family more clearly is an important benefit of having a stepfamily.

In our experience, there is a sequence to resolving emotional issues in stepfamilies. First, problems too disturbing to deal with directly are often displaced onto the stepfamily and attacked in effigy, as it were. When someone in the biological family realizes that the problem predates the stepfamily and lies within the biological family, the enlightened individual has greater self-understanding. That individual may then be courageous enough to discuss those insights with his or her biological family.

We are not saying that all or even the majority of the tensions that adult stepfamilies experience are caused by unresolved problems in one's biological family. Some of the most intractable difficulties stem from competition and clashes built into step roles, as well as the involuntary nature of stepfamily rituals. Still, many of the most inexplicable, most strongly felt problems in stepfamilies seem to predate them. As soon as the biological family realizes that the stepfamily is often a shadow of itself, family members may become more tolerant of difficult behavior in both their step- and biological families.

Whatever the cause, remember that stepfamilies, like biological families, are systems of interdependent parts. When one person in a family system begins to behave differently, change inevitably occurs elsewhere in the system, and, oftentimes, for the better.

We encourage you to talk with your biological family about the experiences you have had with your stepfamily during holidays and other family celebrations and commemorations. Talking with your own family can broaden and deepen your initial insights.

If holidays, weddings, and other family events are stressful, illness creates its own special tensions. In the next chapter, we shall show how health issues can bring stepfamilies closer together or tear them apart.

CHAPTER 16

Health and Illness: Thank Heaven the Caretaker Is on Duty

Over the years, children's roles vis-à-vis their parents gradually reverse. Once taken care of, the children eventually become the care*takers*. Now, instead of Mom worrying when one of the children has a tummy ache, the children worry about Dad's arteries. The role of caretaker is both coveted and burdensome. As a result, an adult daughter may resent her new stepmother because the daughter wants to be Daddy's caregiver. At the same time, she is grateful that someone else is assuming much of the hard work and responsibility for his care.

Rationality is not the name of the game in stepfamilies—or any other families, for that matter. The same daughter who was angry and resentful over her new stepmother's coming between her and her "needy" father may simultaneously and paradoxically welcome that newcomer's arrival. So may all the other children, male and female. Why? Because, to put it bluntly, the newcomer will take the burden of their aging father off their shoulders.

As Sophia, age fifty-four, told us:

Since Mom died two years ago, Dad has lived in that house all alone. He's healthy enough and active, and he doesn't seem to mind. We keep in touch with him by phone, and we visit whenever we can, but we've been worried about him. We're not sure what he's eating, and he's had some heart problems.

So when we learned he was seeing Margaret, it was a blessing. We wanted him to have someone, because we knew he was lonely. When Margaret moved in with him that was even better. Now, he would have someone right there to take care of him.

There are many between-the-lines meanings in Sophia's statement. On the surface, we're hearing from a loving child genuinely concerned about her aging father's welfare. There is also the suggestion that Sophia is relieved that Daddy is no longer her problem.

Maybe, it would all be much less confusing if Margaret weren't also Dad's lover. Wouldn't it be great if she were just a paid nurse? Then, Sophia and her siblings wouldn't have to feel bad about Dad's violating their mother's memory or having sex in their mother's bedroom. Besides, when Dad passed on, the siblings could just pay Margaret for her nursing services, and she would leave. As adult children soon learn, however, when their parents find new loves late in life, things just aren't that simple.

Here are the words of fifty-year-old Joanna, remarried for five years at the time of the medical crisis she describes:

I was the one who called 911. And they ended up putting in a pacemaker. Tom's fine now, but he almost . . . I think his heart was twenty-nine beats. It was really low, and I ended up in the emergency ward with nobody else there and having to decide how am I going to call his daughters and not frighten them, but inform them. There were so many thoughts that went through my mind. How to be sensitive to the situation, to reassure them and give them information without frightening them while I was so scared myself.

So, he's lying unconscious in a little room. They let me use the phone, and I think I said something like "Barbara, this is Joanna, and your father is just fine. He's going to be just fine, but he had a problem, and we're in the emergency ward." But first I said, "He's just fine." And something about his needing a pacemaker. Then, I waved to one of the doctors.

You know how miserable they are in the emergency ward, but I waved and caught the eye of one of the doctors and asked him if he would talk to . . . I told him it was "a daughter." They didn't understand our relationship, you know they were rushing around. So, anyway, he talked to her, and then, each day and night, I would call her and tell her how he was doing.

Health problems often change a stepfamily's dynamic overnight, as it did in the case of Joanna and Barbara, her thirty-year-old stepdaughter. An unexpected phone call and a worried voice may lead to the first heart-to-heart communication between an adult child and a stepparent. Prior to this time, their conversations may have consisted entirely of small talk.

In health crises, the biological parent may not be available to mediate between the stepparent and the adult children. Since the ailing parent is the only one who knows everyone well, that can be a real loss. In most stepfamilies, most of the time, the biological parent is the one who knows the most tactful way to approach his or her children, particularly at stressful times.

Perhaps, the stepparent and the stepchildren haven't had time to get to know each other well. Maybe, they have protected themselves emotionally by limiting their interactions to pleasant discussions of trivial or neutral topics. When illness strikes, suddenly everyone must begin talking about important, sometimes grim, matters in an atmosphere filled with tension.

Typically, the stepparent is the one on the scene when the biological parent becomes ill. The adult children are very concerned, need information, and want answers. The stepparent is probably apprehensive about being second-guessed or ganged up on by the biological family.

These are occasions when hurtful questions and comments are often let fly. "Why didn't you *tell* me he was having surgery?" a child may ask. "Why didn't you get a private duty nurse?" "Have you gotten a second opinion?" Or a child may declare, "That's the worst hospital in the city!" All of these responses to a parent's illness are understandable, but none is very helpful. Such comments may be more than the worried stepparent can deal with, under the circumstances. Instead of laying blame, the family must try, as quickly as possible, to mobilize to help the ailing parent. But how to do that when there is so much potential for misunderstanding?

FROM THE ADULT CHILDREN'S POINT OF VIEW

As an adult child, you understand that your aging parent is likely to develop a serious illness at some point. You also know that your parent will probably be slower to regain his or her full health because of advancing age. At some level, you have even faced the inevitability of your parent's death. That's what you know, but it has very little to do with what you feel.

Whether because of divorce or death, your other biological parent is not on hand to give you daily update's on your ailing parent's condition. As neurotic as your biological parents may be, you have learned over time how to interpret what they say and the tone in which they say it. You can read them. You also feel, as their child, that you have an inalienable right to ask the same questions over and over again when your parent isn't getting any better. Unfortunately, you probably don't know your stepparent nearly as well, and you can't pester him or her with the same freedom you might a biological parent.

It boils down to this: When a parent has remarried, the inevitable problems surrounding illnesses and death become more complicated. Your stepparent is on the scene and likely to be managing your parent's care. Your stepparent, though intimate with your parent, may be a comparative stranger to you. All the medical information now seems to be filtered through your parent's new spouse, and you don't know how hard to push in order to talk directly with the doctor or even to your own ailing parent. When the intermediary is a stepparent who is emotionally reserved or excessively formal, you may feel that you are not being told the whole truth about the illness. And, tragically, that may true. In the worst possible case, you will lose your parent, and you will not have the opportunity to say good-bye.

You don't want to be in the position of thirty-six-year-old Jack, who told us:

I only saw my father after he was dead. His wife waited twenty-four hours to call us. Okay, I might not have gotten to Boston in time, but she had no right to decide that for me.

You probably want to participate in decisions about treatment or withdrawing supportive care. Your participation may involve everything from discussions about a terminally ill parent's quality of life to certain financial decisions.

Even when no stepparent is in the picture, serious health problems put a terrible strain on adult children. On the one hand, you recognize your parent's ultimate right to decide if he/she has the financial and emotional means to try a cutting-edge or experimental treatment. Organ transplants and complex cardiac devices are costly. A decision to pursue an expensive treatment can indirectly pressure all the family members to contribute money or equally precious personal time for a parent's care. A parent's long illness will most often significantly deplete his or her finances.

On the other hand, the decision of a parent with, say, cancer to pursue no treatment except alleviation of pain may be at variance with your values and needs. You may see that course as defeatism on your parent's part or lack of caring for the rest of the family. You may see it as desertion or abandonment, rather than stoicism. You want an opportunity to understand how your parent came to make whatever choice he or she makes. You want your opinion to be given a respectful hearing, at the very least.

Finally, if the worst happens, you want to participate in the planning of the funeral or memorial service. You want to be confident that whatever burial arrangements are made reflect your parent's wishes and the traditions of your biological family. Your understandable desire to be involved one last time with your parent now may be complicated by your stepparent's desires, values, and even tastes. Your stepparent may have different religious views from your biological family, which can be particularly upsetting when dealing with death and other final matters. You may want half your parent's ashes buried in the old family's cemetery. Your stepparent may be horrified by the idea.

Serious illness and death make all of us feel that we have limited control. The presence of a stepparent may exacerbate that feeling. Adult children with medical backgrounds who want to be involved in the parent's care will feel the most frustrated about not being in charge.

Some illnesses come on gradually, but many strike suddenly and require immediate action. Forty-year-old Martha told us:

At first, I couldn't believe what was happening to my father because I'd just seen him the other day, and he was completely healthy. His wife, Cindy, was trying to keep calm over the telephone, but I knew it was bad. My father had had a heart attack, and they were trying to dissolve the clot, but it didn't seem to be working, and they were talking about doing an angioplasty to keep the artery open. I was stuck at home with young kids and couldn't go there to be with him. I felt really glad he was remarried. Because, even though Cindy isn't someone I could ever feel was really family to me, I knew she was like a watchdog about my father's health. She subscribes to a dozen wellness newsletters, and she nagged my father into joining an expensive health club. I knew she would protect my father and had the guts to demand that the doctors give him the medical attention he needed.

When it comes to a parent's health, most children are grateful for a stepparent who really cares. Twenty-eight-year-old Carol told us:

I took my dad's new wife out to breakfast because I like her and wanted to get to know her better. I told her I was happy that she was in my father's life. She said she really appreciated my saying that. She asked me if I sometimes felt that their marriage was getting in the way of my relationship with my dad. She's a therapist. She said she didn't want me to feel excluded since she had come on the scene. She knew that my dad and I were always so close, and she asked if she was getting in the way. I began to laugh. No, I wasn't jealous. My dad had a serious heart attack when I was quite young. I told her my dad used to call me all the time when he was anxious about his heart, but since she was in the picture, he didn't. It was such a relief. I didn't have to worry about that anymore.

It goes without saying that adult children are busy with their own lives. If you are in the "sandwich generation"—providing for your own spouse and children at the same time you are concerned about your parent's well-being—you undoubtedly appreciate having a stepparent who keeps you informed. You recognize the thoughtfulness of a stepparent who makes sure you have an opportunity to speak to the doctor during a medical crisis. Being able to speak to your parent and the doctor helps you to confirm for yourself that your parent is getting the best possible care. It also allows you to feel almost as if you were on the scene as an active participant in your parent's care.

A stepparent who shares emotional and factual information with adult stepchildren can create a real bond, perhaps for the first time. Although a parent's illness can shatter a stepfamily, it can also result in the building of trust among all of you in a way that few other experiences can do. The tensions of day-to-day stepfamily life can seem trivial, indeed, when compared with a beloved parent and spouse's health.

Sharing little victories, like a day when a parent is without pain or has finally completed an arduous course of radiation therapy, can create a new kind of family unity. A parent's illness may be the occasion for putting some, if not all, of the Five Furies to rest.

Genevieve, sixty-three years old, told us ruefully:

I only got to know my stepmother in the last month of my dad's life. I moved in with them to help care for him. We really bonded during that time. It made me regret the years I'd avoided her. And I told her so. We hugged. She said, "Let's not look back. Let's just go forward together." I was really ashamed. For the first time, I saw her as my father did.

Respond in kind if your stepparent is acting in an inclusive way. Don't brush off a stepparent's attempt to include you in the collective effort of caring for your sick parent. Even if it isn't your style, think about sending snail mail notes that can be pinned up in your parent's hospital room. Consider it as a gift if your stepparent is so competent that it isn't necessary for you to rush to your parent's bedside, or miss work, or neglect other important responsibilities at the first sign of illness.

WHEN ILLNESS TURNS CHRONIC

New problems arise when a parent's illness is progressive and that parent doesn't regain his or her former vigor. When there is talk of long-term care and alternative living arrangements, conflicts between stepparent and adult children often become serious.

The tension is predictable. All the participants are dealing with the terrible threat of loss that irreversible illness brings. This is what happened to forty-year-old Alex:

My sixty-eight-year-old mother's seventy-eight-year-old husband was accustomed to my mother being active and providing the meals and the entertaining and all the infrastructure he needed to carry on his life for the last fifteen years. When it appeared that she was not going to recover from her stroke and would need assistance walking, bathing, and dressing, he announced that he had found a long-term nursing home for her. He called me and said that they had visited the place together, and my mother agreed that it was the best place for her. I was furious. I figured he didn't take long to dump my mother once it was clear that she could no longer be of service to him. I swallowed my anger and asked to meet with both him and my mother in their apartment to talk over this decision.

When we met, I questioned him strongly about other possible alternatives. I did my homework and gave him the names of several assisted-living facilities with apartments that they could move into together and where my mother could get additional assistance. He had a look made of stone on his face. He clearly wanted to continue to live in their apartment. Alone. He told me he wasn't ready for "that kind of place" yet, but he would visit my mother every day. My mother's eyes were full of tears, but she said slowly with slurred speech that the nursing home was very nice. I knew that she was worried that if she complained he wouldn't visit her there every day.

I couldn't get over his selfishness, but, on the other hand, I have three children, and I don't have the room or time to help such that my mother could come and live with us. If my father had been the healthy one, he never would have been capable of that kind of cruelty.

This sequence of events, in which adult children witness their beloved parent being monopolized and sometimes exploited by a stepparent, only to be deserted when times are bad, is not uncommon.

Forty-two-year-old Andy told us:

As soon as my mother developed Alzheimer's disease, her husband sued for divorce. It was fine for her to pay for their trips to Hawaii, but when she got sick, he was out of there. He was looking at huge nursing home bills and wanted out before she got to that point.

Andy's story reminds us that everlasting, unconditional love, though promised, can become distinctly conditional under deteriorating circumstances. When someone else makes us aware of the limits of love, we become anxious and are tempted to cast the first stone.

Conflicts between stepparent and adult stepchildren are not the only ones that surface during health crises. Stepsiblings may break into adversarial camps as they face the strains of illness and death. Whatever your role in the stepfamily, you will need extraordinary tact and self-awareness to avoid behaviors that aggravate the tension. Watching a parent die is one of the most grueling experiences we have, and it often causes childish, inconsiderate behavior.

Forty-five-year-old Robert told us:

The day my stepmother died, my father was in a tremendous amount of grief. He was very much in love with her. Meanwhile, my stepmother's kids were literally standing in the house, picking, selecting what they were going to take of her property and when. My stepmother was dead in her bed. She had just passed away, even though she had been sick with cancer for a long time. Her son was saying, "Well, gee, the blue china is gonna look great in our pantry," and her daughter was saying, "Oh, I love the tall wineglasses." My dad was devastated, and finally, I think it was my brother who said, "Are you guys kidding? Don't do this now." Well, my dad has never forgotten it, and you bet he heard it. And that was the beginning of . . . it was then he saw her kids for what they really were, both of them, within the same afternoon.

As terrible as that experience was, it offered opportunities to use the Tack and Tacking skills that we discussed in Chapter 2 to handle the situation in a constructive way.

Robert might *think:* "Those selfish kids. Their mother dies, and all they think about is their inheritance."

Robert might *say:* "Dad, no matter what it looks like today, your stepchildren are not without deep feeling for what has happened. They are probably trying to avoid the finality of their mother's death by focusing on her possessions."

Another disastrous deathbed scene involved Stanley, an eighty-year-old stepfather, and his forty-year-old stepson, Peter.

My mother was dying of kidney failure in a nursing home, where she had been deteriorating for four weeks. Stanley and I cooperated on finding this excellent facility but, otherwise, we had a history of having bitter arguments during the entire twelve years of my mother's marriage to him. I've always believed that Stanley married my mother for her money.

It was strange for us to be at peace with one another, but both of us were standing together weeping at the bedside of my almost comatose mother when Stanley burst out emotionally saying, "If your mother was a dog, I would put her out of her misery." I was horrified. "My mother is not a dog! How dare you say that!"

In another grieving family we interviewed, the principal issue was a child's being denied access to an ill parent by the new spouse. If your parent has been the only glue in an otherwise distant relationship with your stepparent, you may, in fact, risk being completely cut off from your parent if he/she develops a serious illness. That is one more reason for trying to build a good relationship with your stepparent from the start.

Thirty-year-old David told us:

When my father got cancer, his wife, Betty, didn't allow us to get near him. She wouldn't pick up the phone. When we called, we got the answering tape. We came to their door several times. When we did come inside, she said he was resting from the chemotherapy and was too sick to see us. I couldn't believe that he didn't want to see us, but she didn't want to deal with us. She wouldn't share him with us at all, and we thought about calling my father's lawyer to see what he would advise. It was as though she had kidnapped him. Thankfully, my father had a remission, and we have talked about what it was like when he was ill. He had been feeling that we were shunning him during that time.

In such a situation, you might *think:* "It was awful to be kept apart from my dad. His wife is crazy. She wants to pretend that we are not important to him. If he hadn't survived, and it was up to her, we would never have had a chance to say good-bye" (a response that is an example of Fury #2, Fidelity to Family, and #5, Favoritism).

You might *say* to your father: "Dad, the only way I can explain Betty's behavior toward us when you were sick is that she was concerned that you get enough rest so your cancer treatment would work. Or she was so scared that you weren't going to recover that she kept us entirely out of your way because she wanted so much to be with you. But that is behind us. This may be an up-and-down illness, so let's figure out a way where you can be the one to let us know how you are feeling. I don't want us to have to go through another long time when we don't see each other" (Tack and Tacking #1, Reframing the Issue; #4, Tenacity; and #5, Trading and Negotiating).

You might *say* to your stepmother: "I know your time together with my father is very precious. But I'd like to find a way to see my father even when he is sick and relieve you of some of the responsibility of caring for him twenty-four hours a day" (Tact and Tacking #1, Reframing the Issue; #5, Trading and Negotiating).

Fifty-two-year-old Larry told us:

Managing my father's care was the worst struggle I had with my father's wife in the twenty-five years of their marriage. I knew her well, and we had what I thought was a pretty decent relationship. He was in intensive care for two weeks after a brain hemorrhage. Then, he stabilized and started to recover, although his speech was hard to understand. My sister and I figured out what he wanted, and he wanted to go home. His wife, Laura, was impatient and didn't listen. "I don't want him at home." We were so freaked out by that. She kept saying, "There's no way I'm going to do it. I don't hear him asking."

Well, the hospital discharged him finally, and we found a great nurse. She really started to be able to communicate with him. As she got closer to my dad, Laura got more distant. Then, one day she fired the nurse and told us that she was afraid she was going to run out of money. She hired a less expensive nurse for shorter hours, and he only lived ten more days. I was very upset. He didn't survive because nobody was really in contact with him.

Would Larry's interpretation of the cause of his father's death have been different if his biological mother had been at father's side, instead of his stepmother, Laura? Perhaps. But Larry did the wise thing and decided to maintain his relationship with Laura, despite their differences, largely because his step-mother had meant so much to his father. They speak to each other every few weeks and visit several times a year.

When a chronically ill parent remarries, his or her dependency on the new spouse can develop very rapidly. If the new spouse is a physician or a nurse, the parent is even more likely to become dependent on that spouse. As an adult child in such a situation, you may feel that you are no longer a source of support and comfort for your parent, as did thirty-six-year-old Louise:

When my father died, our family doctor, who was a little guy and unat-tractive, started to pursue my mother immediately. I didn't like him. I couldn't even look at him when he had an arm around my mother. My own father had been elegant and handsome and generous. We had been a proud and accomplished family. My mother was so attractive and refined. But she was also very shy and vulnerable and had diabetes, which our family doctor had been treating for years. She was very dependent on him. So, he really had her trapped. She believed everything he said.

My mother married him quickly, within a year. What a comedown that was for her. He left his wife for her. They bought a place in Boston and a place at the Cape. They lived together for ten years. She and I could never talk about things after they married. He managed her life, and she believed he was keeping her alive. She wanted me to agree with her about his being her savior, and I couldn't do it. His children adored my mother. When my mother died of heart disease, she left only a small estate to us. I think all the real estate went to him. Things got a little sticky. I don't know what happened to her jewelry. I never did see her fur coat. It went to his daughter, I think.

What Louise might *think:*

"What an unethical thing for our family doctor to seduce my vulnerable mother, who was his patient, after all. He should lose his medical license for that. And then he gets his hands on all the property my father had left to my mother."

What Louise might have said to her mother:

"Mom, I am glad you are happy again and feel well taken care of by your new husband. I'm still missing Dad and have a hard time right now seeing you with someone else in his place. I know it must hurt you to see me reject your husband. I take responsibility for my behavior and want you to know I am mak-ing a real effort to adapt to your new marriage. In the meantime, could you and

I meet alone for an afternoon to do the things we used to like to do together? I'll pick you up and take you home." (Tact and Tacking #6, Empathy, Apology, and Tolerance; #5, Trading and Negotiating)

WHEN A PARENT BECOMES ILL

If you are an adult child, these are some of the things you should expect when a parent becomes ill and some of the ways you can cope.

1. **In the early phase or acute phase:** Don't be surprised if you begin to feel like an abandoned child. That's a normal response. You need to start gearing up at once for a long, frustrating period of uncertainty, tests, and procedures. Your parent is going to be frightened and needy, and you will want to help. And, painful as it may be, you need to prepare yourself for an impending loss. *Expect all these things and get your own support system in place.*

2. **Determine what you can contribute to your parent's recovery in the short term.** Don't get ahead of yourself and attend a funeral in your mind. First, listen carefully to what your parent and stepparent have to say about the nature of the health problem. Then, offer to do only those things you are able to deliver on—bring food, get medical information, keep other family members up to date, or visit. Maybe, all you can do is keep in touch by phone. Then, do that. Find out the best time to call your parent each day and plan how to end the conversation on an upbeat note. Tailor the length of the call to your ill parent's needs, rather than your own. Let your stepparent know what you intend to do and ask for his or her input. Expect differences of opinion. If you want to speak to your parent's doctor, ask for your stepparent's permission.

3. **In chronic or progressive illnesses:** Do some research on the condition on your own. Find out about the course of the disease and probable outcome on the Internet, at a good library, or by consulting your own doctor. If you discover something relevant to your parent's treatment, say you would like to give him or her some additional ideas, based on what you have learned about the disease. But make it clear that you understand that your parent will make the decisions about his or her care. Even if your research doesn't help your parent, doing it will make you feel better. Besides, it may provide you with information that is relevant to your own health.

4. **Be a voice of both realism and optimism, without being dogmatic or foolish.** Many chronic disorders stabilize at a certain level for long periods. Accept within yourself that your parent may never fully recover. Ask yourself if you are advocating more consultations because the diagnosis isn't clear or because you can't face the facts. Don't recommend an experimental treatment or some other extreme measure to your parent or stepparent that you couldn't or wouldn't do yourself, without making that caveat clear.

5. **Before making suggestions for treatment or rehabilitation, ask yourself if you are you willing to be responsible for some of the expense and logistics of the therapy.** Your parent may be in a position to pay for the treatment, and your stepparent may be able to handle the logistics. Still, you should at least recognize these important aspects of your parent's care before making suggestions.

6. **Ask yourself if you can become your stepparent's ally in making your parent's remaining time as good as possible?** If the answer is "yes," tell your stepparent. We found that the desire to form a positive alliance with a worried stepparent was often felt, but not put into words. Both parties need to be explicit about their intentions. The chance to create an alliance that will benefit your parent might be missed. Remember, no one can read your mind.

   Sometimes, the ill parent leads the way, directing the family to cooperate in managing his/her illness. That, however, is rarely the case. Usually, the spouse steps forward to guide other family members. As an adult child, you can facilitate cooperation by showing your siblings that you are willing and eager to work with your parent's spouse.

   Taking some responsibility, whether as a co-leader or good follower of your stepparent, can be an act of love for your parent. This often involves personal sacrifice. It is also a way to show reciprocity to a parent who has always loved you and cared for you, at a time when he or she truly needs it. You can show your parent your love without making anyone else feel excluded or resentful if you proceed honestly, thoughtfully, and tactfully.

   We are not trying to pretend that the serious illness of a parent is a shining opportunity. Usually, it is extremely harrowing. Rather, we are saying that you can choose to be either constructive or destructive in dealing with your parent's illness and its impact on your stepfamily.

7. **In cases of sudden death,** everyone in the family has to deal with his or her own unanticipated loss. There is plenty of opportunity for self-

blame and blaming others. Your emotions may include anger at the emergency medical staff or your stepparent for not doing enough. You may be angry at yourself for failing to show your parent how much you loved him or her while there was still time. Don't be surprised if you feel angry later at your dead parent for neglecting his/her health or safety and, as a consequence, deserting you by dying.

Irrational and explosive mood shifts occur. A parent's sudden death underscores and heightens whatever tensions already exist in the stepfamily. Because everyone is under pressure and suffering, it is harder to avoid conflicts, and there is not enough time to forge new understanding among the mourners. Because the parent who usually mediated family disputes is gone, arguments about property may escalate. There may be an ugly squabble over who gets the ashes. After all, these are the only earthly remains of a beloved parent and spouse, who has suddenly been snatched away. Religious differences among family members can make the situation even more volatile. If you find yourself in this situation, you can be enormously helpful by assuming your deceased parent's mediator role. Do whatever you can to ease tensions and keep the focus on honoring your parent's memory.

8. **If death has been anticipated for a while,** talk to your siblings about the kind of funeral or memorial service each would like. Consult with your stepparent to see what he/she has in mind. Act as a conduit between your siblings and your stepparent, so he or she knows how the rest of the family feels. Find a way to collaborate.

When a parent dies, the surviving stepparent and the adult children often maintain an attachment to one another, even when there has been enough conflict to warrant estrangement. This is particularly true when the stepparent has no biological children. Perhaps, the stepfamily's *détente* is a case of mutual need. The death may have made everyone realize how trivial the issues were that divided them. Or the widowed stepparent and the adult children may draw closer because they are trying to hold on to the last vestige of the person they all loved.

Sometimes, however, the stepparent and the children simply go their separate ways. This may cause anger and a sense of desertion in family members, who now wonder if their past relationship was simply a sham.

FROM THE OLDER COUPLE'S POINT OF VIEW

At the outset of their marriage, older couples rarely imagine how much of their life together is going to be spent in emergency rooms and doctor's offices. That is probably for the best. Sadly enough, many older couples discover that big chunks of their time are devoted to discussing symptoms, awaiting the outcomes of diagnostic tests, and weighing possible treatments. For the first time, the couple may understand the "in sickness and in health" part of their wedding vows in ways they never imagined when they were younger.

Part of loving each other will be learning how to be a sensitive consultant and how to help evaluate whether a symptom is important enough to seek medical intervention. Like it or not, you may find that a significant aspect of a late-in-life marriage consists of being a caregiver, being taken care of, or alternating those roles.

Sometimes, older couples chose to marry, rather than simply living together, because they realize that they need the legal authority of marriage to arrange the best possible medical care for each other. This includes the daunting authority to take your spouse off life support, if that is what he or she has requested beforehand.

If all that sounds grim, there is another side, as well. Perhaps, the extraordinary sweetness of being in love late in life comes from knowing how short and precious life is. That understanding and perspective help us to bear the loss of physical beauty, which is inevitable in the course of certain medical treatments.

Sixty-seven-year-old John told us:

When Helen and I married, it was a dream come true. We felt it was such great luck to find each other so late in the game. We were both in great shape physically and that was a big part of the attraction. I knew we vowed at our wedding all about in sickness and in health until death do us part, but it didn't occur to me that sickness would come so soon. She developed cancer of the breast in our first year together. We went together to see so many consultants, and all of her strong-minded children had their opinions, too. We finally made the decision together that chemotherapy would increase her chances of a cure. When she lost her hair, I did have a hard time with the change in her appearance even though I admired her courage, but I kept up a good front. Her hair is growing back, but the tamoxifen she has to take to prevent recurrence of the breast cancer reduced her sexual drive and that has been rough for both of us. Now, she's got an ovarian cyst that needs surgical removal.

I miss the life we were going to have together. Her favorite son insists on second and third opinions and argued for the most aggressive treatment for her cancer. But he has dropped out of the picture during the roughest times. He's not the one who goes with her to those appointments and sits through those second and third opinions and the extra lab studies each doctor seems to need. What's worse, somehow, I end up comforting him about his mother's lack of energy and attention to him. This is not what I planned on for my golden years.

From the healthier spouse's point of view, there is a trade-off between getting help and getting interference from stepchildren. There is an uncomfortable imbalance when the adult children want the authority to plan medical treatment without taking the responsibility for implementing it.

As a person with an ailing spouse, you are already feeling overburdened. The added demands of comforting your spouse's children and fielding their questions may tempt you into sharing less information with them. This is especially true when the health crisis takes so much of your energy and attention. But, remember, secrecy is a calculated risk. At some point, the children will probably learn the full extent of the crisis, and anger and resentment at your reticence are bound to follow.

Sometimes, though, having the family know too much in advance can backfire. That's what happened to fifty-eight-year-old Martin:

When Gail had to have her hip replacement, we wrote and told all our kids when and where it would happen several weeks in advance. Since they are all living out of town and working, we didn't expect them to travel here. The day before surgery, my two kids called her to wish her luck. Her own kids never called.

After the surgery was over, I called all our children and left messages to say she was fine and to call me back for details. Her kids didn't call back. Mine did. The following day, her daughter finally called my wife in her hospital room, and I answered the phone. Her daughter spoke to me in an annoyed tone of voice to say that she hadn't been informed as to when her mother was having surgery, essentially accusing us of neglecting to tell her. I lost it. I told her we had definitely told her and written to her about it, before I gave the phone to my wife. After the call, my wife said to me, "I wish you hadn't said that. It just makes it worse." My wife was mad at me for saying the truth, rather than getting angry at her daughter for not showing genuine concern.

It is painful for a parent undergoing surgery to see that stepchildren may be more concerned for them and more thoughtful than their own biological children. In Martin's case, his wife's anger with him is probably due to the fact that he has witnessed the embarrassingly bad behavior of her daughter.

I DIDN'T HEAR YOU SAY "THANKS"

One recurrent theme we heard from older stepparents was resentment over the failure of the spouse's children to appreciate all the stepparent had done in caring for their ailing parent. In light of what we heard, we would modify King Lear's complaint to read, "How like a serpent's tooth is an ungrateful *step*child."

Sixty-eight-year-old Doris told us:

Alfred was hospitalized a dozen times during a ten-year period of our marriage. I was amazed at his ability to withstand all the threats to his life and admired his courage. But I was constantly dealing with the possibility of losing him. Each illness was life threatening. It started with a bowel obstruction, which the doctor in the emergency room wrongly diagnosed as constipation. It turned out to be a malignant tumor that was luckily caught before it spread.

Then, he had abnormal heart fibrillations, which they treated with some medication that thinned his blood and had to be closely monitored. Then, he had a bladder cancer that they removed. I became an expert at pacing the floor of hospital surgical waiting areas. Then, he developed chest pain, and we rushed to the emergency room, where they gave him a clot buster. But it didn't work, and they tried a balloon angioplasty. A few days later, the pain came back, and they put in a metal piece they call a "stent" to hold the artery open. That worked for a few years, but finally he needed four-vessel bypass surgery.

None of his children ever went out of their way to come to the hospital during any of these times because they either lived out of town or the ones nearby were busy with their own lives. Okay, I guess I understand that. They talked to us on the phone, but those conversations turned out to be mostly for reassuring them that everything would be all right. The thing that hurts me the most is the absence of any acknowledgment for my role in prolonging their father's life. Even when we get together for holidays and vacations, they never make the effort to take me aside and thank me for anything I've done to help their father.

We suspect there is a big disconnect between what many stepparents fear is ingratitude and what adult children actually think about the role their stepparent has played. When we interviewed adult stepchildren about their parent's health problems, we invariably heard words of admiration, albeit sometimes grudging admiration, for the spouses who so faithfully cared for their remarried parent.

A number of adult children said how grateful they were to a stepparent who had helped their parent stop drinking or smoking. Even when the new spouse was someone with whom the children had little natural affinity, they almost always recognized the health benefits conferred on the parent by his or her happy remarriage. It's too bad all the stepparents who feel unappreciated couldn't have been flies on the wall during our interviews with their stepchildren.

When there is a large age difference between the remarried parents, it is usually the woman who is younger. In a world where more and more women are in the labor force, many of these women have demanding jobs or professions. Many are just hitting their professional stride and don't want to give it up when the older spouse becomes ill.

The married couple may have already prepared for the older partner's declining health and may be able to make do with hired healthcare workers. Yet, the adult children may be horrified by what they see as a cold, uncaring response on the part of their stepmother. Younger stepparents should not be surprised if their adult stepchildren respond negatively to the couple's turning much of the older spouse's care over to professionals, however well trained.

WHEN ADULT CHILDREN OR GRANDCHILDREN GET SICK

The older generation does not hold the exclusive rights to health problems in adult stepfamilies. Younger people also become ill, and the remarried older couple may find themselves being drafted or volunteering as caregivers for adult children or grandchildren.

A stepparent who is especially devoted to his/her biological children may inspire a spouse to get more involved than usual in the care of his or her own adult children. Still, not every stepparent is a gung-ho caregiver. Moreover, taking care of adult children was not something most stepparents signed on for when they remarried. As a result, the stepparent may resent the loss of the spouse who becomes the nurse to his or her grandchild or adult child.

If this caretaking role is only for a short time, while the younger family remobilizes its resources, the spouse may tolerate it well. Still, this is one of those instances when spouses inevitably wonder, *Who comes first, I or your children?* The older couple's marriage can be seriously damaged if that question isn't answered promptly and satisfactorily.

SETTING THE AGENDA FOR THAT DIFFICULT CONVERSATION

In the matter of illness, as in so much in life, the best strategy is to be pre-pared. Have a plan of action. Every couple needs to have a frank discussion about how they want the other partner to handle a serious illness and whom to notify if the ailing spouse is incapacitated.

Serious illness is a painful topic. This topic may be even harder to talk about than whether it is time to buy long-term care insurance (probably it is) and whether a retirement community makes sense or it is better to stay put. Each spouse also needs to know what funeral arrangements the other wants.

These are definitely daunting topics. So, it is hardly surprising that couples frequently postpone such discussions. Nonetheless, you should deal with these matters sooner rather than later, especially if either of you has adult children. There is less room for misunderstanding and conflict in the stepfamily when each partner can tell his or her children that decisions on these matters have been made. In addition, couples who marry late in life may find themselves facing compli-cated medical problems even before their relationship is firmly established.

Most of us don't want to think about illness and death, and so many of us don't. If you and your spouse haven't yet had this conversation, you need to do so. You don't really know what your spouse wants until you discuss it. Even if you have lived together for years, you may discover you are completely wrong about your spouse's desires. You need to tell each other.

For example, you may not know that your spouse wants all his or her chil-dren notified immediately in an emergency, even before the doctor has done an examination. Unless told otherwise, you may have assumed your spouse wanted to wait until a diagnosis was made and treatment recommended.

Actually, when you sit down to talk with your spouse, you may find this conversation isn't so terrible, after all. There are only so many decisions that have to made. You may find that you can psych yourself up for it. There are four basic questions involving illness.

1. **What** medical conditions warrant notifying the rest of the family? Distinguish the big stuff from the little stuff, the serious and life threat-ening from routine procedures.

2. **Whom** should you notify? Make a list—biological children, stepchil-dren, siblings, special friends, and other family members?

3. **When** should everyone be notified? Should you call at the first sign of illness or when the situation has stabilized?

4. **How** do you want the communication made? Do you want to tell everyone yourself (unless you're incapacitated), or do you want to leave it to your spouse, doctor, or a medically trained friend or family member?

Let's examine each question in more detail.

What?

Most couples don't think it appropriate to notify their adult children when scheduling routine diagnostic procedures, such as colonoscopies or mammograms. They rarely want to sound the alarm for nonthreatening illnesses, including a mild case of flu. Most couples don't feel it's worth alarming others over routine illnesses and tests. They also may feel that it is an invasion of privacy. On the other hand, when serious or life-threatening illness occurs, the word should go out promptly.

Who and When?

Most older couples soon learn that it is unwise to notify just one family member about any serious health issue without telling everyone in the immediate biological family of the ailing partner. Telling everyone prevents feelings of rejection, exclusion, and other negative responses that only add to the burdens of illness. Telling everyone is almost always the best strategy. If the ailing spouse is close to his or her adult stepchildren, one or both of you may want them notified as well.

Some families use e-mail, which is fast and easy and helps with problems caused by time-zone differences. Having everyone on a single group address also allows everyone to see who else has been notified.

Inclusion is a wise principle when you want to promote cooperation. Still, using the phone to make sure everyone is included can backfire. An unexpected phone call about a parent's health usually rattles the recipient, which is one reason most families don't notify everyone about the small stuff.

If either of you develops a life-threatening illness and is incapacitated, do you want your spouse to tell your children immediately or do you want to wait until morning or until the diagnosis is clear? If you haven't told each other what should be done in advance, your spouse may become the target of a great deal of anger on the part of your children. Even if the children cannot get to the hospital, or don't want to come, they may never forgive your spouse for failing to alert them.

When a significant illness is diagnosed, do you agree that you should inform your adult children, once you and your spouse have had some time to deal with the diagnosis yourselves? Often, telling the children as soon, as simply, and as calmly as possible prepares them for what may be coming down the road. Keeping them in the dark may lead to their being blindsided cruelly in the future. If that happens, adult children are liable to be furious, and probably justifiably so.

Most of the time, surprises engender mistrust and anger at parents, be they biological or stepparents. Adult children will wonder why you and your spouse felt the need for secrecy. Candor and inclusion may be even more important in stepfamilies than in biological ones. After all, trust in stepfamilies is often more fragile, if only because it has had less time to develop.

Do you or your spouse want word sent out to the adult children any time that a hospitalization is necessary? Or is one or more of the children a medical professional, whom you want consulted first and whose assistance you can enlist to tell the others?

Inclusion is great in theory, but there is a real possibility that bringing the children in on the discussion will be more of a burden than a help, at least initially. This is particularly true if you expect yourself to comfort and reassure everyone at a time when your own emotional resources are already stretched thin. Why not surrender the role of comforter? The best you can do is try to anticipate likely consequences of whatever strategy you choose. Forewarned is forearmed.

Try to simplify the communication process. Set up a telephone tree or calling chain so that you need notify only one family member, who can then call the next. That way, the whole burden of notification doesn't fall on you as you try to deal with more urgent concerns. Remember that the others may be hurt that they were not the first to be notified. Still, family members are usually more than willing to help in these emergencies.

Under what circumstances do you or your spouse want the other to discontinue life-support efforts? Have you and your spouse given each other formal permission to do so? Have you done the legal paperwork? Do you want a priest, minister, or rabbi present? What kind of funeral arrangements do you want? Do you want to be cremated and your ashes buried at sea or flown into orbit? Do you want to be buried together or in a family plot near your parents? Do you want a memorial service? Do you want donations made to a favorite charity in lieu of flowers or a more elaborate ceremony? Decide and be prepared to tell others in the family what you and your spouse's wishes are. That means your wishes on everything from resuscitation to the music at your memorial service.

How?

Usually, the ill parent should tell his or her children about a serious illness, unless, of course, that parent is already incapacitated. The ailing person usually knows the most about his or her illness and can tell the most complete story. This means not just the facts, but important information on his or her perceptions of the illness and how he or she is coping. Clear, candid information is extremely critical in helping the children give appropriate support to their parent.

Two people can have the same medical problem but have very different views on managing it. For some, the illness dominates; for others, they dominate the illness. Some people want their spouse there when they talk to other family members. Some may want to meet with their children with a doctor present, but without their spouse.

COPING STRATEGIES WHEN YOUR SPOUSE IS ILL

Besides talking about health issues before illness strikes, how can you best cope with a spouse's illness? Here are some suggestions:

1. Decide what help you would like from family members. They are going to ask you, "What can I do?" You should have a ready reply. This is no time to be a martyr, even if you sometimes feel like one. You can delegate many tasks: tracking down relevant old records from other hospitals, donating blood, running errands, finding out the costs of home nursing assistance, investigating possible nursing homes, or sitting with you in the surgical waiting room. All these tasks must be done. Allowing your spouse's children to do some of them will both help you and educate them about dealing with serious illness. Be ready to act as captain of the team, but make it a team, not a solo performance. When other people are brought into the decision-making and caregiving process, they have a greater investment in solving the problem. Those who have helped will be much more likely to support your decisions.

2. Sometimes, an adult stepchild will push for second opinions or other consultations that you do not believe are necessary and that may not be covered by your health plan. If your spouse is well enough, he or she should make the decision. If your spouse is too ill to decide, it's your call. You may be open to the child's plan if he or she is willing to participate with time, effort, or money. If you are opposed to the child's

plan, get a wise friend to be your advocate. Have your friend sit in with you on family discussions if you are afraid you're going to be steamrolled.

3. Be sure that the biological children have access to their sick parent and encourage communication, as long as your spouse desires and can handle it. Respect their input and their wish to contribute their wisdom for their parent's recovery. Don't be afraid to have them relieve you in the hospital from time to time.

4. You and your spouse are so emotionally involved in the illness and its treatment that you may be absorbing only 3 percent of what the doctor is saying to you. Don't hesitate to ask someone whom you both trust to sit in and ask questions when you meet with the doctor. That person should be intelligent and calm. You should also ask a calm, reasonable, optimistic family member or friend to sit with you in the waiting room during surgery or other long hospital procedures. You, too, need support and comforting.

IF YOU ARE THE SICK PERSON

1. As long as you can, stay in charge of what is happening to you medically. If possible, inform your children yourself about the state of your health. Ask your spouse to do it only if you cannot. If your spouse must take over, try to make it clear to your children that this is your wish. If your spouse is unable or unwilling to take over, designate someone else whom you trust to direct your care and communicate with the family. It could be one of your children. Often, a family member with a medical background is the best choice.

2. Find out who is the most medically astute person in your family or friendship circle. Consult with that person or persons and ask your spouse to do so, as well. A friend or family member who is a physician can be a lifesaver in a health crisis. That person is a good resource for determining what questions you should ask or for helping you identify appropriate specialists.

3. Let your spouse know what you have asked your children to do to help. That way, your spouse and the kids won't be tripping over each other or duplicating efforts. Be as tactful as you can under the circumstances. Even though you are sick, their feelings are still easily bruised. You

will benefit the most from an efficient, coordinated effort on the part of all your loved ones, with no time or energy wasted in squabbling.

4. Inform your stepchildren about your medical problems, preferably in person. It almost always helps if the spouse who is doing the caregiving has the informed support of his/her biological children.

COLLABORATION, NOT COMPETITION

Competition sometimes seems built into the relationship between stepparents and their spouse's children. Illness doesn't make that competition disappear. Still, because you have a loved one in common, the potential for cooperation also exists, although it is often overlooked. The shared desire for a parent to recover can strengthen alliances within the extended family. If family members make a genuine effort to mobilize their energies and talents, the ill parent can only benefit, and the stepfamily may emerge from the crisis closer than ever before.

The cleanup at Ground Zero after the World Trade Center tragedy took significantly less time and money than originally predicted. That happened because labor unions and government agencies collaborated instead of acting, as they so often do, as adversaries. The crisis created by a parent's serious illness can cause a similar realignment within the stepfamily. Work together to help the parent get well. In the process, everyone can benefit.

Enough issues arise in adult stepfamilies to fill an encyclopedia. We have described some of the thorniest problems and proposed strategies for dealing with them. In the next chapter, we'll offer some final thoughts on how to survive and thrive in an adult stepfamily. Think of it as a miniguidebook to adult stepfamilies.

PART IV

Destination Reached: A Pocket Guide

CHAPTER 17

The Brave New World of
Adult Stepfamilies

Adult stepfamilies, we repeat, are not for sissies. Neither are they for dummies. These stepfamilies—composed of a couple who marry late in life and their adult children—require courage, determination, wisdom, patience, empathy, compassion, humor, and much more.

Even at the height of matrimonial bliss, problems surrounding stepchildren can open a dangerous fault line in the new marriage. From that beginning, permanent fissures can snake through the new spouses' relationship even before the couple has had a chance to find a solid footing.

Over time, though, and despite these early shocks, most stepfamilies are like fine wines. They age pretty well. Yet, like those wines, stepfamilies need tending and turning to ensure that they are aging properly. Don't expect your stepfamily to succeed without a consummate effort on everyone's part. And don't be surprised if not all the members are equally committed to doing the hard work necessary to ensure a happy outcome.

Let's remember that the adult stepfamily was not created by consensus. The parents enthusiastically and largely unilaterally decided to take this late-in-life journey. The adult stepchildren were dragged along for the ride. These are hardly the most auspicious conditions for starting a new family, especially when the children are adults, who have been making their own decisions for quite some time. When parents remarry, the children find themselves in an unfamiliar role, a role they never prepared for or sought. It's not surprising that so many adult stepchildren respond with bewilderment, anger, and an unpleasant sense of having lost control of their own destinies.

THE NEW COMING OF AGE

For the parents to be quite oblivious at first to their children's response is equally natural. To the children, the parents often seem like impulsive, irresponsible, self-obsessed teenagers, blinded by their new love and blind to their children's distress. Buoyed by passion and optimism, the parents may be insensitive—perhaps, for the first time ever—to the feelings and needs of their children and grandchildren.

We were surprised to find that virtually every newlywed parent we spoke to felt nonplussed by the complex emotional responses of their children and stepchildren. Most were amazed, at first, that the children were not absolutely thrilled about the marriage. Living in their own bubble of happiness, these parents repeatedly expressed surprise that their children, busy with their own families and demanding professions, were so exercised about their parent's new relationship. Nor did the problems end with the parent's remarriage. Often, that's just where they began.

WHO'S THE REAL BAD GUY?

Remember from Chapter 2 the sister and brother who complained about receiving a postcard nonchalantly informing them that their father was honeymooning in Las Vegas with a bride whom they'd never met. They were still angry at him long after he had died. Initially, the children were furious at *both* their father and his new wife. Eventually, you may recall, they realized that their father's offhand announcement was consistent with the thoughtless way he had always behaved, long before their stepmother had entered the picture. They also knew that their father had always used his potent charisma to bend everyone to his will. Once they focused their rancor on its proper subject, they began to see their stepmother in a new light.

The stepson, age fifty-seven, told us:

When we met Isabella, we actually found that we liked her. She was a terrific woman. We began to wonder what she saw in someone like our father, who had a lifelong habit of putting himself first. He had put himself ahead of our mother and ahead of us all of our lives, but, still, he was the only father we had. By then, we realized that he was an accomplished seducer, who was used to getting whatever he wanted by pouring on the charm. In fact, we actually felt very sorry for his new bride, and that increased over the years. Eventually, after many years of marriage counseling and therapy, Isabella left Dad. We wondered how she had stood him so long.

In this case, the too-casual wedding announcement was not a stepfamily problem, but a variation on a problem from the sister and brother's biological family. Their father was the weak link in the new stepfamily, and it was sad, but not surprising, that the adult children remained angry at him even after his death. They probably would have been furious with him for many similar reasons even if he had never remarried.

THE ART OF APOLOGY

Someone with a "lifelong habit of putting him[or her]self first" is not a good candidate for advice from us or anyone else. But there is a lesson in that story of the postcard from Las Vegas. If you are a newly remarried parent who thought you could avoid family problems by eloping, don't bet on it.

The good news is that there's still time to make amends. As soon as you can, call the family together to apologize. Better yet, meet with each family member and explain how you arrived at that not-so-wise decision. Don't overdo the breast-beating, just tell it like it was, then get on with your happy new life.

Empathy is your best weapon in your battle to create a happy stepfamily. If you're the errant parent, remember how you felt when your adolescent kids stepped over the line and did something "unforgivable," only to apologize later and ask for your forgiveness. Sooner or later, didn't your heart melt? If you're the "sinned against" adult child, shocked by your parent's failure to include you in such an important event, take a few quiet moments to remember your own adolescent misdeeds and your parents' ultimate forgiveness. Forgiving makes the world whole again. This is your chance to reciprocate by forgiving your parent for being so thoughtless just this once. Forgive that postcard from Vegas just as Dad forgave you for that dent you put in his new car twenty years ago.

When those we love acknowledge their failures of judgment and ask our forgiveness, it behooves us to give it, even to our parents. The act of forgiveness has great therapeutic powers, both for the forgiver and the forgiven.

INEVITABLE COMPLICATIONS

There are few certainties in later-in-life remarriages. Unpredictability exists, even when parents have painstakingly laid the groundwork for their upcoming marriage. Even when the adult children already know and like the prospective stepparent, there is still no guarantee that all will go swimmingly in the future.

Stepfamilies, like most families, seem to move from crisis to crisis. Once the ceremony is over, there are still potential trouble spots everywhere. What will happen to the family home? How will the new marriage affect the children's inheritance? What will happen if the parent becomes seriously ill? Relatively improbable events and small matters can seem important in the emotionally charged context of a new stepfamily. At your new stepson's wedding, will you have to talk to your new spouse's former spouse? Will you be in the family wedding pictures? Does your new spouse expect you to invite his former wife to Christmas dinner "for the children's sake"? How should you select gifts for children and stepchildren with different tastes and different expectations about their cost? Are you and your spouse going to continue to support his (or her) irresponsible daughter? Is your spouse willing to pick up part of the tab for your son, who has finally decided to go back to graduate school?

THE BENEFITS ARE REAL

Every stepfamily has its own set of challenges and perils. Every stepfamily has to find the right answers in its own way. It isn't going to be easy. It takes hard work on everyone's part to make a happy, or even a peaceful, stepfamily. Yet, when a stepfamily succeeds, the benefits far outweigh the costs for everyone.

They may seem far off, but be assured, the benefits are definitely out there. They include a stronger, richer extended family; more kin to love and to be loved by; and more helping hands during family celebrations and medical crises. Still other benefits accrue: invaluable insights into yourself and your biological family; examples of different, sometimes better, ways to live that stepfamily members bring to the mix; new chances to reconcile with old family members; opportunities to "get it right this time" with a new spouse, children, or stepparent; the gift of a complete family, if you are a spouse who has never married before or never had biological children; greater financial security, perhaps; and—something we could all use—increased wisdom and maturity. Keep such benefits in mind when you are tempted to do or say something that might slow the growth of your promising new stepfamily.

These benefits, of course, don't simply arrive in the mail. Like most valuable gifts, they need to be earned, and not just once. They need to be earned over and over again. Stepfamilies require massive amounts of patience, tolerance, and good will.

You can maximize the chances that your stepfamily will succeed by assuming one or more of the positive roles we described—by becoming a Joiner, a Guardian Angel, a Unifier, or some combination of all three. When things are going badly in your stepfamily, you may be tempted to throw in the towel and opt for one of the negative roles—the Indifferent One, the Distancer, or the Destabilizer. Resist that temptation. It can only lead you into trouble. Try to take note of the roles others are playing. Your good example may be enough to persuade a Distancer, say, to reconsider and start joining in, if, initially, only for the duration of some particularly pleasant stepfamily function.

We are not proposing that your whole life must now be devoted to analyzing and solving stepfamily problems. Far from it! If you are an older spouse, you deserve to invest most of your energy and time in enjoying your new relationship. Life, as we all know, is always too short. Sometimes, however, there may be one particular family member who is particularly annoying and destructive. If you have tried your best and failed to come to terms with that person, you may have to let go. Give yourself permission to give up on that relationship, if only in your heart. At family gatherings, be civil, even pleasant if you can muster it. But remember that none of us has the magic power with which to change others.

Even if you are a trained therapist—and most of us aren't—it is not your job to cure the ills of your new relatives. That's not what family life is all about, even in stepfamilies. In our research, we found that the people who were happiest in their stepfamilies were those who had modest expectations and simply dealt with new problems as they arose. The happiest ones also seemed to have the knack for seeing humor even in the small potholes along the stepfamily highway. It's an added plus if you have the ability to laugh at yourself!

No matter how old or new your stepfamily is, tensions will keep cropping up, just as they will in biological families. For example, stepchild, suppose a stepparent invites you to a family get-together, but only at the last minute, weeks after you have learned about the upcoming party from your stepsiblings. Surely, you will feel hurt. Our advice: Get over it! An example for the stepparent: A stepchild who unexpectedly reminds the stepparent that he or she is not *really* family will still cause pain, even if the marriage is ten years old. That's their problem, not yours. Most families have hurtful members, who have a special gift for pushing painful buttons. Your best option is just to sit as far away from these harbingers of gloom as possible!

Remember, one or more of the Five Furies—Fear of Abandonment and Isolation, Fidelity to Family, Favoritism, Finances, and Focus on the Self—afflicted virtually every family in our study. So, don't be surprised if the Furies visit yours. All five Furies, however, can be contained, and none has to cause permanent scarring.

In fact, the Furies teach us important lessons. Some of the most valuable learning in adult stepfamilies comes from analyzing situations in which we found ourselves shaken by a visit from the Furies. Our negative reactions to stepfamily members can be valuable clues to our own unsolved problems. Often, what we see as just a stepfamily conflict turns out to have its real origins in some old wound we suffered long ago.

Such self-learning can help us improve our relationships with our original families, as well as with our stepfamilies. Besides, such personal insights often free up energy within ourselves—energy that can be used for more constructive purposes than dwelling on the past.

THE DANGER OF TRYING TOO HARD TO MAKE ONE HAPPY FAMILY

Here is one last cautionary note. Happily married stepparents sometimes feel that they must succeed in creating a happy stepfamily, no matter what the cost. There are several reasons for this. First, it may be meant as an act of love for your spouse. Second, it may be motivated by a desire to show generosity and goodwill. Third, you may feel morally committed to maintaining a positive, can-do point of view. But be cautious lest you overdo it. Such motives may end up causing cracks in the marriage. Sometimes, your efforts can become obsessions that convert stepchildren from simply being cool, distant acquaintances into becoming a reason for ending your marriage.

Here's an example. George, a seventy-four-year-old man, was in this quandary:

My stepsons and I got off on the wrong foot from the beginning. They consistently avoided meeting me for the first year of my relationship with their mother. I tried to forget about that and make a fresh start when she and I married two years ago. I made efforts to be pleasant, sociable, and accommodating, without overdoing it or stepping on any toes. I've offered to help them with practical problems, like lending one of them my car in a pinch or giving them tickets I can't use to a ballgame. They have responded by treating me with a sneering and sarcastic attitude or ignoring me completely. My wife is present when they behave this way, but she doesn't seem to get it.

When I talk with her about it privately, she looks away from me and says she agrees it is unfair, but doesn't know what to do. I think she's afraid of telling them what she thinks to their faces because she's afraid they will turn their backs on her if she criticizes them.

I am sick and tired of being treated with resentment and as if I'm not worth civil manners when I'm in their company. My marriage is in jeopardy if we can't resolve this. I've never had any bad intentions towards them and just want to live a good life with the woman I love.

What, then, can George or you do when feeling rejected by your spouse's adult children? Your friendly behavior only seems to encourage a response of contempt and disrespect. Appeals to spouses for help can make things even worse. Their dual roles as spouse and parent are in conflict. Parents may fear that criticizing their adult child's behavior will evoke further hostility and rejection. They dread causing permanent damage to their relationship with their child, which they are trying so hard to preserve in the face of their remarriage.

Pressuring a spouse to deal with a stepchild's rejecting behavior is seldom an effective method. On the other hand, having a conversation with your spouse about feeling discouraged by repeated rejections or insults can be quite helpful. When you married, you made a commitment to share the ups and downs of life. Speak from the heart about your own feelings, but be careful not to be destructive to your partner's feelings. Use your Tact and Tacking skills and be sure you plan to give yourself the best chance for success. Pick an agreeable, quiet time and place for this important conversation. Don't start to discuss it while you are still feeling angry or hurt.

Ask yourself what you want to accomplish. What would you consider a successful conversation? One measure of success is getting to the point where your spouse becomes able to express—to your satisfaction—*your* problem in *her/his* own words. (The same measure can, of course, apply to discussions between stepchild and stepparent.) Remember, even at the point that the other person understands your dilemma, he or she may still disagree with your conclusions. After you've had your say, reverse the process. Get your spouse's take on the problem. You both might get some new ideas after listening to each other's observations.

After such an important conversation, wait awhile to see if there is a discernible change. If your spouse does not spontaneously step in and tactfully intervene the next time the offensive behavior occurs, it's time to move to another option. This takes courage, but by now you know that being a member of an adult stepfamily requires that kind of strength.

Continuing to pressure an unwilling spouse for protection is never wise. Even if you win, you lose. Your spouse is very likely to resent being forced to choose sides in what feels like a whose-side-are-you-on showdown. Without intending to do so, you may unconsciously create a situation in which a stepchild, who previously could be managed as a Distancer, is now transformed into a Destabilizer.

SOME THINGS CAN'T CHANGE: DON'T BREAK YOUR HEART TRYING

Here is something worth thinking about before you try even harder to convert an unwilling spouse into an ally in your struggle against his/her own biological child. Parents who can't set limits on their child's rude or cruel behavior are either not able to recognize such behavior when they confront it, or they recognize it but are loath to say anything about it. The reasons: embarrassment, tone deafness to feelings, and/or, most likely, guilt.

Guilt is multifaceted. A parent may feel a deep sense of guilt about saying "no" to almost any behavior coming from that child. Or guilt may result from feeling responsible for the failure of the old marriage. Or a parent may feel guilty about never having been able to love that particular child sufficiently. Parents acting out of guilt often believe, falsely, that giving in to that child will eliminate those painful feelings.

All of these habitual reactions were in existence long before you came on stage. Remember, denial of hostile behavior and/or feeling excessive guilt are enduring attitudes, highly resistant to change. Both often have unconscious roots. Remember, too, that you signed on as a partner. You have not been invited to act as a therapist, nor do we recommend that you try. That's why it's a good idea to find out, tactfully, and before your marriage, the answer to this not-so-simple question: "Do you find it hard to say 'no' to your children?" You'll probably marry anyway, but knowing the answer in advance should help you to manage your expectations.

HAVE YOU TALKED ABOUT IT WITH CHARLEY/CHARLENE?

What can you do with a difficult stepchild, short of putting out a contract on your adversary's life? Sooner, rather than later, either accept the degree of distance that will intervene between you or make your own solo efforts to change it. You may want to gird up your loins and invite a rejecting stepchild to some special event that he/she enjoys. Ask your spouse for suggestions. Your spouse will probably be glad and relieved to hear that you are trying a positive, independent effort to reach out. Reaching out to the "enemy" is difficult. It takes courage. Keep your expectations realistic. You don't have to have a wonderful time together. Settle for a pleasant, civil time, a time where you can get to know one another a bit better. It won't all be solved on the first try. It takes years, not days.

You might ask a stepchild who typically doesn't speak to you when he/she visits to help you serve drinks, help serve the food, or clean up with you. You may be able, in this gentle way, to show this person it is possible to create a civil relationship.

HAVING YOUR TALK, AND THEN WALKING YOUR TALK

If nothing changes, the next thing to try is a more direct one-on-one discussion. Be sure your spouse knows what you are planning. Describe it for what you want it to be: a constructive approach to your problem. Have lunch or coffee in a quiet place, preferably away from your home. Here are some talking points that may be useful.

- "We've known each other for almost a year (or whatever), but I don't feel we've yet become comfortable with each other. It would please me if we really got to like each other, but I'll settle for feeling comfortable. What do you think? Are you uneasy, too? I'm pretty anxious about bringing this up."

- "I wonder whether I'm doing some things that you don't like?" Then, listen carefully and respectfully to the response. Try not to jump in to defend yourself when your behavior is described.

- If your stepchild tells you what is difficult for him/her after you have listened carefully, put it in your own words and reflect back. "Did I get it right?"

- Look at the situation as one in which the relationship isn't working. *Both* of you need to figure out how to improve it. "What works for you?" may be the best response to criticism of the way you have done something.

- If you get either no response to any of your questions or denial of any problem, go on to state how you feel. For example, "When you come to our home, I'm not sure whether you are going to say "hello" to me or even include me in your conversation. I'd like to be included. I'd like to know what's going on in your life. We've been thrown together by circumstances, but can we try to make it work the best way for both of us?"

By the way, all of these talking points are equally appropriate for an adult stepchild to initiate with a problem or difficult stepparent.

That's about it. You may not make any progress in the relationship, but you will have been brave. You will have let it be known that you are here to stay and open to talking about changing things for the better. After all, what are your choices? Withdrawal can be a form of self-protection, but it can also be an attempt at punishment that is almost always ineffective. Martyrs and victims don't win medals in stepfamilies. On the other hand, someone who has gallantly tried and failed to engage in a positive way can then move on without guilt. Everyone knows that it takes two to tango. Yet, sometimes, we keep trying to dance it alone.

MANAGING EXPECTATIONS

How tempting it is to fantasize about changing the "wicked stepmother" or "indifferent stepfather" or "selfish stepchild" into a model family member. Forget it! You can only change your own behavior, attitudes, and feelings. So, stop thinking about the transformation you would like to see in the most difficult stepfamily member. It's not going to happen. Instead, decide on something you would like to change in yourself and work on that. Maybe, you want to stop trying to win the affection of the stepfather, whom you see as indifferent. Denying him so much power in your life will make you feel more empowered.

That doesn't mean that you shouldn't pay keen attention to your stepparent or stepchildren. Far from it. Like the members of your biological family, your stepfamily will probably value your thoughtful attention. Nonetheless, remember, you are all adults. By definition, grown-ups have to live and learn their own lessons, and the healthiest ones continue to do that throughout their lives.

IDENTIFYING THE SAVING GRACES

We have urged you to look for the Saving Graces in your stepfamily. Like the Furies, the Saving Graces are always there, beneath the surface. The Saving Graces tend to be quieter than the Furies, and so you may have to search harder to find them.

Over time, the Saving Graces allow us to see that our new, larger, more complex family is full of possibilities—for new relationships, happiness and support from unexpected quarters, and for learning more about ourselves and the world. The Saving Graces are the gifts we get in return for dealing with the heavy demands of the adult stepfamily. The Saving Graces include all the increased resources that a stepfamily can bring to us—additional caches of emotion, support, knowledge, even financial help.

Dealing with the slights of new family members who are not as emotionally advanced as you are helps you to learn patience. Knowing that such petty cruelties are common in stepfamilies (biological families, too, for that matter) can lessen their sting and reinforce your determination to be kinder to others. Sorting through the stereotypes of stepfamily life, with all their ancient cultural baggage, will teach you that it's almost always the role that needs to be fixed, not the person in it. And, we hope, you will learn to look beyond the stereotypes to the real people who are struggling, just as you are, to make the best experience of this unfamiliar, new family unit.

The first Saving Grace you may notice is how the remarried couple blossoms in a fulfilling new marriage. Replenished and reinvigorated, the couple may become better biological parents, as well as stepparents. Another Saving Grace may appear as stepfamily members gain new wisdom and maturity in dealing with the "other family." This is what we mean when we say that gaining a stepfamily holds up a mirror to the original family.

The expanded family may offer fresh opportunities for friendship and mentoring. This can be a special joy for stepparents without children of their own and for stepchildren who did not have competent parents or who lost a biological parent through divorce or death.

If you are an only child, a stepfamily can offer you a second chance to have siblings. Or the stepfamily may mean a chance to have more functional, kinder siblings than the ones your biological family gave you. Particularly for adult children who have long worried about a lonely, aging parent far away, perhaps the greatest Saving Grace is the knowledge that your parent has another chance for a loving, caring, and enriching relationship.

We are not asking you to ignore the downside of stepfamilies. Far from it. In fact, you must learn how to stand your ground and set boundaries in your new stepfamily, just as you did in your biological one. Don't fight it. Grow from it.

TACT AND TACKING

We have described a set of strategies for resolving family problems that we called Tact and Tacking. They ranged from reframing issues to allowing time to solve some problems; from standing back and taking the dispassionate role of an observer to trading and negotiating; from exercising tolerance and forgiveness to simply letting go of your anger and avoiding the known hot buttons of other family members. Sometimes, no strategies work, and you must simply hold on, remaining calm, sensible, and supportive of the people whom you love the most. Usually, though, Tact and Tacking skills are effective not only in dealing with stepfamily members, but in other interpersonal situations, as well.

Besides, as we have noted throughout this book, the stepfamily is a system. Consequently, any change in one part of the system ripples and reverberates throughout all the other parts. It is often easier to see how someone else's bad behavior has roiled the entire system than to see the impact of your own tentative efforts to make things better. Nevertheless, every positive step you take matters, too, even if the changes are subtle and progress is maddeningly slow.

YOUR STEPFAMILY IS NOT YOUR LIFE

One lesson that we may not have stressed enough is the importance of giving up the epic saga of your grievances with your stepfamily. Although repeating the tale again and again may be all but irresistible, remember that re-opening the wound doesn't help it heal. Instead of broadcasting your sad story, confide in a buddy you can trust, preferably someone who also is struggling in an adult stepfamily. The catharsis can be exhilarating and therapeutic, especially if your friend occupies the same role in his or her stepfamily as you do. It can be even more helpful to have a friend who occupies the opposite role, the role of your stepfamily *bête noire*. He or she may be able to give you insights you have been too hurt or angry to get from your own stepfamily.

A friend who can listen compassionately and offer sensible, noninflammatory advice is an invaluable resource. You may even learn from observing how your friend missed a chance to create an alliance or repair a rocky relationship in his or her stepfamily.

We have talked repeatedly about the importance of buddies. Here, we should issue a caveat. A buddy's value is in helping you dig yourself *out* of a hole. Don't use conversations with your friend as an excuse for digging the hole deeper and deeper. Don't allow yourself to become addicted to the sharing of stepfamily horror stories.

From the ever-growing pool of potential confidantes, steer clear of the visibly neurotic ones and the people whose relationships tend to be dysfunctional. They may be good commiseraters, but they have little to offer in the way of constructive, cool-headed counsel.

Over time, sharing your stepfamily experience with someone in the same situation and/or a wise therapist, along with a good deal of introspection, can help you to tame the Furies. Some of our interviewees reported that they were helped enormously by professionals trained in family dynamics, but such help usually required more than a few sessions. Psychotherapists, clinical psychologists, marriage counselors, social workers, community or church groups, and other support groups may provide all the impartial, knowledgeable help you need. Moreover, if, ultimately, you can help someone else as a result of your hard-won experience, by "paying it forward," all your struggle and self-examination will seem that much more worthwhile.

FAMILIES ARE SYSTEMS AND SYSTEMS CAN BE FIXED

When you change how you react to someone, that person has to change strategies, as well. Once any family member learns to tame one or more Furies, other members of the family system can also benefit. When anyone becomes skilled at recognizing the Saving Graces, that family member is modeling constructive behavior from which everyone can learn. Eventually, the use of Tact and Tacking strategies will result in much smoother sailing for the entire stepfamily.

In the opening pages of this book, we compared living in an adult stepfamily to traveling in a foreign land. The comparison seems even more telling as we come to the end of this book. The marrying couples, for the most part, enter this foreign country with happy, often naïve anticipation, expecting beautiful vistas, intriguing architecture, exotic food, and a new language that they look forward to learning. For the adult children, most feel they prefer an itinerary of their own choosing.

As the voyage begins, the adult stepfamily often encounters rough seas. Sometimes, there seems no antidote to the green gills of seasickness. Once they set foot in the foreign country, most family members discover that their journey entails unexpected adventures: wrong turns that confound and frustrate them, signs they can't translate, food that disagrees with them, currency exchange rates that require constant renegotiation, and strangers who, for no good reason, don't like them.

If they hang in there, the family members also discover a new world, rich in unimagined pleasures: a landscape beautiful in its own way; new customs that perplex and delight them; freedom to redefine themselves and relinquish old, narrow identities; and the possibilities of new friendships and eventually even loving familial bonds.

There is a secret to enjoying, learning, and growing in this complicated, distinctly foreign territory. The secret lies in surrendering not to your fantasies and preconceptions, but to the reality of this new land of adult stepfamilies as it really is.*

---

*Here we are paraphrasing the advice of Bernadette Murphy in her review of Merrill Joan Gerber's *Botticelli Blue Skies: An American in Florence.* (Madison, WI: University of Wisconsin Press), 2002, in the *Los Angeles Times,* November 26, 2002, p. E 10.

GLOSSARY

THE FIVE FURIES: RECURRENT FEARS AND CONCERNS THAT BEDEVIL STEPFAMILY MEMBERS

1. **Fear of Abandonment and Isolation:** the fear that you will lose a relationship that you depend upon for emotional and/or financial support and the fear that you will be pushed aside and left in a lonely limbo.

2. **Fidelity to Family:** worry about changes in loyalty. These worries occur when members of the original family fear that a) the parent will lose his/her old loyalty after remarriage; b) the children will be unfaithful to a divorced or deceased parent by supporting their remarrying parent; c) the spouse will be overly committed to his or her old family; d) the stepsiblings will have too much influence over their parent.

3. **Favoritism:** concern about who is now number one. Whose wishes get top priority when choices have to be made?

4. **Finances:** for adult children, fear that they may lose money and/or property that they expected to be theirs; for parents, fear that their children care more about their inheritance than about the parent.

5. **Focus on Self to the Exclusion of Others:** anger that a parent or adult child is concerned only about himself or herself and no longer cares about the needs of others.

THE EIGHT TACT AND TACKING STRATEGIES: STRATEGIES THAT STEPFAMILY MEMBERS CAN USE TO DEAL WITH THE FIVE FURIES

1. **Reframe the Issue:** Turn a sow's ear into a silk purse. Look for a kinder interpretation of negative behavior. This strategy helps you to see the same set of facts, originally viewed as negative, in a more positive way.

2. **Let Time Pass:** This strategy involves letting the passage of time decrease the intensity of negative feelings.

3. **Become an Observer, Then a Participant Observer:** This strategy allows you to gain some emotional distance on your new stepfamily by assuming the role of a cultural anthropologist.

4. **Use Tenacity, Stick Up for What You Believe.** This strategy requires you to maintain and defend your core values (the personal rules of behavior that allow you to maintain your integrity).

5. **Trade and Negotiate; Give and Take:** This strategy involves learning how to negotiate until you both achieve win-win results.

6. **Use Forgiveness, Empathy, Apology, and Tolerance (FEAT):** This strategy involves the attitudes and behaviors directed toward others.

   - Forgiveness is maintenance of a positive relationship, despite your having been treated in an unfair or harmful way.

   - Empathy is the capacity to identify with and show compassion for another person.

   - Apology is acknowledgment and admission that your own behavior has been wrong.

   - Tolerance is the ability to see that views contrary to your own may have validity.

7. **Practice Transformation Through Wisdom:** This strategy calls for making changes within yourself as a result of new insights and understanding.

8. **Practice Turning Away from the Problem and Letting It Go:** This strategy calls for recognizing what cannot be changed and not allowing it to dominate your thinking.

THE FIVE SAVING GRACES: THE HIDDEN TREASURES THAT CAN BE FOUND IN ADULT STEPFAMILIES

1. **Fulfilling Remarriage and the Consequent Surge in Parental Happiness:** This grace enhances the parents' ability to nurture their biological and stepchildren and their families.

2. **Facilitating Objectivity, Maturity, and Wisdom:** This grace allows all members of the stepfamily to become wiser and more realistic about themselves and others. This capacity develops as members of the new stepfamily renegotiate family roles, adapt to a new group of players, and learn from the process of creating a new, adult stepfamily.

3. **Friendships with a Stepparent or Adult Stepchild:** This grace promotes relationships based on friendship, and, maybe, eventually love, between stepparents and stepchildren.

4. **Fraternity of Siblings and Stepsiblings:** This grace allows you to draw closer to your biological siblings, as well as to stepsiblings.

5. **Freedom from Filial Responsibility:** This grace helps adult child to feel less guilty about being unavailable when their parents need them.

INDEX